T. S. Eliot

T. S. Eliot

A Short Biography

JOHN WORTHEN

Haus Publishing

LONDON

Copyright © 2009 John Worthen

First published in Great Britain in 2009 by Haus Publishing,
70 Cadogan Place, London SW1X 9AH
www.hauspublishing.co.uk

The moral rights of the author have been asserted

A CIP catalogue record for this book is available from the British Library

ISBN 978-1-906598-35-8

Typeset in Garamond by MacGuru Ltd
info@macguru.org.uk
Printed in England by J F Print Ltd., Sparkford
Jacket illustration courtesy Getty Images

Contents

Illustrations

Introduction

A currency of misinformation – not just new material – may require new biography.[1] Writing and thinking about T. S. Eliot's life and work are bedevilled by gossip, to a large extent provoked by the biography of his first wife, *Painted Shadow: A Life of Vivienne Eliot* (2001), but fuelled too by the biopic *Tom and Viv* (1994)[2] and by Anthony Julius's book *T. S. Eliot, anti-Semitism, and literary form* (1995). There has been a great deal of knowing talk about Eliot's first marriage, about its 'sexual problems' and 'sexual failure',[3] as well as about Eliot's 'homosexual predilections'.[4] It also appears generally believed that, during his first marriage, he was in love with an American woman called Emily Hale;[5] and it is widely taken for granted that he was anti-Semitic.[6]

❧

Given Eliot's own attitude towards biography,[7] such a situation is particularly ironic. One of his earliest critical *bon mots* had insisted that the 'progress of the artist is ... a continual extinction of personality', and he had done his best to distance, as far as he could, the idea of 'the man who suffers' from 'the mind which creates'.[8] Accordingly, as early as 1925, when he was only thirty-seven years old,[9] he stated that he wanted no biography of himself, despite his remark to Virginia Woolf that 'he was more interested in people than in anything'.[10] In 1938 he would instruct a potential literary executor to 'suppress everything suppressible' and to 'discourage any attempts to make books of me or about me': 'I don't want any biography written'.[11] At the end of his life, he explained that he did not want his executors 'to facilitate or countenance the writing of any biography of me'.[12]

His attempts to prevent biographical speculation have, however, spectacularly misfired. He once sardonically commented on the degree to which Jonathan Swift's 'most interesting private life' had contributed to his literary reputation,[13] and few twentieth-century poets have been judged more interesting than Eliot. His own rejection of biography may have been a sign that he knew just how fascinating he had become, in particular during the years he spent with Vivien Haigh-Wood, whom he had married in 1915.[14] Vivien and he had at times quarrelled horribly, and her life was dominated by illness: as she once remarked to a friend commiserating with her, 'Am ill (still ill) not ill again (always ill)'.[15] Partly in consequence, she had been terribly dependent upon her husband, while Eliot had felt burdened and exhausted by Vivien. But for him the years of his marriage had been marvellously creative and productive: his relationship with Vivien lay behind the composition of what is arguably his major work, written between 1917 and 1930. This book will demonstrate his reliance on, and his continuing attachment to, the woman from whom he separated in 1933 and who died in 1947.

For Eliot's poetry is of surprising significance in charting his intense inner existence. Whereas his polemical and social writing has in many ways dated, a great deal of his imaginative work continues to be powerful, and opens up his immensely complex life to our scrutiny. Eliot himself hoped that his poetry was 'aboriginal', less controlled and more revealing than his prose; he not only believed that poetry was a 'disturbance of our quotidian character'[16] but once declared that the function of the poet was 'to bring back humanity to the real'.[17] It certainly brought *him* back to the reality of his own experience.

❀

This short biography of Eliot looks hard at his poetry because, as he said himself, 'in the writing of verse one can only deal with actuality'.[18] He often returned to the subject of biography – as when, for example, in 1927, scoffing at those who 'reconstructed' his biography out of passages he had quoted from others or had 'invented out of nothing because they sounded well', he confessed to 'having my biography invariably ignored in what I *did* write from personal experience'.[19] Naturally he wrote directly out of his own experience at times, in ways that illuminated his life. And although the unpleasant things that we all experience may demand 'a self-silencing by way of an impersonal writing',[20] Eliot believed that the only thing that 'constitutes life for the poet' is 'the struggle ... to transmute his personal and private agonies into something rich and strange'.[21]

Eliot had also cultivated an extraordinary detachment, to which the 'personal and private agonies' of his first marriage certainly contributed. A man who knew him well was impressed – and depressed – by the 'detachment of spirit' Eliot demonstrated in everyday life, as well as by his habit of reaching decisions based on 'pure intellectual justice, pronounced with great caution'.[22] Such were the indications of his careful, detached, self-silenced and at times deliberately impersonal and deeply-hidden self: a very important part of the person he wanted to be.[23] As early as 1925, his sympathetic friend Virginia Woolf observed how 'there is a kind of fun in unravelling the twists & obliquities of this remarkable man'; in 1933 she would imagine him as a 'dark well'.[24]

It had all the same been the achievement of his poetry up to 1930 not to muzzle the revelatory personae and the personal, suffering voices which interrupted, came into conflict with, and at times overruled the controlled and controlling self with which he attempted to govern his everyday life, his critical life, and – after 1927 – his religious life. His poetry *demanded* that such revelatory and at times violent, rich, strange, unpleasant and amoral voices should be heard. This biography will concentrate upon their versions of the actualities of Eliot's life.

I

Where one starts from[1]

I n old age, Eliot would cheerfully if implausibly refer
to himself as 'an American who wasn't an American'.
Although born in the south – St Louis, Missouri, on
26 September 1889 – he was by no means a southerner: his
family, as he was aware from the start, 'looked down on all
southerners and Virginians'. Both sides of his family came
from New England and it was on the coast there that the
Eliot family continued to take its summer holidays; first at
Hampton Beach in New Hampshire, later at Gloucester on
Cape Ann. When Eliot was eight, his father had a large house
built at Eastern Point, near Gloucester, in full view of the sea,[2]
for the family's holidays (they would stay each year from June
to September). Eliot spent nineteen summers there, in all,[3] and
loved the place: the great granite rocks, the wind, the sea, the
sunlight.[4] He became a devoted bird-watcher and also learned
to sail. The place would frequently feature in his poetry, as
in 'Ash-Wednesday', written some thirty years later, with its
images of the 'granite shore' and the 'white sails' that 'still fly
seaward';[5] in his fifties he could recall 'The fresh season's rope,
the smell of varnish / On the clean oar, the drying of the sails'.[6]

Ten miles or so up the coast lies a group of rocks a mile and a half out at sea, impressive granite teeth, which became the title of another of his poems – the Dry Salvages.[7] Sultry, smelly, industrial St Louis was however where he spent most of his time as a child and an adolescent: 'for nine months of the year my scenery was almost exclusively urban, and a good deal of it seedily, drabby urban at that'. The 'urban imagery' of his early poetry drew heavily upon St Louis, upon which he superimposed 'Paris and London'.[8] The great river Mississippi (joined by the Missouri just north of the city: hence the particular brownness and disturbance of the water) ran through St Louis, 'sullen, untamed and intractable', with its cargo of 'human bodies, cattle and houses'.[9] Even 'in the nursery bedroom'[10] the river could never really be avoided. St Louis people, too, felt different from those he associated with the north-east, or with other centres of culture; he once remarked 'I was fortunate to have been born here, rather than in Boston, or New York, or London'.[11] Although people might be proud of their New England descent, he reckoned they should be glad not to be the 'contemporaries'[12] of their formidable ancestors. There was enough in Eliot's life to encourage him to adopt the mask of the Boston Brahmin[13] – superior, smug, intellectual and distant – without adding cultural location to the mix. Anyway, for the period of his childhood and adolescence he remained a southerner,[14] 'a small boy with a nigger drawl'. He would later take pains to get rid of the Missouri accent 'without ever acquiring the accent of the native Bostonian.'[15] Eastern Point, its fir trees, 'the bay and the goldenrod, the song-sparrows, the red granite and the blue sea'[16] survived as a kind of cherished dream landscape for the rest of the year.

Eliot's oddly mixed upbringing (he liked explaining) meant that he ended up feeling 'never anything anywhere'. In 1934, in Virginia, he would actually refer to himself as 'a Yankee',[17] but he also enjoyed thinking that he was 'more a Frenchman than an American and more an Englishman than a Frenchman'.[18] Behind the pleasing, rehearsed conceit of such a formulation lies a serious point: that he had come to enjoy being – by other people's standards – 'never anything anywhere': always an outsider. In 1919, having lived and worked in England for five years, he remarked to an English friend that he felt he was still only 'a *metic* – a foreigner'[19] (the Greek word means an alien allowed residence in the city because of his utility); in the late 1930s, when England had been his home for more than twenty-five years, he would adopt the Greek form of the same word ('μέτοικος') as his signature to an essay.[20] It was a status he took pleasure in claiming: it gave him a distance, it contributed to the detachment he cultivated and to the authority he came to desire. A friend realised that 'He wasn't a bit like an Englishman' and once told him how there was 'this indestructible American strain in you'. He responded: 'I'm glad you realised it. There is.'[21]

❀

The Eliots could trace their English origins back to the village of East Coker in Somerset, but in America they had been distinguished by their religious enthusiasm and their good works. Eliot's paternal grandfather, William Greenleaf Eliot, had – like his own grandfather – been a Unitarian minister; Eliot's father Henry Ware Eliot was a kindly, rather rigid-minded but successful president of a brick-making company, troubled by deafness and as a result not very accessible; his mother Charlotte was an immensely energetic ex-schoolmistress, poetry-loving, domineering and deeply caring. She had been forty-five when she gave birth to her seventh child and second son,[22] so that Tom Eliot (he was very rarely 'Thomas' except in some official signatures and book inscriptions[23]) grew up with elder sisters who were between twelve and nineteen years older than he was. His brother Henry was his nearest surviving sibling, nine years older. Tom Eliot – always slight in build, dark-brown haired, with jug-handle ears – was probably closer to his young nurse, Anne Dunne, of whom he was very fond,[24] than to any of his sisters or his brother, though he eventually grew deeply attached to them. A photograph from 1896 shows him at the front gate of the family house, a very small boy surrounded by four most impressive female figures.[25] His upbringing was indeed 'rather overwhelmed'[26] by women.

Being mostly sedentary was practically inevitable for Eliot. He had a congenital double hernia (an abdominal rupture, in Eliot's case on both sides, where parts of the intestine protrude through the bowel wall). The condition troubled him on and off for much of his life until an operation finally dealt with it. The child of caring and careful parents, from a very young age he wore a leather or canvas truss designed to contain and compress the hernia (as a child he was astonished to come across the picture of a naked boy without a truss: he had assumed that all boys had them). As soon as he learned to read he became very bookish; a family legend would, much later, hint how – not having spoken until he was six or seven – 'he remarked one day to his mother that they were having a dreadful snow-storm'.[27] A great deal more reliable is the photograph of him as a boy showing him curled up in his chair on the porch of the Eastern Point house, not watching the white wings of sails but totally absorbed in his book. It would not have been a coincidence that when his twenty-five-year-old sister Charlotte painted him around 1900, she pictured him dutifully reading a volume of Shakespeare,[28] even though, years later, he confessed that the only good thing about reading Shakespeare was 'being commended for reading him; had I been a child of more independent mind I should have refused to read him at all'.[29] The books he read needed to be of the right kind, of course. When he was small, he had made his mother anxious 'because he devoted too much attention to the novels of Mayne Reid'[30] – stories about savages and the Wild West; *Tom Sawyer* and *Huckleberry Finn* would be forbidden for not being serious enough.

Thirty years later, Eliot wrote a now rather neglected poem about the growing-up of an uncertain, bookish small child who sounds very like himself; a child who eventually emerges into adult life 'Irresolute and selfish, misshapen, lame, / Unable to fare forward or retreat ... / Denying the importunity of the blood'.[31] The 'family temperament' of 'Fear

1. T. S. Eliot, oil-painting by Charlotte Smith, *née* Eliot, *c.* 1900–01.

and Conscience'[32] was legendary; there was 'the Eliot way' of seeing 'only the immediate difficulties and details'[33] and their fear that climbing irons would be needed to conquer a molehill.[34] When he was young, Eliot himself suffered innumerable agonies and apprehensions, as when

> we travelled by train from St Louis to the East ... I always feared that it would pull out in front of our eyes, or that my father, busy with seeing the luggage put aboard, would miss the train. I found a variety of calamities to worry about.[35]

He was deeply conscious of his own anxieties, as well of an emotional immaturity which lasted at least into his twenties, perhaps longer.

❀

The demands of the family's Unitarian faith – modified by a dose of Emersonian transcendentalism – had had crucial consequences for the small boy. Unitarian congregations shared no common creed beyond an insistence on the single nature of God and a denial of the Trinity; all other belief depended upon the local minister and local congregation. Central to the faith was the idea of the individual taking on responsibility for self-control and discipline; religious ideas were rooted in rational thought rather than being drawn from external authority (the churches had no structure of bishops or elders). Religious principles were developed from conscience, thinking and experience, and appeared – especially to the growing child – perfectly bewildering 'imperatives of "is and seems" / And may and may not ...'[36]. Principles and moral choice were everything; learning what was wasteful or time-wasting or vulgar was extremely important, while 'decisions between duty and self-indulgence'[37] were crucial. There was, naturally, no smoking or drinking in the Eliot house (though he subsequently smoked for most of his life: he gave up in 1954), while he recalled how 'I was brought up to believe it was a selfish indulgence to buy candy for *oneself*!'[38] Not behaving well was the unforgivable sin for members of the Eliot family: Eliot once reminisced how 'his parents did not talk of good and evil but of what was "done" and "not done"'.[39] Unwritten moral imperatives, closely allied to demands for impeccable social behaviour, can easily start to become 'the damage of a lifetime' for an impressionable child. Being rational, thoughtful, courteous, sensible and self-denying, while in all possible ways 'Denying the importunity of the blood',[40] was the code at the heart of Eliot's upbringing. The Unitarian tradition of his family ensured that he learned to conduct himself with scrupulousness, dedication and rigour, traits which in spite of his innate kindliness led, at times, to an 'almost savage intoler-ance'[41] of others and of himself.

Unitarians were, nevertheless, famous for their active involvement in the improvement of society, and the Eliot family had a distinguished tradition of public service.[42] William Greenleaf Eliot had lived and preached in St Louis but had campaigned for alcohol prohibition not only in

Missouri, but also in the USA as a whole. He had also worked for the Western Sanitary Commission, establishing hospitals; he had helped to found Washington University in St Louis; he had founded schools for boys and girls in St Louis (including Smith Academy, the school Eliot attended), but – in keeping with his religious faith – he had always believed in education for the best possible result, not just for general improvement: 'One best was more than many good.'[43] Eliot's father, by becoming a business man, might have been seen as having stepped aside from the family tradition, but Unitarians always believed in good works, not to say excellent works, and a dedicated and efficient employer could also be a highly moral individual.

His father, however, effectively cut his family off from their old friends and social contacts in St Louis by choosing to stay on until 1908 in the old house on Locust Street (where Eliot had been born), with the Unitarian Church of the Messiah just a few blocks away along the same street. This was long after the rest of the area had deteriorated into 'slums among vacant lots'.[44] Henry Ware Eliot doubtless did this out of loyalty to his own widowed mother, who lived in the house next door; but it meant that – with his siblings so much older than himself – the young Eliot was deprived of a good deal of companionship. His hernia meant that he could not participate in most games, still further isolating him.

An upbringing thus both lonely and strictly controlled helped emphasise what Eliot later called his 'intellectual and puritanical rationalism',[45] his insistence on conscience and on moral judgement, a 'lifelong moral strenuousness which was unbending'.[46] Becoming the poet he did would in many ways go clean against his nature as it had been formed when he was young; the American poet Ezra Pound, in 1920, would sympathetically comment that he believed that Eliot had suffered from the 'disease' of American moral Puritanism 'perhaps worse than I have – poor devil'.[47] Eliot's upbringing fostered both an unforgiving frame of mind and a determination to excel. Nothing but the best was permitted either for (or from) the growing child: he remembered being reproved as a child for using 'the vulgar phrase "O.K."'.[48] His upbringing meant that Eliot always felt a preternatural burden of responsibility; in 1914, when he was twenty-five, he would talk to the young and flighty Brigit Patmore about how old he felt: 'so old that it makes me despair'.[49] That was the legacy of a burdened conscience and of years of responsible choice. The need to excel meant that when, later in life, he felt unable to cope with everyday demands ('always behind hand, never up to date'), he grew deeply unhappy ('always tormented'). When Virginia Woolf looked hard at him in December 1920, she saw 'A mouth twisted & shut; not a single line free & easy; all caught, pressed, inhibited; but great driving power some where'.[50] When she described him in August 1937 as 'uneasily egotistic',[51] she was acutely aware of what his upbringing had brought to him, and how he had grown up a 'very self centred, self torturing & self examining man'.[52] A contemporary who shared a similar upbringing commented on its savage if effective combination of 'Moral passion (Shut up) and business efficiency (Get on with it)'.[53]

The young Eliot grew up with a highly developed ability to be friendly but with no intimate friends; his beautiful manners, now and later, were a way of controlling his friendships. As he later wrote about Matthew Arnold, 'He had no real serenity, only an impeccable demeanour'.[54] It takes one to know one. Eliot's playfulness was pronounced; he could write and fantasise with huge wit and charm, and even at his unhappiest could be 'so very funny and charming and domestic and nice to be with'.[55] But he was also very serious, especially when responding to his parents' demands. When he was sixteen, his mother would describe him as having 'always been a student', and the list of reading he had completed by that age is impressive; his Latin (begun at twelve or thirteen) and Greek (a year later[56]) as well as his French were all excellent – he won the Smith Academy Latin Prize for 1903–04 – while he had read all of Shakespeare, and had been commended for doing so. His mother went on to describe him as 'although quiet ... most friendly', 'very modest and unassuming, yet very self-reliant too'.[57] It is an interesting list of contrasts – quiet but friendly, unassuming yet self-reliant – and it already sounds very like the Eliot of later years.

One of the great gaps in our understanding of Eliot is the part played in his life by his mother.[58] His siblings thought that, of all of them, he was the one most like her. She certainly did everything she could for him. A sequence of letters she wrote in 1905, when Eliot was sixteen, the year in which she found a place for him at Milton Academy up in Massachusetts, so that he could be profitably occupied during the year before he went to Harvard, is remarkable for their scrupulous care about what her son might study, and their tenacity in sorting out every detail of everyday life.[59] The way that she cosseted him – the frail, youngest child, now growing tall and thin[60] – is something her letters also reveal. After Eliot had been at the school for eight months, she wrote questioning whether he should really be allowed to swim in a nearby quarry pond. One of his father's sisters had, years earlier, been drowned in such a pond. Diving into it would obviously be dangerous. There was a risk of typhoid infection. And were the boys allowed to decide for themselves how long they should remain in the water?[61] She might have been enquiring about a seven-year-old rather than about a young man who was, by now, seventeen years old. In 1919, when he was thirty-one, she offered to make him some pyjamas; he replied 'I should love to have pyjamas made by you ... it would seem to keep us nearer together.'[62] The fact that, deep into his thirties, Eliot continued to tell her in detail about his health in his letters ('I always sleep on my left side because I breathe more easily'[63]), suggests how intensively Charlotte had mothered him, how fully he had responded, and how ingrained their intimacy had become.

His relationship with his father is more mysterious; but as Eliot himself later suggested, Henry Ware Eliot was a lonely person and 'hardly knew himself what he was like'.[64] He was affectionate but in some peculiar way damaged, so that it often seemed as if his deafness were the result rather than the cause of his detachment. An eloquent 1914 letter reveals the attitude towards sex which he would have tried to inculcate in his children:

> I do not approve of public instruction in sexual relations. When I teach my children to avoid the Devil I do not begin by giving them a letter of instruction to him and his crowd. I hope that a cure for syphilis will never be discovered. It is God's punishment for nastiness. Take it away and there will be more nastiness, and it will be necessary to emasculate our children to keep them clean.[65]

Henry Ware Eliot does not appear to have been able to enjoy much in life, or respond to much, with the exception of worldly achievement, of which his youngest son unfortunately did not bring him much; Eliot only became a great success after his father was dead.

❀

Eliot's first surviving poetry dates from when he was sixteen; it is accomplished, utterly second-hand, full of puns;[66] most of it is just what one might expect to be written by a very clever, bookish boy to impress his teachers – and amuse his elders and betters. He was also good at writing strict, appropriate verses, as is shown by his poem for Graduation Day at Smith Academy in 1905; and he was also able fluently to reproduce the styles of other poets (for example Ben Jonson), in which his great range of reading obviously helped.[67] In every way his writing was impeccable, as he himself knew very well: he once referred to himself as an Emersonian

> First born child of the absolute
> Neat, complete,
> In the quintessential flannel suit.[68]

The pose, the style, the elegance are all suggested there.

His mother was immensely proud of him, in particular because he was doing what she had failed to do. As she told him in 1910, she wanted him to 'receive early the recognition I strove for and failed';[69] she would have loved to go to college and had always had excellent marks academically. Her son's success was of great importance to her, though it was (naturally) his academic work of which she thought most highly and in which she primarily believed. She herself was a poet, even if she specialised in writing poems about thinkers and moral heroes; her long and thoroughly tedious poem *Savonarola* contains the telling lines 'My Art was but a means whereby to climb / To higher things'.[70] (The nicest thing Eliot ever did for her poetry was to have the poem published in 1926, with an introduction by himself.) In 1916, she would declare that she was perfectly happy with her son publishing poetry – 'if not too much of the ephemeral "vers libre"' – just so long as he was sure to make 'Philosophy his life work'.[71] Philosophy was to her a good example of a 'higher thing'.

His mother elicited from him the most emotional

expressions in his surviving early letters. When his father died in 1919, his first letter to his mother stated 'I do long for you': he wished she could 'sing the Little Tailor to me'.[72] That suggests the continuation of an extreme – even stifling – closeness: he wanted very deeply not just to be mothered, but to be taken far back into childhood. Working hard in order to please her and to demonstrate his love to her became Eliot's habit from very early on. However, in the long run pleasing such a mother would be a problem, especially for a man selecting a literary and not an academic career. And how would she respond to any partner he might choose?

Eliot was a man who very often made others feel foolish: Brigit Patmore, for example, remarked that none of the great literary men she had known – Yeats, Lawrence, Huxley, Pound – 'ever made me feel quite as inadequate as I was when with T. S. Eliot'.[73] Eliot in turn seems also to have been made to feel both ungrateful and inadequate by his mother; and we can guess that such a tendency would have started early, and continued to the end of her life. He told her in September 1920 that 'I depend dearly on your letter every week'; she would punish him for not writing by not writing herself.[74] The fact that, within a few weeks of her death in 1929, he should have published his despairing little poem 'Animula', about the psychological and spiritual disaster for a child who has been subjected to an upbringing that sounds remarkably similar to his own, suggests how deeply ambivalent he had by then become about his mother and about their love for each other.[75] Teaching students at Harvard after his mother's death, too, Eliot remarked that D. H. Lawrence's book *Fantasia of the Unconscious* was 'better than all the psychoanalysts' in its devastating analysis of 'mother-love'.[76] It is impossible to say just which parts of Lawrence's book impressed him, but presumably the descriptions of a 'mother-supported, mother-loved' boy who 'flares up like a flame in oxygen. No wonder they say geniuses mostly have great mothers. They mostly have sad fates.' Such a boy will find women a terrible puzzle: 'he is linked up in ideal love already, the best he will ever know.'[77] The most savage of Eliot's remarks about Lawrence seem to have resulted from his enraged realisation of the other man's similarity to himself in just this respect, along with an instinctive refusal to accept that the life of a working-class man who would write so personally about the body's fulfilment might in any way have run in parallel to his own.[78]

Pose and Poetry

U p to the age of twenty-six, Eliot was concerned to do everything that might have been expected of him by others (though he would later write how bad it was 'to think and want the things that your elders want you to think and want'[1]). He had been a complete success at Smith Academy and then at Milton, and – in spite of having 'loafed' at Harvard during his Freshman and Sophomore years – had done well enough in his Junior year to get his BA in June 1909 and to graduate MA in June 1910 at the end of his Senior year. He had become a striking presence at Harvard, as his figure filled out a little: no longer gangling, he was 'a singularly attractive, tall, and rather dapper young man',[2] always elegant and well-dressed, with his hair slicked down and parted in the middle. His Harvard friend Conrad Aiken remembered him as 'fabulously beautiful and sibylline', with a mind that was 'best of all'.[3] A photograph of him tucked down under the boom of his sailing boat, one summer holiday during his Harvard years, conveys a striking combination of elegance and keen concentration.

What was perhaps more important to him was that he had

2. T. S. Eliot in the *Elsa* off Cape Ann, *c.* 1907.

started to publish poetry and reviews in the *Harvard Advocate* (he was elected to its board in 1910); it had been in the magazine's library towards the end of 1908 that he had discovered Arthur Symons' book *The Symbolist Movement in Literature* and was thus introduced to the writing of the French poets Rimbaud, Laforgue, Verlaine and Corbière. They came as a kind of revelation: it was possible to write intelligent poetry that was not simply moralistic. He bought Laforgue's *Oeuvres Complètes* in 1909[4] and his own poetry changed direction utterly; he began to write whimsical, mannered poetry in the style of Laforgue ('Humouresque' and 'Conversation Galante'[5] can both be dated to November 1909), and realistic (if still elegant) urban poetry about the streets of Cambridge, characterising for example a street piano as 'garrulous and frail'.[6] Most of his poems were short, witty, cleverly rhymed ('patience' with 'considerations'[7]), combining a pose of laconic detachment with acute descriptions of 'the squinting slums, the grime and smoke and the viscid human life within the streets'.[8] He inscribed the new poems, as he wrote them, in a small leather-bound notebook, now the only source of most of his early work.[9] What he included in the notebook marked what he felt to be a fresh start in his poetry writing.

Interestingly, though Eliot preserved his poems in the notebook, he attempted to publish very few of them, even while still at Harvard, and in most cases he did not go back to them later for re-working or revision. He saw them as belonging to the time and place when they were written, and thought they remained confined to it. Only two longer poems

– 'Portrait of a Lady', started in February 1910 and completed in November 1911, and 'The Love Song of J. Alfred Prufrock', started in 1910 but mostly written in July 1911 – seemed from the start worth not only preserving but also revising and re-working.

By the time he had finished these poems, he had left Harvard and Cambridge and had gone abroad. His first trip to Europe took place during the academic year 1910–11, and was a proof of his desire to broaden his horizons, academically and culturally, though it was very much against his mother's inclinations (she commented: 'I do not admire the French nation, and have less confidence in individuals of that race than in English'[10]). Eliot had developed a directly contrary idea: a pleasing fantasy 'of giving up English and trying to settle down and scrape along in Paris and gradually write French'.[11] This indicates that, as early as 1910, he had started to wonder about the academic career in America for which everyone assumed he was predestined.

He travelled over to Europe in October 1910 and spent most of the next six months in Paris, living in a pension on the allowance his father gave him, taking French lessons and studying at the Sorbonne (where at the start of 1911 he heard Henri Bergson lecture). He made some important new friends, including the writer Alain-Fournier and a lodger at his pension, the medical student Jean Verdenal. His relationship with Verdenal has given rise to a huge amount of speculation. Their friendship has regularly been turned into a 'gay relationship', although 'unlikely to have been a physical one'.[12] There is practically no evidence of the two men's feelings for each other – all that survive are a handful of Verdenal's letters to Eliot – but largely because some critics and biographers have wanted to subvert the idea of Eliot's correctness and respectability, it has been argued that 'in this gay relationship alone', Eliot 'felt, for the first time, accepted and understood by another human being'.[13] There is no evidence for the word 'gay' whatsoever, apart from what may be deduced from a very limited knowledge of circumstance, and no evidence either that Eliot had any such feelings of acceptance or understanding. Neither Eliot's very serious dedication of his first volume of poems to Verdenal,[14] nor a remark he made in 1934 about a friend he saw in Paris carrying a branch of lilac,[15] can bear the weight of interpretation that has been loaded on to them.

What does however survive is the evidence in Verdenal's seven surviving letters to Eliot that they talked at great length (in French) about books, art, music, philosophy, meaning and idealism;[16] that Verdenal was a person of acute intelligence, both self-doubting and perceptive, with an eye for image and ear for poetry; and that he looked back to his time with Eliot as one when his friend stimulated him to particular intellectual effort and perception. Eliot may well have felt the same; certainly, when Verdenal was killed in the war in 1915, Eliot wanted to commemorate such an interesting and sympathetic person having been (in his savage 1934 phrase) 'mixed with the mud of Gallipoli'.[17] Verdenal's death marked the kind of loss of the civilised and the civilising that would come to characterise the war for Eliot.

❀

After leaving Paris, Eliot travelled widely in Europe, going to London in April 1911 and Germany in the summer (a lot of 'Prufrock' would be written in Munich) though he was back in Paris at the start of September for a couple of weeks. During the year he also inserted the first three of his four 'Preludes' into his notebook, more poems for preservation: urban studies, originally American. The night reveals, to a restless sleeper, 'A thousand sordid images' from which – the poem suggests – 'your soul was constituted'.[18] This is not simple 'realism' by any means. The 'you' – perhaps the dramatisation of another person, more likely a version of a first person – takes us straight into the problem of who and what is actually being revealed, in an Eliot poem.

For a narrative engineered around varieties of pose and posture was characteristic of him. Towards the end of his 1911 poem 'La Figlia che Piange', written soon after his return from Europe, the narrator imagines losing the subject of his poem, who has profoundly compelled his imagination, but his final regret is the possibility of losing 'a gesture and a pose'.[19] The poem is really about ways of looking at the world; it is not a poem about another person.

All Eliot's life he was notorious for his ironic adoption of attitudes.[20] His very earliest successful poetry constantly engages with the idea of the pose. 'Portrait of a Lady', a longish poem which is a short masterpiece, includes a posing lady and an even more posturing narrator, who – having felt superior throughout to the patent absurdity of the cultured middle-aged lady's attitudes and speeches – finds himself unexpectedly confronted by her regretful good sense, as she wonders 'Why we have not developed into friends'.

> I feel like one who smiles, and turning, shall remark
> Suddenly, his expression in a glass.
> My self-possession gutters. We are really in the dark.[21]

All the narrator can offer himself, in an attempt to restore his necessary self-possession, is yet another series of poses:

> And I ... must borrow every changing shape
> To find expression – dance dance
> Dance like a dancing bear,
> Whistle like a parrot, chatter like an ape;
> Let us take the air, in a tobacco trance.[22]

As Eliot commented in 1926, 'the existence of a pose implies the possibility of a reality to which the pose pretends'.[23] Many of Eliot's early poems hinge on the contrast between the pose and the actualities of experience. The finest example is 'The Love Song of J. Alfred Prufrock', probably still his best-loved poem. He had taken the drafts of some Laforgue-like passages to Europe with him (the one starting 'No! I am not Prince Hamlet'[24] was one, later judged by his friend Ezra Pound not to be up to the standard of the rest, and only retained in the poem because Eliot was attached to it). Eliot finished the poem in July 1911. Here, for once, the Browningesque device of the narrator (one who gives himself away a good deal more than he knows) is linked with the pathos of a lonely, middle-aged man whose ideas of love, security, inhibition and extravagance are delicately and sympathetically created, along with his self-consciousness about the figure he cuts. It is, in fact, Eliot's first piece of successful dramatic verse. Prufrock's failed encounters are almost exclusively with women: women in artistic circles who 'come and go / Talking of Michelangelo', women at parties whose eyes 'fix you in a formulated phrase', women whose arms 'are braceleted and white and bare', women who – if you made any kind of advance to them – would be bound to say 'That is not what I meant at all. / That is not it, at all'.[25] Instead, Prufrock fears that he will simply grow old, wear respectable white flannel trousers, walk upon the beach. Mermaids will, of course, sing – and being mermaids might conceivably lure him on to the rocks: but, after all, he is not so very likely to be the victim of a grand passion. 'I do not think that they will sing to me.'[26] All he can do is live in hopes that something romantic and exceptional will happen to him, while knowing that if he *really* confronted his experience, or his emotions, such things would actually kill him.

❀

As early as November 1910, another kind of poem had also started to appear in Eliot's poetry notebook, one that he appears to have taken just as much care to preserve as anything else he entered; and although he later excised the original pages from the notebook, he did not destroy them. On the back of section I of 'Portrait of a Lady' some of Eliot's so-called 'Columbo' verses appeared, and some more are written on the back of 'Portrait of a Lady II'. Indeed Eliot sent further examples of them to Ezra Pound in 1915 and 1917, to Conrad Aiken in 1916, to James Joyce in 1921 and another stanza to Pound in 1922. A stanza from 'The Whore House Ball' demonstrates some of their characteristics:

> "Avast my men" Columbo cried
> In accents mild and dulcet
> "The cargo that we have aboard
> Is forty tons of bullshit."
> The merry men set up a cheer
> On hearing this reparty
> And the band struck up "The Whore House Ball"
> In accents deep and farty.[27]

'The Triumph of Bullshit' also came to be inscribed in the notebook. Eliot would cheerfully adapt such verses to local conditions. A couple of months after the outbreak of war in 1914, for example, when living in London, he sent some new Columbo verse about the sinking of a German warship to Aiken: 'But the cabin boy was sav'd alive / And bugger'd, in the sphincter' (rhyming with 'sink'd her').[28]

These verses have had an odd press. Lyndall Gordon has attacked them as 'puerile aberrations ... There's a sick fury here, an obsessional hatred of women and sex, punitive in its virulence'.[29] Carole Seymour-Jones is impressed by their 'consistent homosexual theme',[30] assumes that 'Eliot boldly exhorts his reader to buggery'[31] and concludes that 'Eliot's obscene verse testifies to the violence of his feelings, and it is hard to believe that they were never acted upon'.[32] Gabrielle McIntire, though, finds the verses primarily significant for their 'rendering of the history, legacy and cultural memory of early European colonial expansion'.[33]

All three writers overstate their cases. In the first place, jokes, especially loud and embarrassing ones, always appealed to Eliot (more than one visitor to the Faber offices in the 1930s would find himself invited to sit on a cushion which emitted a farting noise when compressed) – and that was when Eliot was highly respected and respectable. Secondly, there was an Anglo-American tradition, applying to male students and extending to upper-middle-class men, of exactly such verses and songs and jokes; a colleague at Faber in the 1930s recalled how Eliot 'would often tell quite ribald stories'.[34] The role Eliot was adopting (as he adopted so many: 'I must borrow every changing shape / To find expression') was that of the ordinary, slightly crass heterosexual male who unthinkingly enjoyed such things.[35] He may really have enjoyed them too; with Eliot it is impossible to be sure (he would probably not have been quite sure himself, either).

The obscene verses are also indications of the extent to which he was taking on the role of the typical male student of his time; other verses, inscribed during his year in Europe, were five stanzas of the enormously long Tinker ballad which generations of students compiled: the Tinker who 'came across the sea / With his four and twenty inches hanging to his knee'.[36] Such verses allow Eliot to be extravagant linguistically while developing an exact ear for colloquial rhyme – as in the verse in which Bolo's queen

> Was awf'ly sweet and pure
> She said "I don't know what you mean!"
> When the chaplain whistled to her[37]

The obscene verses are striking, too, as the subversive work of someone who enjoyed presenting himself as wonderfully refined in almost every other aspect of his life. Subversive obscenity, like elegant cultivation, was arguably also a pose, but it was one in which he was happy to trade for much of his life. In 1921 he would comment on the 'sense of relief' one feels in hearing 'the indecencies of Elizabethan and Restoration drama' (which leave one 'a better and a stronger man');[38] in 1927, he would refer in a letter to 'the purest tradition of British Obscenity',[39] and he was still sending cheerful obscene verses to Pound in 1934.

❦

The fantastical pose of staying in France as a kind of literary aesthete, however, turned out to be just that: a fantasy. Although 'perceptibly Europeanized',[40] Eliot returned to

Harvard in the autumn of 1911 with, in his own words, 'the intention of becoming, in time, a professor of philosophy'.[41] He enrolled in a course on Indic Philology, began to study Sanskrit and to read Indian philosophy. He remained in touch by letter with Jean Verdenal (their correspondence continued at least until the end of 1912.) In 1912 Eliot was appointed Assistant in Philosophy at Harvard; in 1913 he decided to write his doctorate on the philosopher F. H. Bradley.[42] Very few poems resulted from these years; a pattern had already been set in which periods of considerable poetic activity would be followed by periods when he wondered if he would ever write poetry again.

On the other hand, it is also clear that he was not happy. Three years later, he would describe this period at Harvard as the time when he had 'begun to worry';[43] what we would now call depression beset him. In March 1914 he met the English philosopher Bertrand Russell, who was a visiting Professor at Harvard, but it took more than a year for a poem ('Mr Apollinax') to result from the encounter, and to memorialise Russell's 'dry and passionate talk' and the extravagance of his merriment: 'He laughed like an irresponsible foetus'.[44]

For a new and distressing problem was fast coming towards Eliot: whatever was he going to do with his life? Ever since coming back from Europe in 1911 he had continued to be a model son, pupil and student, and had as a result been rewarded with academic friendships and fellowships appropriate to his achievements. An academic future (perhaps at Harvard) as a philosopher, probably specialising in comparative religion, appeared secure – assuming that he wanted it. But he was in a mood in which he hated academic life more and more. He wanted to be independent; he wanted to write; and he feared that the life he was now leading at Harvard made it impossible for him even to do as well in his poetry as he had done with 'Prufrock' three years earlier. Another chance to escape – albeit temporarily – came in the spring of 1914 when he was successful in an application for a Sheldon Travelling Fellowship from Harvard, which would allow him to take his philosophical interests where they could best be answered, academically.

He was writing about Bradley, and the world expert was Harold Joachim, at Merton College Oxford (Bradley was resident at the same college but almost completely inaccessible). Not surprisingly, Eliot took the chance of returning to Europe for the academic year 1914-15: at least he would be his own master again, and Europe was where he had written his best poetry. In April 1914, his father sent him a touching little note (significantly, perhaps, his only surviving communication to his son) on Eliot's success in obtaining the Sheldon award. Eliot had presumably remarked that the fellowship meant that he would no longer have to be such a financial burden on his father, and his father – pleased with the fellowship 'rec ... on act[45] of the honor' – remarked that it was the parent who was indebted to a son as dutiful as Eliot.[46] The almost comical brevity of the note, its contracted words and signature ('Yrs. P.'), were characteristic of a man who did not believe in wasting words or time: but within the extremely strict limits he allows himself, he is both affectionate and tender. On the other hand, Eliot would have found the idea of duty deeply depressing. All he could currently imagine of a future was one in which he would not be in the least dutiful to his father or his mother (or indeed to his potential career as an academic philosopher). Yet he had no money of his own, and there was no way he could live by his writing: he was still almost unpublished. And the last thing his father was likely to do was to subsidise a career for him as an independent writer. All he could do was take the fellowship and hope that something would turn up while he was in Europe.

❀

The temptation of Europe deepened significantly when his original plan of studying for the summer in Germany was interrupted by the outbreak of war in August 1914. He was obliged to travel at once to England, where he lived for a month in London before going on, as originally decided, to take up his fellowship at Oxford. After what he now felt had been missed opportunities for escape in France in 1911, a longer than planned-for stay in London was no hardship; it was a place where his work as a poet who wrote in English would obviously be better appreciated. By the end of September – partly because of the influence of his friend Conrad Aiken – he had got in touch with Ezra Pound, then living in London, had shown him 'Prufrock', and was getting himself introduced into circles of writers; early in October, Pound called him 'worth watching'.[47] This was exactly the kind of contact he had come to Europe to foster.

So far as his family and Harvard friends were concerned, of course, he had every intention of returning to Harvard at the end of the academic year, presenting his doctoral thesis and applying for an academic post. That was the career that his family expected of him, his upbringing foretold and to which his now considerable experience as a philosopher would naturally have led.

But the academic year 1914–1915 showed him for the first time in active rebellion against home, family and past. He knew very well that he was considering something his family would find unforgivable – his father even more than his mother, perhaps. What right did he have to abandon his long-developed and expensive education, along with all his carefully nurtured academic prospects in North America? He needed to ensure that his American family remained in ignorance of the impending crisis in his affairs; nothing in his surviving letters home suggested that anything out of the ordinary was happening.

In fact he was seeing as little of Oxford as possible. He was instead spending long periods of time in London, in the company of Ezra Pound and 'some of the modern artists whom the war has so far spared'.[48] He attended Pound's Thursday dining club at Belotti's restaurant in Soho whenever he could; he met Yeats in January 1915;[49] letters to a non-family-member reveal him attending 'cubist teas'.[50] It was Pound who helped most, introducing him everywhere. And it was Pound who assisted him hugely by sending 'Prufrock' to the distinguished editor Harriet Monroe for the American magazine *Poetry*, and then insisting to her that it was 'the best poem I have yet had or seen from an American' (she did not think very highly of it: Pound had to struggle 'for six months'[51] to get it accepted). His protestations ensured that it finally appeared, uncut, in the June 1915 issue. Eliot called Pound 'kindness itself', although his original attitude to Pound's own poetry (which had been shown to him in Harvard in 1908) had not changed: 'his verse is well-meaning but touchingly incompetent',[52] he had told Aiken in September 1914.[53]

Even though *Poetry* 'pays – which is everything to me'[54] (it paid him eight guineas), one successful poem in a prestigious magazine does not make a career. How could Eliot earn his living in Europe? What was a poet to do, to make his way in literary London? Reviewing – even if Eliot could manage to get it (and he was almost unknown) – would not have paid the bills. And not a single review by Eliot actually appeared in print in England before he started to write for the *Manchester Guardian* and the *New Statesman* in the middle of 1916, eighteen months later.

In one way, Eliot was lucky. During his year spent (in theory) in Oxford, his fellowship was paying some of the bills. It was incumbent on him to keep his teachers at Merton College (and the University of Harvard) happy with scholarly attendance and philosophical essays when required. And he managed to do this, in spite of what he later experienced as a 'maddened feeling of failure and inferiority'[55] in consequence of having got himself stuck in the academic world, when he wanted to be a poet, and knew that he ought to be spending all his time making contacts with editors and journalists. (He would later say that all he learned at Oxford was 'self confidence' and 'how to write plain English'.[56])

❀

By the spring of 1915, it had become imperative that he reach a decision. Harvard was putting pressure on him to decide what to do next and (assuming that he could *not* live as a poet) he saw only two alternatives: either to return to Cambridge (Mass.) to teach, submit his doctorate, become a professor, doubtless get married and have children, spend his life in America, 'and compromise and conceal my opinions and forfeit my independence for the sake of my children's future'[57] – that was by far the most likely possibility, and it is clear how much he hated it. His only other prospect was that of returning to America, somehow working, saving money, retiring early and returning to Europe as a kind of independent aesthete, occupying 'a table on the boulevard, regarding the world placidly through the fumes of an aperitif at 5 p.m.'.[58] Not surprisingly, such a fantasy did not appeal to him either. During April he went on desperately worrying about what to do, spending all the time he could in London 'among poets and artists',[59] hoping that his way forward might somehow become clear. He learned that he would have five poems – including his 'Preludes' and another lengthy urban poem, 'Rhapsody on a Windy Night', written in France four years earlier – published in the second issue of the radical Vorticist publication *Blast* in July 1915. That was an English publication and a different kind of success. And – again with Pound's incomparable assistance – *Poetry* took three more short poems (old ones) and one new one for October 1915, which brought in some money as well.

Living and trying to work in an England now digging in for a lengthy war, in which prices were going up and publishing was very likely to take a downward turn, Eliot would have known that even such publications were nothing like enough on which to found a career. And he was worried about his recent poetry. He feared that he had written nothing as good as 'Prufrock', now four years old. As if to confirm that judgement, *Poetry* decided at a very late stage not to publish the new poem he had sent them ('The death of Saint Narcissus'),[60] although it had been set up in type. They may have been put off by the eroticism of the verse, the way that (for example) the saint's flesh is 'in love with the burning arrows'.[61] It was not an auspicious start to what Eliot must have hoped was – somehow – going to be a professional career.

3

Marriage

I t was in this state of uncertainty that, in the spring of 1915, Eliot met a twenty-six-year-old Englishwoman called Vivien Haigh-Wood, who had recently broken off her relationship with another young man. Eliot already knew her slightly, having been introduced to her in Oxford (she knew his old American friend Scofield Thayer via Thayer's sister Lucy, had visited Thayer in Oxford, and on at least one occasion had observed Eliot sitting in his rooms 'quietly reading'[1]). He then encountered her again, apparently at a Saturday night dance at a London hotel. According to Brigit Patmore, Vivien was

> slim and rather small, but by no means insignificant. Light brown hair and shining grey eyes. The shape of her face was narrowed to a pointed oval chin and her mouth was good – it did not split up her face when she smiled, but was small and sweet enough to kiss. Added to this ... she shimmered with intelligence.[2]

The girls Eliot usually met in such places were, he thought, 'charmingly sophisticated (even "disillusioned") without being hardened',[3] but this one was different. She was 'a person of immense charm and vivacity, and quickness of uptake':[4] he would later pay tribute to her mind, calling it 'immensely clever and precocious',[5] and was reported as saying that she was the only woman he knew 'who had a mind like a man'.[6] Vivien was actually employed as a governess in Cambridge; it would have been natural for Eliot to go and see her there on a visit to his philosophical contacts.[7]

His own much later account says that all he had wanted, in 1915, was a 'flirtation or a mild affair' but that he was 'too shy and unpractised' to manage either.[8] This account probably under-estimates the degree to which he found himself attracted to Vivien, and the way in which he seems immediately to have grasped at her as the solution to his difficulties. Ford Madox Ford's dictum (published, incidentally, in March 1915) is appropriate:

> there is no man who loves a woman that does not desire to come to her for ... the cutting asunder of his difficulties. And that will be the mainspring of his desire for her.[9]

That seems to have been almost exactly Eliot's experience. In July 1915, indeed, he would say about Vivien that 'She has everything to give that I want, and she gives it'.[10]

A couple of years later Aldous Huxley would describe Vivien as 'an incarnate provocation' and conclude that it was 'almost entirely a sexual nexus between Eliot and her: one sees it in the way he looks at her'.[11] She also struck the hostess Ottoline Morrell as 'of the "spoilt-kitten" type, very

second-rate and ultra-feminine',[12] meaning sexy and flir-
tatious. When he saw her and Eliot in June 1918, Huxley
summed her up as 'vulgar, but with no attempt to conceal her
vulgarity';[13] Bertrand Russell also thought her 'a little vulgar,
adventurous, full of life', and was strongly attracted to her.[14]
But Eliot's attraction was not only sexual. He was seduced by
her liveliness, her poise and gracefulness as a dancer, and by
her apparent ease with herself. He, by contrast, was profoundly
and at times cripplingly self-conscious, as well as physically
rather slow and painstaking: a friend remembered his 'formal
and elusive body',[15] while his always troublesome hernia would
have made sexuality and nakedness both difficult and embarrassing. Much later in life he would make clear how very much
he envied the person for whom everything done or attempted
'comes out of a completeness in himself':[16] a completeness
which he himself never felt. Vivien seemed possessed of everything he did not have; and he had met her at one of those
'essential moments' in life, which he later described as 'the
times of birth and death and change'.[17]

❦

Just four months before meeting Vivien, Eliot had told Aiken
about his 'nervous sexual attacks' in cities, almost certainly
meaning the way that prostitutes excited him. As with many
French writers of the late nineteenth century, his writing had
constantly returned to the subject of the street walker; his
urban poetry had been full of them, from the 'leering houses

that exude / The odour of their turpitude'[18] to the 'women spilling out of corsets'[19] standing in entries, the woman 'Who hesitates towards you in the light of the door',[20] as well as the one 'with reddish hair and faint blue eyes' who was 'An almost denizen of Leicester Square'.[21] When Jean Verdenal had written to him in 1911 about the 14th July celebrations in Paris, he had described for Eliot's pleasure a merry-go-round, with 'the rise-and-fall of the horses curving the soft busts of the whores' as 'a heavy, sticky breeze drifts warmly past'.[22] What Verdenal is sharing with his friend is distinctively heterosexual; but what is equally clear is Eliot's own almost complete innocence in such things. He writes about such women knowingly, but confessed to Aiken in 1914: 'One walks about the street with one's desires, and one's refinement rises up like a wall whenever opportunity approaches'. He wished he had 'disposed' of his 'virginity and shyness'[23] earlier. He had probably never slept with a woman before he found himself attracted to Vivien.

※

Sexual desires for upper-middle-class[24] heterosexual people in 1915 would conventionally, of course, have led to marriage. Vivien at any rate was not the kind of person to have an affair. At the age of twenty-seven, with the wartime male population of the country already diminishing and a relationship recently ended, Vivien probably felt in real danger of being left on the shelf;[25] whilst Eliot was fastidious, puritanical and inexperienced. Mutual sexual inexperience may have led them into a situation which one or both believed had compromised them – so that marriage had to be offered, and was accepted[26] (Eliot was haunted by the Paolo and Francesca episode in Dante's *Inferno*, and Francesca's striking confession: 'but one moment alone it was that overcame us'[27]). It is also true that if Eliot found himself very much wanting Vivien, he would have known that the only way forward was to marry her. What is more, the *idea* of marrying her and solving the problems of his life at one glamorously uncharacteristic stroke, so that he would never have to go back to America at all (just as he had fantasised about leaving America for France in 1911), had become a startling possibility.

'I came to persuade myself that I was in love with her', Eliot wrote nearly fifty years later.[28] In 1915 he did not need to persuade himself. Vivien's arrival in his life seemed heaven-sent. Ezra Pound got involved in the decision too, telling Vivien that Eliot was a great poet, and must be saved for poetry by staying in England, rather than being swallowed up by an academic career in America. But Eliot was an attractive, not to say exotic (and beautifully mannered) young man, and Vivien would not have needed to feel that she was saving a genius from extinction to accept Eliot's proposal.

❀

Eliot did not tell his father or mother about Vivien, or about his decision, until they had actually got married on Saturday 26 June 1915, at Hampstead Registry Office. One good reason for their marrying with such speed was so that Vivien's dearly loved younger brother Maurice – now a Second Lieutenant – would be able to attend: he was leaving for France with his regiment later the same day. A sexually compromised woman (if that is what Vivien was) might also have wanted respectability restored to her as soon as possible. But the most likely reason for the suddenness of their marriage was to escape the objections which both sets of parents would have mounted. Eliot might have been respectable but he had no job and no immediate prospect of one; on his marriage certificate he was obliged to describe himself as 'of no occupation'. The Eliots in North America could hardly have escaped viewing their youngest boy's marriage as one made 'as the saying is, to disoblige his family'; and by fixing on a woman like Vivien, 'without ... fortune, or connections', he managed to do it extremely thoroughly.[29] A couple of days after the wedding, Ezra Pound – in his usual way, determined to be helpful – wrote a long and rather embarrassingly rambling letter to Eliot's father about how Eliot should stay in London as a poet and critic and would in the end be able to make his living; and how he needed some financial assistance to start with (Pound suggested $500 for the first year). The letter was intended to help Eliot survive; it almost certainly confirmed Henry Ware Eliot's belief that his son had fallen in with a bad set of people, and should not be encouraged to go on with them. P. Vivien had financial expectations of her own; she 'quite honestly expected to get something when she married', but she and Eliot 'didn't get it fixed up ....'[30] Her father allowed her just

£50 a year. Eliot's father, however, was shocked. He stopped Eliot's regular allowance, although he agreed to go on paying his son's rent, while his mother put huge pressure on her son to come back to America and, at the very least, see his teachers and sort out his future with Harvard. (Eliot had already told his Professor at Harvard, James H. Woods, that he would 'have to be in America this summer'.[31])

And, rather surprisingly, given that Eliot was in a thoroughly rebellious mood, Charlotte Eliot's pleas for him to return were successful, which suggests just what kind of pressure she and Eliot's father had brought to bear on him. Sometime in the first fortnight of July, Eliot agreed to come to America, and he sailed on 24 July 1915. The fact that he travelled without Vivien tells its own story – his family remained deeply hostile to the very idea of her – even if the reason that Vivien offered was that German submarines had made the journey too dangerous[32] (on 7 May 1915, the submarine U20 had sunk the British passenger-ship *Lusitania* off the coast of Ireland, at the cost of over 1,100 lives, including those of more than 120 American citizens).

During Eliot's time with his family (they were at Eastern Point for the summer, as usual) he also went down to see his professors at Harvard; and under their combined influence, he agreed after all – in spite of Vivien, his marriage and his hoped-for career as a writer – to remain in the USA to finish and take his doctorate,[33] although he did not rule out going back briefly and bringing Vivien to the USA. Before leaving England, he had obtained a job teaching in a school in High

Wycombe, to the west of London, starting in September (his original plan had been to return to Europe on 1 September), but since his plans had now changed, he wrote to the head-master handing in his notice.[34] He had, in effect, abandoned his attempt at escape. The wiser counsels of the Eliot family and his teachers (and those voices within him, too) had prevailed, and his mother's dictum that she retained 'absolute faith in his Philosophy but not in the vers libre'[35] had won the day. Presumably he wrote to Vivien telling her what he had now decided to do.

He did not, all the same, make a good impression on the entire Harvard faculty. Professor G. H. Palmer had remem-bered him as a graduate student with a 'mind of extraordinary power and sensitiveness', but recalled being 'deeply disap-pointed by the change' when they met in August 1915. Palmer concluded that Eliot had 'allowed himself to be turned into weak aestheticism by the influence of certain literary cliques in London': 'that love of beauty, which might have been his strength, had turned out to be his weakness, by reason of a certain softness of moral fibre'.[36] Eliot must have told Palmer about getting married and writing poetry rather than devoting himself to philosophy, and the older man had made clear to him 'as plainly as he dared the dangers he was running'.

In mid-August 1915, however, Eliot received a telegram informing him that Vivien was 'very ill in London'. He felt he had to go and see her before returning to Harvard for the start of term. But, having got him back in England, Vivien success-fully prevented him from returning to America. We know very little about this crucial moment in Eliot's life, but only a few years afterwards he gave her full credit for it: 'she kept me from returning to America where I should ... probably [have] never written another line of poetry'.[37] He would also, rather ruefully, later pay tribute to her 'persuasive (even coercive) gift of argument',[38] while she was very aware of her own ability 'to shove him ... and I *do* shove'.[39] Within a fortnight of his return, Eliot and Vivien were taking a 'second honeymoon', this time in Eastbourne. It may have been an attempt at a fresh start – perhaps necessary if their first honeymoon had been cut short by his American trip – but for Vivien it was perhaps another way of being persuasive.

By 9 September, Vivien had given Russell to understand that this second honeymoon had all the same been 'a ghastly failure'. She may have realised how close Eliot had come to abandoning England (in which case it is hardly surprising that she was now giving him a hard time), but it was also the case that she was attracted to Russell, who had seen a good deal of her while Eliot was away ('He is all over me, is Bertie, and I simply love him', she had confided in Thayer on 2 August[40]). Her remark may well have been primarily a way of urging Russell on by disparaging her husband: and of provoking Eliot to respond too. In 1938, Eliot would write with intimate knowledge about a wife unhappy with her husband who 'is trying to play one of her comedies with him' – because she knows that 'to arouse *any* emotion in him is better than to feel he is not noticing her'.[41] That sounds like an accurate version of Vivien's life with Eliot. She habitually kept men on tenterhooks, not (as Russell thought) because she was cruel but because she wanted their response so badly. Russell later wrote sententiously about her that 'She is a person who lives on a knife edge, & will end as a criminal or a saint'.[42] This may mean no more than that she had flirted with him in a way that surprised him, though it is clear that in 1915 Russell remained thoroughly unsure about what Vivien wanted. She was clearly 'really very fond' of Eliot.[43] But she wanted to be loved.

Her feelings for Russell indicate something else that would astonish (and in a way also attract) Eliot about Vivien: that she was in no way conventional. Russell would call her 'half-Irish, & wholly Irish in character', meaning tempestuous and given to contradictions, and he would fasten on the idea that she needed 'some kind of religion, or at least some discipline, of which she seems never to have had any'. Eliot – ten years later – would declare himself deeply impressed by Russell's insight: 'everything has turned out as you predicted'.[44] He would write with real fascination a couple of years later how 'the unmoral nature', when 'suddenly trapped in the inexorable toils of morality' can be 'forced to take the consequences of an act which it had planned light-heartedly'.[45] Vivien may well have undertaken marriage to Eliot 'light-heartedly', as 'one of her comedies', but had found herself trapped in the conventional 'toils of morality'; her later behaviour with Russell showed how unconventionally she would eventually respond. At this early stage, although he deeply admired her capacity for freedom and her inspiriting, compelling lack of restraint, Eliot had no reason to fear that Vivien would actually betray him:

and he would also have wanted to believe Vivien's assurances about how 'unattractive'[46] she found Russell. Now and later he felt extremely grateful to Russell for taking so much time caring for them both, in very practical ways, with accommodation and also by handing over debentures in an armaments company which – given Russell's resistance to the war and to conscription – he felt he ought to dispose of: the income from an investment of £3000 would have been wonderfully helpful to the Eliots.

❀

It turned out that the teaching job in High Wycombe, which Eliot had high-mindedly turned down while in Massachusetts, was still available, if he wanted it. He took it for a term (it paid £140 a year, with free lunch) before taking up a post at Highgate Junior School, teaching pupils up to the age of 13, in January 1916. The Highgate job was slightly better paid – £160 a year, with dinner and tea – and meant that he did not need to rent an extra flat but could live with Vivien in London. And although for a few months he went on planning to go back to the USA, he did not go. By dint of working extraordinarily hard in his spare time (he called it a 'winter of work'[47]), he was able to submit his doctoral thesis to Harvard in April 1916, which demonstrates that he had not yet decided to burn his boats. To do so would probably have meant a complete break with his parents, and that he could not bear.

But, once again because of Vivien, he did not return to

America for the examinations necessary to obtain his PhD. All he could do was offer the excuse to Professor Woods in May that, in wartime, he preferred not to take the risk: 'I do not like to leave my wife here, or venture the waves myself'.[48] There had been no tragedy on the scale of the *Lusitania* during the previous 12 months, but he was clearly determined not to go to America. The thesis was regarded as one of very high quality but, without his own attendance, he was unable to take his doctorate. His father was furious. 'Mrs. Eliot and I will use every effort to induce my son to take his examinations later',[49] he wrote to Woods. For the third time, Vivien had managed to prevent Eliot from doing the things that his 'elders' wanted him to do – and the responsible, careful, dutiful side of him wanted to do, too. He settled in Europe, he told a friend four years later, 'in the face of strong family opposition'.[50] That was putting it mildly.

He and Vivien – although very happy at times (she never forgot the way they 'used to walk about London at night. I loved it so ... So many mad mad nights'[51]) – were, by the standards of both of their upbringings, desperately hard up from the autumn of 1915 onwards. Eliot's teaching did not bring in much, her allowance was very small, and the poetry and journalism he was trying to do brought in even less, while Vivien (Eliot discovered: her August telegram may have been the first serious indication of it) needed constant medical attention, as indeed she had for years; it seems unlikely that Eliot had fully realised this before marrying her. She suffered from colitis, high temperatures, insomnia, migraines and physical exhaustion,[52] as well as bouts of depression. It seems likely that she was suffering from some disastrous and undiagnosed hormonal imbalances; she had also become drug dependent in her teens because of various doctors' prescriptions, probably dosing her with bromides and chloral.[53]

Russell helped them out by letting them have a small room in his flat in London – so small that Eliot had to sleep in a deckchair in the hall – and also wrote reassuringly to Eliot's family in America that, when he had obtained his PhD, Eliot should be able to get academic work in England. There is no sign that Eliot ever actually tried to get such work, though between the autumn of 1916 and the summer of 1919 he worked as a University extension lecturer, a scheme in which part-time itinerant teachers took University-level teaching to people who could not attend University. But whether he and Vivian could survive without his getting a full-time job was another matter.

❀

So much misinformation has been taken for granted about the marriage of the Eliots – in particular in the play and film *Tom and Viv*, in *Painted Shadow*, and also via some of Eliot's own later recollections[54] – that it is important to try and stick with the known facts and dismiss the wilder assumptions. Eliot's suppressed 1918 poem 'Ode', for example, has been assumed to be entirely autobiographical about his own wedding-night experience in 1915:[55] menstrual blood and premature ejaculation have been knowingly discussed as the facts of the case, and 'the physical failure' of the marriage is taken for granted by even responsible biographers: a 'sexual failure ... had undoubtedly occurred'.[56] By far the most depressing fact about his marriage was revealed by Eliot himself in 1939, in a letter to his friend John Hayward, when he remarked with horrible candour that he had never slept with a woman he 'liked, loved, or even felt any strong physical attraction to'.[57] We have to assume that the women included his wife (she may even have been the only person he had been to bed with before 1939[58]). If that is the case, then it is a grim recollection indeed. It seems possible that – after his first alarming surrender to Vivien in April 1915 – by the end of June, Eliot had found himself no longer very much attracted to her, but for one reason or another obliged to go through with the marriage. Virginia Woolf found it actually impossible to imagine that he and Vivien had ever had sex together,[59] while Russell commented dryly that Vivien had

> a great deal of mental passion & *no* physical passion, a universal vanity, that makes her desire every man's devotion, & a fastidiousness that makes any expression of their devotion disgusting to her. She has suffered humiliation in two successive love-affairs, & that has made her vanity morbid ... At present she is punishing my poor friend [i.e. Eliot] for having tricked her imagination.[60]

Her 'present' punishment was probably to refuse to have sex with Eliot (confirming that he still wanted to sleep with her). But she went on wanting his 'devotion', and this would be consistent with her demands on him over the years which followed. She would continue to criticise Eliot's restraint, his intellectual detachment, his strictness and self-containment, all of which she always hated (she would sigh and refer to 'The frightful time I have with Tom'[61]). The less responsive he was to her feelings, the more she would have tried to attract him and provoke him.

Between 1915 and 1922, at any rate, Eliot did feel, enormously strongly, the responsibility that he had taken on with Vivien. He had 'a profound & quite unselfish devotion to his wife', as Russell noted.[62] It is important to stress that, in these early years, although her physical illnesses were turning out to be almost constant, she was in no way damaged by the 'psychological ailments' that most commentators have come to assume she suffered from the start.[63]

Eliot's brother Henry, in 1921, would conclude that to some extent Vivien's illnesses were put on, or at least exaggerated, and had more to do with her relationship with her husband than anything else; Henry ended up believing that Vivien's appeals to Eliot out of illness had become her best way of provoking her husband's feelings.

> I have a feeling that subconsciously (or unconsciously) she likes the role of invalid, and that, liking as she does to be petted, 'made a fuss over', condoled and consoled, she … encourages her breakdowns …[64]

There was certainly something in that – just such an illness had brought Eliot back from the USA in August 1915 – but Vivien was also a chronic invalid, especially in the 1920s, when the marriage increasingly became a succession of physical crises, new doctors, new treatments, Vivien being despatched to various country cottages with attendant nurses, gradual recovery, eventually new breakdown.

Eliot felt profoundly guilty with regard to her. He would tell Pound in 1922 that he felt 'responsible toward her in more than the ordinary way'; the reason being that he had 'made a great many mistakes, which are largely the cause of her present catastrophic state of health'.[65] He may have been blaming himself for the huge 'mistake' of marrying her in the first place, though he probably also meant that he had ignored or underestimated ill-health or symptoms which had turned out to be significant. The main problem almost certainly remained the way that he felt he had ignored her; had not just been intellectually detached but, for all his care and caring, and his sexual demands, had at times been actually indifferent and at other times leaving her alone far too much. His biggest 'mistake' lay perhaps in helping turn an independent-minded active young woman, full of immediate emotional response, into the 'nervous self conscious bundle',[66] paralysed by her own illnesses, whom Virginia Woolf described in 1925, and to whom Eliot was now regularly ministering as sick nurse, in addition to his other responsibilities. And then he also had to endure her 'Dostojewsky kind of cruelty'.[67] If at times she hated him – his indifference, his self-containedness, the way 'his mind is so accurate and dissecting and fits in every idea like a Chinese puzzle'[68] – she had no compunction in telling him so, nor of finding ways of ridiculing him for being so different from her.

There was also something about pain – Vivien's pain – which he found irresistible. Brigit Patmore saw this in 1915: 'And pain – he loved not only his own, but the pain of others.'[69] He would later write with real understanding about how Baudelaire '*attracted* pain to himself': 'He could not escape suffering and could not transcend it.'[70] This was something Eliot knew about himself long before he met Vivien: he had written in 1911 about the fascination of the 'infinitely gentle / Infinitely suffering thing'.[71] His sympathetic love for Vivien confirmed it. Not only her cruelty but her suffering – and his own suffering, consequent on hers – seemed for a long time a natural part of their relationship.

One particularly unfortunate fact about their marriage, which was not necessarily a result of their sexual life, was the fact that they never had children. This mattered, so far as we know, especially to Eliot, and his later poetry was rife with references to hidden children.

❦

We cannot overestimate the importance of Eliot's first marriage. It was responsible for his decision to stay in England, in the teeth of the opposition of his family, and against all his own natural tendency to behave sensibly, rationally and responsibly. Staying and writing were what he partly wanted to do, but it was Vivien who demanded (and ensured) that he actually did it. As she wrote in 1922, 'I fought like mad to keep Tom here and stopped his going back to America.'[72]

She also did more to shake up and upset his existence than anything or anyone else ever did. To judge by his remarks at the time (and by what he subsequently wrote), she became more important to the writing of his major poetry than any other experience in his life, and other people who knew him drew the same conclusion: one close friend commented that Vivien, 'rather like Ezra [Pound], was an immense help to Eliot – to Eliot as a poet ... I doubt he'd ever have written *The Waste Land* if it hadn't been for Vivien'.[73] Eliot's sister-in-law Theresa, of whom he was very fond, commented grimly that 'Vivien ruined Tom as a man, but made him as a poet',[74] while a woman close to them both in the early 1930s, although terrified by Vivien, called her 'his muse all the same'.[75] And when his first substantial book of poems came out, he would inscribe the copy he gave to his wife for Christmas 1925: 'For my dearest Vivien / this book, which / no one else will / quite understand.'[76]

This was not because she had encouraged him to write. It is striking how, after his marriage, his poetry-writing suffered another of its periodical lapses;[77] as he put it in January 1916, 'I *hope* to write, when I have more detachment.' Vivien did, however, admire his work enormously, and his January 1916 letter continued: 'I have *lived* through material for a score of long poems, in the last six months.'[78] It was life with Vivien (he called it 'a wonderful life'), which made the difference. Naturally cautious and reserved – Virginia Woolf would describe his 'sensitive, shrinking, timid but idiosyncratic nature'[79] – Eliot had managed to marry someone outgoing, exciting, impulsive and careless, who laughed and wept and shouted and demanded, who was always ready to talk, and to play games in various accents and voices; who also loved – and was very skilled at – dancing; Eliot too learned to dance properly. He had always found it hard to quarrel with people, or to be blunt with them: Vivien recalled how 'He hates and loathes all sordid quarrelling and gossiping and intrigue and jealousy ... I have seen him go white and *be ill* at any manifestation of it.'[80] Vivien coped with such things without any difficulty. Eliot believed in firm, reasonable negotiation and diplomacy, and in the event of failure would give way to utter despair (in which state he would feel 'let the wolves get him'[81]). But Vivien told people (him included) exactly what she thought: she fought and struggled. She challenged him constantly, in particular his carefulness and restraint, his 'subtle, splitting mind',[82] his passivity and despairs, and people remembered this about her (and sometimes against her). She was sexually provocative, and made him feel and react: she saw to it that he '*lived* through' new experiences. I suspect that he first allowed himself to feel and show real anger with her, something he had previously always suppressed; later in his life, people were certainly aware of his capacity for savage rage. In 1933 he would write how our lives 'are mostly a constant evasion of ourselves', but it seems that, married to Vivien, he could not help confronting himself and those 'deeper, unnamed feelings which form the substratum of our being'.[83]

And as a writer he wanted, in fact, 'to capture those feelings which people can hardly even feel'.[84] It would be hard to imagine Eliot being able, for example, to write his prose poem 'Hysteria' – with its sexual fantasy of being both attracted and swallowed down by a laughing woman, into the 'dark caverns of her throat, bruised by the ripple of unseen muscles'[85] – if he had not married Vivien. Nor perhaps would he have set down the compellingly rhythmed lines of *Sweeney Agonistes* about the murderer who keeps the body of his victim 'With a gallon of lysol in a bath': 'This went on for a couple of months / Nobody came / And nobody went / But he took in the milk and he paid the rent.'[86] Such violent fantasies (among other things) were what life with Vivien encouraged him to articulate. His poetry stopped being full of beautifully shaped and self-defeating ironies; he found ways of writing about sex and violence, which carried on from his early poems 'The death of Saint Narcissus' and 'The Love Song of St Sebastian' but were now far less gothic and self-regarding. Such things suggest the huge discrepancy between the richness and excitement of what he felt at the time and what he came to write in the 1960s about the simple 'misery with Vivien'[87], which he experienced within a year of his marriage.

What effect their marriage might have had on Vivien is harder to gauge. In September 1915, she apparently felt that Eliot had 'tricked her imagination';[88] she had not only imagined he would be different, but believed that he had deceived her in *not* living up to her fantasy of him. She had married him, she said, in order to stimulate him, and this may very well have been something which Eliot himself had said to her, to explain why he wanted her. Ottoline Morrell, meeting Eliot for the first time in the spring of 1916, shrewdly suspected that he would need 'stimulants or violent emotions' of some kind to break open his straight-jacket of convention-ality,[89] and he may well have found Vivien both a stimulant and one who provoked violent emotions in him, although – to Ottoline – Vivien was only a 'frivolous, silly little woman'.[90] Russell did not actually believe that the Eliot marriage would last: 'I think that she will soon be tired of him.'[91] That was not true, however. For all her rages and difficulties (and Eliot's too), Vivien spent seventeen years married to Eliot. She was deeply impressed by him: 'Tom is *wonderful*,'[92] she wrote in June 1916. In spite of her regular anger with him, she gave herself up to him to a degree that actually alarmed her friends.[93]

But she did need ('at frequent intervals') time on her own: 'a sort of retirement', she called it.[94] She regularly went (or was sent) to the country or the seaside to try and recover; and this of course was very expensive. Russell, again, helped them out by paying for a hotel for them in Devon (he took care to join Vivien there while Eliot was still in London), and a couple of years later paid part of the rent for a cottage in Marlow. Vivien herself recalled how '*extraordinarily generous*' Russell had been to her, 'I mean in *giving* things'.[95] According to an understandably jealous Ottoline Morrell (whose lover Russell had previously been), he gave Vivien 'silk underclothes and all sorts of silly things, and pays for her dancing lessons'. The truth to Ottoline seemed to be that Russell 'likes to feel that she depends on him'.[96] The Eliots' lack of money was something that Eliot in particular found humiliating; and the other man's generosity must have been galling too.

❀

A mysterious subject is Eliot's relationship with Emily Hale, a young woman from Boston with whom he had acted in amateur dramatics in America in 1913. He had told her he loved her before he left for Europe in 1914 but at that time she did not share his feelings 'in any degree whatever';[97] he saw her again in the 1930s and 1940s, and corresponded with her for much of his life. In the 1960s, Eliot described how – when he married Vivien – he 'was still ... in love with Miss Hale'. On the other hand, he also immediately stated that he was not sure whether that was true: it might have been simply his response to his 'misery with Vivien'.[98] As we have none of their correspondence, it is almost impossible to say anything to the point about his relationship with Emily Hale before the 1930s.[99] He did (via Thayer) send her roses before she appeared on stage at the start of December 1914;[100] in 1916 he was taking a general interest in how she was. In 1919, he would tell a common friend how he wanted her to know how keenly interested he was 'in everything that happens to her'.[101] And he kept her letters, as she kept his. But they lost touch at times; on hearing from her in 1927, for example, Eliot remarked that he had not heard from her 'for years and years'.[102]

Following Lyndall Gordon – who argued that when Eliot married Vivien he was 'of course, in love with someone else',[103] that as late as 1952 he 'still loved Emily Hale',[104] that their relationship might be summed up as a 'love story',[105] and who structured her own first account of Eliot's life in the 1930s entirely around his feelings for Emily[106] – many recent scholars and biographers have seen Emily as the real, lost and secret love of Eliot's life. Ronald Schuchard, for example, has stated as a fact that Eliot's love for Emily was renewed no later than September 1923.[107]

It seems rather more likely that Emily Hale was just the kind of refined, humane, serious, fussy and intelligent New England woman whom, as a Harvard Professor, kindly, detached and inhibited, Eliot might well have married and with whom he might have had children: the woman whom Virginia Woolf encountered in November 1935 and described as a 'dull impeccable Bostonian lady',[108] and with whose insistencies Eliot would get so irritated in later years.[109] The whole point of Eliot's decision to stay in England was so that he could get away from conventional academic America, in order to devote himself to a career as a poet and a writer, and to be the awkward, unconventional, opinionated and in many ways uncomfortable outsider which he preferred being. In 1933 he would define the artist as the person who is 'heterodox when everyone else is orthodox, and orthodox when everyone else is heterodox': 'the perpetual upsetter of conventional values, the restorer of the real'.[110] Emily Hale – who would be a college-teacher all her working life – would have been an ideal wife for an orthodox academic; and if, a year after his difficult and at times tumultuous marriage to Vivien, Eliot had gone back to thinking of the sweeter and younger Emily with nostalgic tenderness, that would have been only natural.

And he may well have gone on mourning her loss: in retrospect, Emily would rather easily have become a symbol of what he felt he had given up by marrying Vivien. But we should remain suspicious of accounts of Eliot as a man who between 1914 and the early 1930s was 'really' in love with Emily Hale. The inscription from Dante that he put in the copy of *Ara Vos Prec*, which he sent to her in 1923 certainly suggests that he was now consciously going his own way:

> "... Commended to you to be my *Treasure*,
> in which I still live, and I ask no more."
> Then he turned round ...[111]

He was alive in his own work; but the last three words (preceding the moment when Brunetto vanishes out of sight) are a clear indication of the direction Eliot had now consciously taken, away from Emily Hale.

And back in 1915 his feelings for her – whatever they were – had played no part at all in what he wanted to do. With Vivien's strenuous support, he had decided against life in America; he intended to be a writer and in particular a poet. He would remark in February 1919 – thinking about his recently deceased father – that in his experience everybody (with the exception of simple fools) was 'warped or stunted'.[112] From his point of view, that was simply how people were, himself included. What mattered was what one did about it. And he had apparently succeeded in changing his whole way of life.

4

Literary life, Sweeney and other selves

E liot explained to Virginia Woolf in September 1920 that it had been a 'personal upheaval' which had led him to embark on his career as a poet; an 'upheaval' which had 'turned him aside from his inclination – to develop in the manner of Henry James'.[1] Such a development sounds an odd kind of career, though presumably it would have involved being a man of letters writing sensitive, ironic impressions of Europe for an American audience, growing ever more eminent and ever more conscious of the niceties of language ('I have a great admiration for him' Eliot had written about James in 1917[2]). What had actually happened to his career was that a potentially financially self-sufficient academic (and the author of a few clever poems) had turned almost overnight into a husband without career or financial support, for whom his work as a writer might be important, but who first simply needed to get a job. The 'personal upheaval' nevertheless suggests that what had happened inside him was what really counted.

To start with, all Eliot could do was go on working just to keep him and Vivien alive. For nearly two years, the Eliots survived on what he earned as a school-teacher and then on the little he earned as a writer and as an extension lecturer between the autumn of 1916 and the spring of 1917. He lectured in Yorkshire and also started to teach a course on Victorian Literature on Monday evenings in Southall. Pound, helpful as ever, included five of his poems in the oddly-titled *Catholic Anthology 1914–15*, published in November 1915, and by 1916 Eliot was starting to earn a little from reviewing and essay-writing. But what he brought in was nothing like enough to support the two of them in the style to which he and Vivien were accustomed. People like them expected a rented flat in a nice area of London, which would cost at least £65 a year (luckily Eliot's father was paying the rent), a maid who also cooked, and decent clothes. And Vivien's health was always particularly expensive in terms of doctor's bills and the cost of accommodation in places where she might go to recuperate; 'I am really a wretched crock, and always have been', she would remark early in 1918.[3] It looks as if nothing less than £300 a year would have made them comfortable, and with Vivien's £50 and Eliot's salary of £160 they would have fallen far short. To make matters worse, his teaching jobs (school and extension lecturing) made Eliot so tired that writing in the evenings, which he had planned to do, turned out to be very difficult – and poetry almost impossible. A few scraps apart, his next poem of any length written between June 1915 and March 1917 would be 'The Death of the Duchess', completed in September 1916: a London poem, drawing on Webster's *The Duchess of Malfi*, and moving between beautiful, gentle satire on the inhabitants of Hampstead ('in the evening, through lace curtains, the aspidestra [*sic*] grieves') and terrifying lines such as

> I should like to be in a crowd of beaks without words
> But it is terrible to be alone with another person.[4]

The poem turned out to be one of the thoughts-in-progress towards a long poem for which Eliot was now developing ideas, and he never tried to publish it; he simply kept its two manuscript pages for later.

❀

What he wrote, instead, was material designed to advance his career in the London literary world: mostly reviews of literature, though Russell got him some reviewing in the philosophical magazines *The Monist* and the *International Journal of Ethics*.[5] But Eliot also wrote reviews for the *Manchester Guardian*, the *New Statesman* and the *Westminster Gazette*, all of whom paid better than the philosophy journals, even though – within six months – he had broken with the *Westminster Gazette* on account of its editorial policy, and had written a satire on the editor for encouraging his readers to hate the Germans: readers who would thus be

... redeemed from heresies
And all their frowardness forget;
The scales are fallen from their eyes
Thanks to the Westminster Gazette.[6]

The poem remained unpublished, although shown to friends.[7] But in spite of its ephemeral usefulness, it was also significant as the first of Eliot's poems to be in quatrains: a form which he had never previously employed, but would use a lot during the next couple of years. The idea had come from Ezra Pound, who had seen what the French poet Théophile Gautier had done with the form, and had in his usual helpful way passed on the tip to Eliot.[8] The sweet simplicity of the quatrain (always rhyming the second and fourth lines, sometimes the first and third as well), combined with the outrageous things that could be said within the tightly controlled structure, is what makes the poems so striking. Eliot grasped at the idea joyfully; according to Vivien, in April 1917 he would write '*five*, most *excellent* poems in the course of one week'.[9] She was obviously reading avidly everything he wrote.

The Eliots' struggle to survive went on; their financial problems often in danger of dominating their lives. At the start of January 1917, Eliot tried asking his father for a year's rent in advance. One reason (the one he gave his father) was the possibility that the USA would shortly enter the war against Germany, and communication between the USA and England might become more difficult.[10] The other (which he did not give) was the fact that he and Vivien needed any money they could lay their hands on. During the autumn of 1916, Eliot had been lecturing as well as school-teaching, but it left him in no better state to write material that would help earn their living. He gave up teaching and their income plummeted. By the early spring of 1917 he had got into a state when (according to Vivien) 'he felt that life was simply not worth going on with',[11] and resorted to desperate measures. A friend of Vivien's family gave him an introduction to Lloyds Bank in the city of London, and on 19 March 1917 he took a post in the department dealing with foreign banking (his French and German came in handy), which initially paid £125 a year: 'not a princely salary, but there are good prospects of a rise as I become more useful'.[12]

It must have been with a heavy heart that he took such a job: one which offered him, as a writer, just two weeks holiday a year. After all, it had been his determination to be a writer that had kept him in England; wouldn't he have done better to have stayed in academe? Vivien also felt guilty: 'I shed *tears* over the thought of Tom going into a Bank!'[13] But Eliot was determined to make the best of it: 'It is a great satisfaction to me to have regular work, and I can do my own work much the better for it'.[14] He would also explain how he believed that 'regular work [was] good for people of nervous constitutions'[15] (i.e. people like himself). He was not the only one to be pleased; his father wrote a 'cheery little letter'[16] about his son's new career, doubtless happy that the boy had at last seen sense and got a proper job. It turned out that Eliot had a real aptitude for the work, and he also felt hugely relieved to have made secure at least some of the income he and Vivien needed. Nearly twenty years later, he would give the boys at his old school, Milton Academy, a piece of advice: 'Whatever you do ... don't whimper, but take the consequences'.[17] He and Vivien never made light of their troubles and as a result their letters often made most depressing reading; but Eliot was learning to take the consequences.

That summer of 1917 his contacts with Richard Aldington, a fellow poet about to join the army, led to the publication as *Prufrock and Other Observations* (the title a typical piece of dry wit)[18] of a volume of his poems by the Egoist Press – an offshoot of the *Egoist* magazine. It would have earned him almost nothing, the printing being secretly subsidised by Ezra Pound (who luckily got his money back later), but the reputation Eliot gained by it was extremely important. Eliot also took on the job of assistant editor for the magazine (once again it was Pound who saw to it that Eliot got the post – and himself paid half the salary of £36 a year). As well as working at the bank, he was continuing with his evening lecturing (now Mondays and Fridays), so reading a great deal as well as working extremely hard with editing and reviewing; while Vivien seemed to be ill more and more often. Eliot felt under enormous stress, trying to do so many jobs at once, as well as to do his writing whenever he could. In mid-June 1917, Vivien went to see Pound to explain why a piece promised for the *Little Review* had not appeared: 'Mrs Eliot has just been in ... says T.S.E. has done <u>no work</u> for weeks, that he returns from the bank, falls into a leaden slumber and remains there until bedtime'.[19] He and Vivien struggled on, both regularly collapsing with exhaustion; in December, Aldous Huxley described him appearing 'as haggard and ill-looking as usual'.[20]

Vivien had a brief affair with Russell in Surrey in October 1917.[21] She was spending nearly three weeks in the country cottage, for her health's sake; the affair may have been a way of trying to reassure herself that she was indeed still attractive to men (almost certainly the reason why Huxley had found her sexually so provocative earlier in the year). We must assume either that Eliot did not object to her relationship with Russell or (far more likely) that for the moment he knew nothing about it. But at some point late in 1917 or early in 1918, it seems that he *did* find out about the affair, and was horrified.[22] In the words of his poem 'Gerontion', 'After such knowledge, what forgiveness?' There are some further, haunting lines in his 1919 poem 'Gerontion', culminating in an unpleasant pun:

> I would meet you upon this honestly ...
> I have lost my passion: why should I need to keep it
> Since what is kept must be adulterated?[23]

Any passion which Eliot himself had ever experienced might then have felt pointless, what he retained having been 'adulter-ated' down to nothing by Vivien's adultery; in 1921 he would tell Virginia Woolf that 'humiliation is the worst thing in life'.[24] 'Gerontion' – the monologue of the aged man (one of Eliot's favourite poses) – is packed with sexual longings that now all belong to other people: it is the cautionary monologue of a man who, in old age, is taking care that nothing should ever again happen to him. His life is reduced to reflections in 'a sleepy corner': his one affair of the heart has come to 'lose beauty in terror, terror in inquisition' – which suggests a savage inquisition of an unhappy partner and also perhaps the loss of that partner. All that might have been loving has, at any rate, turned to recrimination. Later in 1919 Eliot would grimly refer in passing to the 'awful separation between potential passion and any actualization possible in life'.[25] He came to believe (when Vivien was no longer able to influence him) that his own preference was for 'ecstasy not of the flesh',[26] and his later contemptuous denunciations of sex may well have been directed back to Vivien's behaviour, first with him and then with Russell. Thirty years later, writing about what he called 'ordinary passion' in *The Cocktail Party*, he would have a character describe it as 'The mixture of motives that poison each other, / The leaping vanity, the recoiling disgust / And all that kind of thing'.[27] That actually sounds very unlike 'ordinary passion' indeed, and is deeply ironic or surprisingly revealing: perhaps both.

What he came to feel about Vivien was far more complex than righteous anger. There seems little doubt that he ended up hating himself for his original sexual attraction. He was already inclined to subscribe to a Bradleyan belief that experience – including 'external sensations', which would probably include sex – is entirely 'peculiar and private';[28] and a knowledge of Vivien's betrayal would have made him clam up still tighter, even if she had insisted to him – as she probably did – that it had been his own weariness and neglect which had driven her into the arms of another man.

❀

It has to be said, however, that this period also marked the start of Eliot's most brilliant period in his long career as a writer. The essays for which he is still best known as a critic – 'Reflections on Vers Libre' (1917), 'Tradition and the Individual Talent' (1919), 'Hamlet' (1919), 'The Metaphysical Poets' (1921), 'Andrew Marvell' (1921) and 'The Function of Criticism' (1923), all written between 1917 and 1923 – blazed with memorable ideas and phrases, were beautifully constructed and full of epigrammatic observations.

In the most famous of them all 'Tradition and the Individual Talent', Eliot had started to insist on the way in which a poet must 'develop or procure the consciousness of the past'[29] if he is to be a poet at all. He was making the point that knowledge of tradition actually enabled the poet to be contemporary: it was 'what makes a writer most acutely conscious of his place in time, of his own contemporaneity'.[30] In Eliot's own case, a tradition of romantic poetry had weighed upon his upbringing, as he had gone through the 'usual adolescent course with Byron, Shelley, Keats, Rossetti, Swinburne'.[31] His fascination with the poetry of the seventeenth century has been seen as his way of getting out of the clichés of romantic poetry into poetry where *thought* mattered as much as feeling. But it was also a way of seeing that he had other forbears, in another tradition, of intellectual and at times philosophical poetry, which paradoxically allowed him to feel he really belonged to the twentieth century, whereas the romantic tradition seemed to bind him irrecoverably to the past. (His extension lectures on Victorian and Modern Literature in the winter of 1917–18 would have made this still clearer to him.[32]) Eliot was not trying to put the clock back, in his stress on tradition: he wanted to alter the way we think about the past, and what we value about it, by becoming surer about what it is that we value in what he called 'the conscious present'.[33]

And in England between 1914 and 1923, Eliot managed to free himself from the romantic literary past while remaining unconstrained by the various fashionable artistic movements that came and went – Georgianism, Imagism, Vorticism, Dadaism. It was his prose that perhaps best allowed him to keep a level head about what he really valued in current writing, and the aspects of the past to which he felt loyal. He was able to do such work in spite of the state of his health or his marriage; the fact that Vivien believed so deeply in him and in his talents would have been an enormous help. She was, a friend remarked, 'a very intelligent listener';[34] she went to hear his lectures when he was giving them in London ('I enjoy them immensely'[35]) and she had confessed in 1916 that although she believed his prose 'very good', 'I look upon Tom's poetry as real genius'.[36]

※

By their own account, he and Vivien simply stumbled on through the winter and into the spring of 1918; Vivien told a friend how 'Tom is impossible at present – very American and obstinate!'[37] He was by now engaged in yet another new kind of verse writing, one based on the previous year's quatrain experiments, but with a new force and offensiveness: very American writing, in its own way, and – as usual – untouched by fashion.

It is clear from the early part of Eliot's life that he had always enjoyed risqué jokes, obscene writing, smoking-room talk; the Columbo and Bolo poems were still in his old notebook, along with bits of the interminable Tinker. Between 1917 and 1927 he felt obliged to articulate in his poetry some most unsavoury characters, ideas and experiences. His poem 'The Waste Land' would offer, for example, only depressing, violent or loathsome sexual experiences; and Eliot would insist that his 1917 poem 'Burbank with a Baedeker, Bleistein with a Cigar' was *very serious!*'[38] despite the way that it demonstrates a lucid and deeply unpleasant anti-Semitism in locating the Jew Bleistein in 'the protozoic slime'.[39] It has been argued that it is the character Burbank in the poem who is guilty of the anti-Semitism, not the poem (or the poet).[40] But even that unconvincing argument cannot defend the version of Bleistein given in 'Dirge', probably scrawled out by Eliot in Margate in November 1921, in which the body of the Jew is seen disintegrating under water so that his teeth ('gold in gold') come into view.[41] Eliot did not like Jews, and though the list of those he did not like in early twentieth century society would be a long one, there can be no doubt that – by the standards of the word coined in the 1880s – these lines are anti-Semitic.

❀

Anthony Julius offered a double-pronged attack on Eliot, which was the subtler for disguising its attack as a species of admiration. In his 1995 book, he argued that

(1) Eliot wrote anti-Semitic poetry and prose, which makes him an anti-Semite; (2) Eliot's anti-Semitic poetry is original and imaginative, and therefore cannot be dismissed as an inconsequential blemish in his oeuvre.[42]

Critics who have argued with Julius have mostly come off a poor second,[43] because they have engaged with him on the grounds of Julius's own choosing: an unwise procedure when dealing with a man whose trade is argument. I prefer to ask whether the author of undoubtedly anti-Semitic lines in poems should so simply be called the author of anti-Semitic poetry, and whether his composition of such things makes him an anti-Semite. Julius takes the answers to such questions for granted, and would, I am sure, accuse me of pedantry. But if I were to argue that a poem were – for example – depressing, or uplifting, it would not be enough for me to point to gloomy or cheerful lines in it, and take for granted that my case was proved. The whole poem has to point in the direction of the description; a depressing poem must have an overall effect, to justify such a description of it. We need to ask whether Eliot's so-called 'anti-Semitic poems' really *are* – as poems – anti-Semitic. To deal with the poems which Julius puts in the dock,[44] I would say that 'Burbank' is, that 'Dirge' is, that 'Gerontion' is not, that 'Sweeney Among the Nightingales' and 'A Cooking Egg' are certainly not. Although Julius's arguments against 'Burbank' are clear and coherent, those against 'Sweeney Among the Nightingales' are based on a series of misreadings and assertions.[45] The anti-Semitic lines in 'Gerontion' are nasty but their presence does not infiltrate or colour the rest of the poem. They do not make the poem anti-Semitic. Julius puts them all in the same category, which is unwise if he wishes his arguments to be taken seriously. Classing them together makes him look as if his desire to obtain Eliot's conviction for anti-Semitism were greater than his desire to read the poetry honestly.

Julius has thus left himself vulnerable to having his case dismissed – or not taken seriously – because he attempted to convict Eliot on too broad a range of work, and because he assumed that Eliot held fixed beliefs and wrote from particular points of view, which his poetry inevitably demonstrated. Julius deserves credit for having shown – with a great deal of historical context – just how offensive and anti-Semitic 'Burbank with a Baedeker, Bleistein with a Cigar' is. But even such things would not make Eliot an anti-Semitic poet unless he had written a body of anti-Semitic poetry. He published one anti-Semitic poem, and another ('Dirge') survived among papers which he did not intend to publish. He made anti-Semitic remarks in a number of places, all of them before the second world war; like many of his contemporaries, he was unthinkingly anti-Semitic, and at times thinkingly so. To turn those facts into the conclusion (or assumption) that he was an anti-Semitic *writer* is wrong.

Eliot's poetry (including 'Burbank with a Baedeker, Bleistein with a Cigar') is however significant because it expressed its feelings – not its points of view, nor its ideas, which were always a great deal less clear than one might expect from a near-professional philosopher – with great clarity and (frequently) violence. It is not surprising that Eliot has been called 'one of the most subjective and daemonic poets who ever lived'.[46] The vivid unpleasantness of the feelings in Eliot's poetry of the period (unpleasant in all kinds of ways which have nothing to do with anti-Semitism: about women, about sex, about class, about the body, as well as about Jews) is one of the most interesting things about it. Such violence was – interestingly – mostly confined to his poetry, which was where he allowed (or wanted) everything to show, and little was inhibited: indeed, the poetry is at times offensive to an extraordinary degree. He created characters, he voiced lines and articulated rhythms which were spoken out of various states of mind, morality and emotion, none of which can be held up as articles of his own unquestioned faith, but some of which were certainly his own, many of which he innately (if not consciously) sympathised with, and all of which in some way he felt. Whether they were expressions of a set of beliefs is quite another matter. Julius assumes that they were. I do not.

❄

Three new poems in 1918 carried on Eliot's newfound, ribald, offensive tradition. To add to 'Burbank with a Baedeker, Bleistein with a Cigar', in 1918 Eliot developed the vicious, amoral and sensual character Sweeney – 'Apeneck Sweeney'[47] as he is called in 'Sweeney Among the Nightingales' – his name perhaps deriving from the nineteenth-century melodrama figure of Sweeney Todd, the demon barber, perhaps from a childhood fantasy ('WHEN OTHERS FAIL / COME TO / DR SWEANY D. D. / INSOMNIA'[48]), perhaps from the simple occurrence of the name in everyday life (there had been two men called Sweeney in Eliot's year at Harvard).[49] Eliot's Sweeney first appeared in the last stanza of 'Mr. Eliot's Sunday Morning Service', seen shifting 'from ham to ham / Stirring the water in his bath.'[50] This wholly prosaic, entirely sensual figure is juxtaposed with very different kinds of being: 'masters of the subtle schools' who are 'controversial, polymath.' And it is Sweeney who is more compelling. In 1934, Eliot would teasingly remark that 'I think of him as a man who in younger days was perhaps a professional pugilist, mildly successful, who then grew older and retired to keep a pub',[51] and there have been efforts to associate him with Eliot's Irish boxing instructor from Harvard days.[52] (Vivien Eliot probably betrayed a more accurate knowledge of his origins in a sly remark in Eliot's magazine the *Criterion* in 1925, when – as 'Feiron Morris' – she asked 'did Mr Eliot ... deduce Sweeney from observations in a New York bar-room?'[53]) James Joyce's Leopold Bloom (first made public in the 'Calypso' episode of *Ulysses* which appeared in the *Little Review* in June 1918) would – if he did not actually provoke Sweeney – have confirmed to Eliot the literary fascination of the *homme moyen sensuel*, even though Sweeney is a great deal more violent than Bloom.

Sweeney then reappeared as the title figure of two of Eliot's quatrain poems, 'Sweeney Among the Nightingales' and 'Sweeney Erect', both written in 1918. 'Apeneck Sweeney' might appear an unlikely creation for a serious, philosophical writer but Bolo or Columbo would have claimed him as a relation immediately. In 'Sweeney Erect' he is fully, forcefully, compellingly described: 'This withered root of knots of hair': 'This oval O cropped out with teeth'.[54] This kind of creation was like nothing Eliot had done before: not just witty but bursting with satire in a deeper (and older) sense: truly satyrical. Such a poetic creation seems characteristic of the writer Virginia Woolf saw and described in 1922 as 'sardonic, guarded, precise, & slightly malevolent'.[55] It is easy to overlook the craft of the writing: 'Knows the female temperament / And wipes the suds around his face'[56] is a small masterpiece just by itself, drawing upon a nineteenth-century cliché about the female[57] but adjusting it to Sweeney's wholly unimaginative knowingness about women. The title 'Sweeney Erect' alludes to Emerson's remark that the self-reliant man 'rights himself, stands in the erect position,'[58] but the poem's erect hero is first seen crawling out of bed: a woman still in the bed is described as epileptic. That is doubtless the Sweeney attitude to a woman reduced to screaming helplessness.[59] The sound which the woman makes alarms and excites the women who immediately come out into the corridor, rather hoping that what they have heard is the sound of an orgasm, but politely using the word 'hysteria'.[60] The poem had started in the grand manner, with instructions to a tapestry maker to depict the details of Theseus' abandonment of Ariadne. But the Sweeney domestic scene has been a great deal more powerful than the language's parodic attempts at the impressive, which are help-lessly dogged rather than superb. The fabled lovers Ariadne and Theseus are also less appropriate parallels for Doris and Sweeney than Nausicaa and Polyphemus in Eliot's poem, virginal charmer and one-eyed monster of the Odyssey.

Such a poem reminds us of the extreme complexity of Eliot's position as a poet, and confirms the way in which he was prepared to let his poetry explore things that his prose (and his prosier self) were primarily concerned to inhibit. Sweeney is a comic character in a very old tradition, one whose pose his creator thoroughly enjoys personifying; but he is also (as Eliot confessed) an ominous portent. He invented an utterly characteristic aphorism by Emerson[61] to sum up the extent to which Sweeney can be seen as us, in our age; the bogus aphorism suggesting the shadow lengthening as human beings grow taller, more developed, more advanced – but with straddling Sweeney putting a stop to any such confident progress. As Eliot commented sardonically in a review of

A History of American Literature published in April 1919, 'Neither Emerson nor any of the others was a real observer of the moral life.'[62] That was what *he* hoped to be, preferring to believe that the excesses of his poetry grew out of what he called 'the damage of a lifetime', resulting from 'having been born into an unsettled society'. Such damage, he suggested, constantly infiltrated 'the moment when one writes'.[63]

Eliot considered his two Sweeney poems 'as serious as anything I have ever written' and – compared with his early poetry – 'much more serious as well as more mature'. The only people who agreed with him, he said, were his wife Vivien and the poet W. B. Yeats.[64] Modern critics have preferred to see poems like 'Sweeney Among the Nightingales' as 'something of a digression from his poetic career',[65] a career in which Eliot's metaphysically anxious and questioning poetry of 1914 would naturally link up with the thoughtful religious poetry he published from 1930 onwards. I suggest that exactly the opposite is true: that the quatrain poems, with their violent images and energies, are not only just as important and a great deal more accessible, but actually a great deal more central to Eliot's achievement as a poet. When he described the importance of Donne's poetry in 1926, he wrote about it in terms that he had learned from writing his own. Words like 'a strange kaleidoscope of feeling, with suggested images, suggested conceits' actually fit his Sweeney poems better than they do Donne: 'the feeling is always melting, changing, into another feeling', 'every image has a peculiar feel to it'.[66] The Sweeney poems represent a real experiment in Eliot's career; was it possible to write serious poetry that contained the energy, ribaldry and laughter of ancient Greek comedy?[67] Seriously funny poetry was almost unknown in modern England. The poetry invites us to know as Sweeney knows, and to feel as Sweeney feels: and that means sympathising with a character who, in the drama which Eliot eventually wrote for him, possesses a wonderfully insinuating, attractive, compelling voice: the rhythms see to that.

'Sweeney Among the Nightingales' also starts to answer the question 'where does sensuality go, in Eliot's poetry?' At times – most of the time, not all of the time – it goes into violence. In spite of Eliot's few and lyrical moments of tender nostalgia and regret in his poetry, often linked with the touch of hair – 'Her hair over her arms and her arms full of flowers', 'Your arms full, and your hair wet', 'Blown hair is sweet, brown hair over the mouth blown'[68] (none of those lines written after 1930) – the sensual in Eliot's quatrain poetry is violent, arbitrary, amoral, compelling, and – in its power to disgust – thoroughly to be relished. So, for example, the woman who has tried to attract Sweeney, 'Reorganised upon the floor', 'yawns and draws a stocking up'.[69] The organs that get 'reorganised' on the floor seem at least preponderantly sexual; the fact that the woman's stocking comes up rather than down is – like the deliberate yawn – only a further enticement. The poem is also a *tour de force* of control, with its last eight stanzas formed out of a single sentence. The 'nightingales' with whom Sweeney associates himself are perhaps prostitutes, perhaps just Sweeney's further fantasies of women whom he has reduced to helpless orgasm.

The last stanza however returns us to the Greek tragedy suggested in the epigraph, where Agamemnon is murdered for unfaithfulness. In this poem his shroud is horribly, grotesquely stained with bird droppings: the same nightingales, perhaps, which were heard 'In ancient days by emperor and clown' (Keats's poem 'Ode to a Nightingale' is never very far away).[70] The famously 'liquid' song of the ever-so-romantic bird here mutates into 'siftings' deriving from the other end altogether.[71]

The poetry, although so clear in one sense, is also difficult in ways that Eliot himself knew. When Virginia Woolf told him in 1920 that she thought it hard because he 'wilfully' concealed the transitions between one thought and another, he responded that 'explanation is unnecessary. If you put it in, you dilute the facts. You should feel these without explanation'.[72] What he stressed, as usual, was the way in which readers *feel* the poetry, not how they comprehend it.

It is in these poems that Eliot's serious playfulness surpasses itself. The quatrain poems are neither domestic fun (like his youthful poems) nor ingeniously obscene (like Columbo and Bolo) but stage an enigmatic, violent, grotesque comedy. Eliot would tell Virginia Woolf in 1920 that his 'turn' was 'for caricature', though he found it hard to convey his precise meaning: 'I dont mean satire'. But he impressed her with his desire 'to describe externals',[73] and that is what he does. Bizarre worlds are conjured up, vivid individuals depicted very precisely ('Rachel *née* Rabinovitch / Tears at the grapes with murderous paws'[74]); feelings of apprehension and violence and danger are powerfully created. Eliot greatly enjoyed the contrast he was able to enact between the upper-middle-class self he enjoyed being ('He's always told the proper lies / And always done the proper thing'[75]) and the shocking, witty and thoroughly unbuttoned self he also enjoyed being, and enjoyed being perceived as by those of his friends with whom he was prepared to be unbuttoned. These were in particular Conrad Aiken and Ezra Pound: in 1922 he wondered whether Joyce might be added to the list.[76] There was also an exhibitionist pose implicit in the production of such Sweeney verses: as if he were saying that he was not just the dry stick people took him for, not simply Mr Eliot the banker at Lloyds, 'with his features of clerical cut, / and his brow so grim / and his mouth so prim',[77] but instead full of outrageousness, suppressed violence and animosity.[78]

❀

All three of the new poems would first appear in collections of Eliot's work; publishing his material was more than ever important, if he were one day to get out of the bank. By the summer of 1918 Eliot himself was hoping for a book of his prose and poems to come out with Knopf in the USA, but his troubles were by no means at an end. This publication took two years to arrange (with the originally planned prose being shed en route), and money (with wartime prices) in England seemed shorter than ever: as Vivien told Eliot's brother, 'We were off our heads all the summer.'[79] By the time the poems came out in America, Eliot would have had published in

England both a small book of his new poems and another book bringing together all his old work and all his recent poetic work.

The second half of 1918 was, however, complicated by his efforts to ensure that – if he were to be conscripted into the American military, as seemed likely – he would not be drafted and sent abroad, leaving Vivien almost penniless and having to fend for herself. Eliot had accordingly tried for a position in the Intelligence Service, and late in October actually resigned from the Bank in order to take up the promise of a non-combatant post in US Navy Intelligence, based in London, 'with a fairly good salary'. But, as he put it, 'Everything turned to red tape in my hands'[80] – and by the time the problems were sorted out, he had lost two weeks salary at the Bank, and the war had come to an end, on 11 November 1918. He went back to the Bank, and as a sign of his value to them his salary was raised to £360 a year shortly afterwards.

But his health was not good and Vivien continued to be worried about him; she had written to his brother Henry late in October 1918 of how 'life is so feverish and yet so dreary at the same time', and that she was distressed how restless her husband was: 'For *months* now, I have waited for T. to be settled'.[81] But things went from bad to worse. In mid-December 1918, Vivien was obliged to get him 'to sign a contract with me' in which he promised – for three months – to do no writing of any kind, except what was necessary for his weekly extension lecture (he was now teaching Elizabethan literature), and no reading except for poetry and novels (and for the lecture).[82] As a result, he had to cut back on the work he had been doing for the *Egoist* and – of course – on poetry.

And then – rather suddenly, on 7 January 1919 – Henry Ware Eliot died. Only the day before, without any knowledge that his father had not been well, Eliot had written to an American friend about his desire to get into print the book which Knopf was currently considering, in order to show his parents what he had been doing since 1915 and to satisfy them 'that I have not made a mess of my life, as they are inclined to believe'.[83] And now he would never be able to prove it to his father; while Knopf's decision to reject the book meant that he could not yet demonstrate it to his mother either. It had been a 'very hard winter to get through'[84] and would turn into a grim spring. To make matters worse, his father's will ensured that family property which Eliot inherited would not, in the event of Eliot's death, go to Vivien: it would revert to his family in America. This was a straightforward snub to Vivien as well as to Eliot: he was the only child whom his father treated in such a way. 'My father disapproved of my residence in England'[85] was Eliot's cool summary of his father's behaviour.

His literary reputation, all the same, was continuing to grow. As an unconscripted American he had had the considerable advantage of having worked in London throughout the war, when most Englishmen of his age had either been in the forces or (in one way or another) on the run; and, unlike Ezra Pound, he had not constantly made enemies. At times he had written most of the *Egoist* himself; it was not surprising that, when literary life began to re-establish itself in London in the course of 1919, Eliot was someone whose reputation quickly burgeoned. As he pointed out in April 1918, 'I am getting to know and be known by all the intelligent or important people in letters'.[86] The critic and author John Middleton Murry – who had also not been conscripted – had managed to get himself appointed to run the magazine the *Athenaeum* as a primarily literary and artistic weekly; and in March 1919 he asked Eliot to become assistant editor, on a salary of £500 a year, saying (Eliot reported) 'he would rather have me than anyone in England'.[87] That was an indication of how far Eliot had come.

Eliot eventually refused the position (given Vivien's state of health, he preferred to stick with the security of the Bank salary and pension: the *Athenaeum* contract was only for two years). But in the spring of 1919 he finally gave up the extension lecturing he had been doing since the autumn of 1916, and started to do a lot of writing of influential essays for the *Athenaeum* – nineteen pieces have been counted from 1919 alone – and to continue reviewing: Ronald Schuchard argues that we cannot underestimate 'the cumulative influential effect of his reviews, almost a hundred in number, on contemporary criticism'.[88] All this had such an effect that, in the autumn of 1919, he was asked by Bruce Richmond to write for the *Times Literary Supplement*. This was an even greater honour. His leading articles (unsigned of course: but everyone in literary circles knew who had written them) were judicious, clever and far-sighted; they cemented his reputation as a man who, he told his mother, had 'far more *influence* on English letters than any other American has ever had, unless it be Henry James'.[89]

❁

This of course makes especially interesting the poetry Eliot had come back to writing – controlled, forceful, disturbing and resonant, quite different from the quatrains he had written in 1917 and 1918. His poetry remained the one place where he could, as it were, be at home and voice what otherwise seemed an entangled mess of hopes, failures and limited successes. To write it, he had to break his contract with Vivien *not* to write; but it was February 1919 before he started, so the three months were nearly up.

'Gerontion' was in many ways a trial run for the big poem that Eliot had been incubating for years: a first person monologue, though from someone not a bit like 'Prufrock'; and deeply influenced by the Elizabethan dramatic writing in which Eliot was now soaked. The lines in fact exemplify 'that perpetual slight alteration of language' which Eliot had praised in Tourneur and Middleton: 'words perpetually juxtaposed in new and sudden combinations, meanings perpetually *eingeschaltet* into meanings' – and which he argued 'evidences a very high development of the senses'.[90] The poem's insistent references to Christianity ('The tiger springs in the new year'), its startling meditations on desire ('the giving famishes the craving'), its complex texture ('deceives with whispering ambitions') all play on 'the senses'. Such lines also add up to a refusal to compromise with readers' preference for clear sense and logical development. What is radical is the poem's technique of presenting a pitiless version of life which is '*not* actually coherent'. The fact that Eliot thought it could stand as a kind of preface to his later poem 'The Waste Land' (in January 1922 he was continuing to ask Pound about the wisdom of adding it on) shows how he believed that the one poem led to the other.

❀

What was especially striking was that – after finishing 'Gerontion' – Eliot does not seem either to have drafted or to have written a single poem for almost two years: February 1919 to January 1921. Though there had been gaps in his poetic work before, there had not been such a dramatic pause since he had been a teenager. It may have been the first of the three occasions during his life when he became convinced 'that I should never again be able to write anything worth reading'.[91] But what was emerging at a deep level was his most famous piece of writing. Over the years since 1913 he had at times drafted lines and passages like those in 'The Death of the Duchess', and had kept the fragments on one side: 'doing things separately'[92] as he called it. But not until July 1919 did he see what he much later called 'the possibility of fusing them together, altering them, and making a kind of whole of them'.[93] The peculiarly unstable 'whole' which began to come together in the spring of 1921 would be the poem that finally made his reputation: 'The Waste Land'.

5

'The Waste Land'

In spite of his achievements, Eliot continued to feel horribly ill and run-down during the late summer and autumn of 1919 – Vivien told her friend Mary Hutchinson in July that 'Tom is *IM*possible – full of nerves, really not well, very bad cough, very morbid and grumpy'[1] – but by November 1919 he believed that he was at last going 'to get started on a poem that I have in mind'.[2] However, he didn't. Although Ezra Pound knew by the summer of 1920 that Eliot was contemplating something 'longer and more serious',[3] in September 1920 it remained only 'a poem that I have in mind', and – still with no other poetry having got itself written since 'Gerontion' – a month later it was still no more than 'a poem I have in mind'. Even when it was partly on paper in May 1921, Eliot referred to it yet again as 'in mind'.[4]

Such references are unique. The poem had remained inescapably both *on* and *in* his mind for years: the fact that, decades later, he would describe his marriage to Vivien as having 'brought the state of mind out of which came *The Waste Land*' suggests that the long-considered poem may not just have resulted from the marriage but, to some extent, was about it too. Eliot would nevertheless have kept such a possibility obscure, even to himself. As he once remarked about poetic incubation, 'we do not know until the shell breaks what kind of egg we have been sitting on'.[5] Or, more generally: 'One wants to get something off one's chest. One doesn't know quite what it is that one wants to get off the chest until one's got it off'.[6] A play was different. That might, for example, be started 'by an act of choice: I settle upon a particular emotional situation'.[7] And an essay could be planned to coincide with a deadline. But Eliot continued to believe that a poem and the feelings in it should be things 'over the development of which he has, as a poet, no control'.[8] This was not a latter-day romanticism. It has sensibly been suggested that 'Eliot was a primitivist as well as a sophisticate, a writer who made guerrilla raids on the collective unconscious. For all his intellectualism, he was averse to rationality.'[9] In 1918, like any primitivist, he had actually prioritised 'thinking with our feelings';[10] he wondered in 1919 how many people would admit to the fact that 'their keenest ideas come to them with the quality of a sense perception'.[11] He would have hoped that – like Tennyson – his feelings 'were more honest than his mind';[12] which was yet another reason not to enquire too deeply into a prospective poem, which he once called 'that dark embryo' within the poet.[13]

For his failure to start writing 'The Waste Land' before 1921, Eliot blamed his efforts to complete his book *The Sacred Wood* (a compilation of the essays he had been writing for periodicals), the months of flat hunting which he and Vivien endured in 1920, then the disturbance occasioned by moving, then the serious illness of Vivien's father and finally Vivien's own continuing bad health.

But he may well also have suspected that the poem was going to foreground anger and disgust with sex, as well as despair about recent history: he was 'greatly distressed' by the 'disorder' of society.[14] It was also going to be a poem written out of a very special kind of experience. He summarised this many years later when describing the moments 'when a man may be nearly crushed by the terrible awareness of his isolation from every other human being': a state of being 'alone with himself and his meanness and futility, alone without God'.[15] He called this the experience of 'dispossession'. The two occasions he recalled from his own life were both of 'dispossession by the dead', when a vivid experience of the past (and of the hordes of unknown dead) became overwhelming: it led to a feeling of utter isolation. He had undergone such an experience at Périgueux in France in August 1919 – he suddenly announced to Pound a few days later, at Excideuil, 'I am afraid of the life after death'[16] – and another such experience had come earlier, at Marlow.[17] Together with Bertrand Russell, the Eliots had rented 31, West Street, Marlow from December 1917, and though attempts have been made to link the experience of dispossession with Eliot's discovery (probably early in 1918[18]) of Vivien's adultery with Russell, there is nothing to support that explanation and a good deal against. An experience of 'dispossession by the dead' has very little to do with anger over a wife's adultery.

Eliot subsequently wrote about the experience of dispossession on a number of occasions. In *The Family Reunion*, Harry describes 'that sense of separation, / Of isolation unredeemable, irrevocable';[19] in 'East Coker', Eliot imagined the 'fear of possession' of old men, 'Of belonging to another, or to others, or to God'.[20] Being 'possessed' – taken over, completely, so that you are dispossessed of your old self and attachments – is terrifying but (for Eliot after 1927) would have been the only real solution to life's problems. In 1940, he would go so far as to announce that 'You must go by the way of dispossession'.[21] That 'way' involved Christian conversion. But long before he counted himself a believer, such experiences of 'dispossession' without any accompanying 'possession' by God had mattered intensely, as some of the central experiences in his life: he desperately wanted to write about them in his poetry.

It was in the winter after his Périgueux experience that he started thinking seriously about 'The Waste Land', but the way in which that poem had been 'in mind' so long meant that when its 'shell' began to crack, early in 1921, it came relatively fast. Like 'Gerontion', it used powerful rhythms, sharply defined individual lines and clearly focused images which often had no obvious relationship with each other (not for nothing had Ezra Pound called 'imagism' the kind of modern poetry of which he especially approved). Attempts to demonstrate how the poem is an artistic whole underrate the extent to which its vision of contemporary life depends upon its experiences (that is, our experiences as readers) *not* being coherent: not, in fact, being our own at all. Its author has 'left out something which the reader is used to finding', and the resulting problem is not solved if the bewildered reader 'puzzles his head for a kind of "meaning" which is not there, and is not meant to be there'.[22]

Instead, as readers of Part I, we are left to realise the horror of being entirely alone in the world, subjected to the multitudes of voices and impressions which afflict the sensitive mind 'on an ordinary day', as Virginia Woolf would describe them in 1925: the 'myriad impressions – trivial, fantastic, evanescent, or engraved with the sharpness of steel'.[23] Vivien Eliot's own account of feeling herself 'beaten upon and worn by the most ordinary amount of human intercourse' suggests that hers was exactly the kind of sensibility for which Eliot was writing.[24] The poem's 'myriad impressions' are at times entirely commonplace – 'Had a bad cold, nevertheless', 'A crowd flowed over London bridge'[25] – but they are insistently, not to say ostentatiously cultural; and it is as if, for the contemporary sensibility, thousands of years of European culture added up to no more than a few quotations. They create no vital link with the past, they lead to no sense of *belonging*. They are just random scraps. '*Öd und leer das Meer*' – 'a handful of dust' – 'I had not thought death had undone so many' – 'hypocrite lecteur!'[26] Social life sounds absurd ('One must be so careful these days'), tender longing ('when we came back late from the hyacinth garden, / Your arms full, and your hair wet') turns to nothing but loneliness, prophetic invitation ('Come in under the shadow of this red rock') is frightening, while violence, as in the Sweeney poems, is comic, grotesque and ubiquitous

('That corpse you planted last year in your garden / Has it begun to sprout?')[27]

Our experience as readers is to realise that we cannot make sense of such voices and impressions. We would like to believe ourselves the heirs of history, literature and culture, but (as in 'Gerontion') we are primarily aware of the past as 'A heap of broken images'[28] and our heads ring mostly with echoes. To use Eliot's own words, we are both 'dissociated'[29] and 'dispossessed' from even the possibility of coherence or meaning or attachment. It has been argued that 'The meaning of a poem for Eliot was a fairly trifling matter';[30] he once suggested that the meaning of some kinds of poem was akin to the 'bit of nice meat' the burglar provides for the house-dog, to keep it diverted and quiet.[31] A 'meaning' might keep the reader diverted and quiet, too, unaware of what the poem was really doing. For

> In true symbolist fashion, Eliot was interested in what a poem did, not in what it said – in the resonance of the signifier, the echoes of its archetypes, the ghostly associations haunting its grains and textures, the stealthy, subliminal workings of its unconscious ...[32]

The genius of this particular Eliot poem lies in the way it turns what he once called the 'personal emotion'[33] of its writer into a feeling for its readers of pitiless desolation and isolation. As he would say about Donne (but had realised about himself), 'the personality' of the poet was really the 'only thing that holds his poems, or any one poem, together'.[34] John Berger has suggested that 'the personal drama of an artist reflects within half a century the crisis of an entire civilization.'[35] Eliot thought it happened a great deal faster; that the really good poet, 'writing himself, writes his time.'[36] Readers of 'The Waste Land' find themselves transfixed by a question like 'What are the roots that clutch'.[37] Such roots barely exist, let alone clutch, among the stony rubbish which is both Europe in the aftermath of the war and a state of mind: but the phrase brings 'what is ordinarily apprehensible only by thought ... within the grasp of feeling'.[38] It provides 'the emotional equivalent' of what Eliot would describe in 1926 as 'highly abstract or generalised ideas'.[39]

Part II foregrounds Cleopatra and the extravagance of the past, in a kind of 'stiffened replica of Elizabethan narrative',[40] but once again the past (both rich and absurd) metamorphoses into a perception of it as no more than 'withered stumps of time'. In the modern era, a couple who sound very like Vivien and Eliot are talking. 'Speak to me', the woman says: 'Why do you never speak. Speak. / What are you thinking of? What thinking? What?'[41] The man's voice races into private recollections which – although allusive – in no way help their situation ('I remember / The hyacinth garden. Those are pearls that were his eyes'[42]). Set against them, people of a lower class argue in a pub; their language may be more fluent (Eliot claimed that it was 'pure Ellen Kellond' – their maid[43]), but it is also simply anecdotal: and it too runs into the sand. The part-title 'A Game of Chess' suggests the patterned moves and the wholly circumscribed area for manoeuvre of both sets of people. Vivien scrawled 'WONDERFUL' in the margin of the typescript, and then 'Yes', '& wonderful', 'wonderful' on the next page;[44] she at least was convinced that Eliot was capturing their particular post-war moment, via the 'different voices' within and surrounding their own marriage.

It was probably the 'Circe' section of James Joyce's novel *Ulysses*, which Eliot had seen in May 1921 (reading it was partly responsible for his comment at the start of June that 'Ulysses ... is prodigious'[45]), that led to Part I acquiring its own long, comic opening narrative (entirely modern and urban – and incidentally American); and at some point after typing up parts I and II, Eliot added the subtitle 'He Do the Police in Different Voices',[46] to stress the dramatic nature of the poem's comic narratives and individual voices. He had hoped that by June 1921 the poem would be in something like its final form, but it was not finished, despite being now about 170 lines long. Eliot cheerfully referred to it as 'a little poem, which I am at present engaged on.'[47]

❧

That was the state of affairs early in June, when Eliot's mother Charlotte, sister Marian and his brother Henry arrived on a long-planned visit to England. Eliot had hoped to travel to America immediately after the war, but a major problem was that – at the bank – even after promotion, he only had three weeks holiday a year. An American journey would have been a terrible rush: five days at sea, two weeks with his family, five more days at sea, back to work. And although we have almost no direct evidence of how Charlotte actually behaved to Vivien, a sentence from a letter Eliot wrote to his brother Henry in February 1920 shows why he might have been keen to delay. He took it for granted that – if he and Vivien were to visit America together – 'mother would never see her'.[48] He did not express this with any particular anger or surprise, simply as a fact to take account of. His mother believed that Vivien had wrecked her son's life by marrying him, and would have preferred to have nothing to do with her. In his surviving letters to his mother, it is striking how often Eliot defends Vivien, or points out how well she has behaved, or suggests how loving she is. He takes a brief holiday on his own, and Vivien falls ill, but she does not tell him how she is, 'so as not to diminish my pleasure in the trip'.[49] They get stuck on a sandbank when out boating with friends: Eliot tells his mother 'Vivien is splendid in a boat, she took off her stockings and jumped off and tried to push'.[50] And then, writing to his mother in January 1920, he slips in the sentence 'I believe she thinks every day about you.'[51] At every turn it is clear how conscious he is of his mother's scepticism about Vivien, and he constantly does what looks like an unavailing best for her. In *The Family Reunion*, written many years later when he was no longer defensive about Vivien, Eliot has a man's mother say decisively, about her unloved daughter-in-law, 'She never would have been one of the family'.[52] That sounds remarkably like the real Charlotte Eliot.

The family's visit to England in 1921 was therefore a

particular problem. It was Eliot's first reunion with them since his catastrophic visit home in the summer of 1915; he had long been desperate to see his mother again, telling her in January 1920 that he was 'frantically eager'[53] to see her, and a few weeks later – in a letter written the same day as he took it for granted that she would not see Vivien in America – he wrote urging her to come to England, and asked her if she could not 'settle down for a time and *live* with us?' He went on to insist that if he could not see her for a proper visit, he would '*never* be really happy to the end of my life'.[54] For a man of thirty-one who had been married for five years, that was a striking statement, but he repeated it on at least three other occasions.[55]

Eliot could not persuade his mother to '*live* with us'. She and his sister went one better; they took over the Eliots' 'cool and civilised' flat (and servant) in Clarence Gate Gardens for three months. Eliot and Vivien (and Henry when he arrived) had to squat in a sequence of borrowed rooms and flats (one an oppressive 'attic with a glass roof'). Vivien spent all the time she could in the country.

The visit was a huge problem for Vivien. She had under-standably always resented the attitude of the Eliot family towards her; they had now dispossessed her of her home, and she found their emotional restraint at all times extraordinary. 'I was extremely anxious to show no emotion before your family at any time', she told Henry in August, at the end of the visit, but 'found the emotionless condition a great strain, all the time'. She had come back to London in order to say goodbye to them, but feared she had made a fool of herself even so, not behaving like a 'lady' but 'just like a wild animal', and ending up 'in a fit'.[56] Presumably she had burst into tears and sobbed. Eliot himself was torn between his love for his mother, his loyal obligation to Vivien, his desire to meet the expectations of his family, weekends spent showing them around London and the country, his need during the working week to maintain his long hours of concentration at the bank, and the continuing demands made on him as a reviewer and essayist. There was no way he could write poetry. 'He Do the Police in Different Voices' seems simply to have stopped: not a single surviving fragment of typescript or manuscript can be dated to the period of his family's visit.[57]

A photograph taken at Itchenor in Sussex that summer provides us with a beautiful study in contrasts.[58] Eliot is the man apparently at ease, looking confidently at the camera. Beside him is hunched his businessman brother Henry in full three-piece-suit and tie, handkerchief in breast pocket. Eliot at least has taken off his tie and waistcoat, while his pose – arm spread over the wall, long legs folded over each other, cigarette as ever between his fingers, book carelessly stuffed into his jacket pocket – shows that he is on holiday from such cares as beset Henry. For the moment, Henry is a parody of the restrained, careful and buttoned-up Eliot self, and Tom offers a pose as relaxed (aggressively and challengingly relaxed) as he is ever going to find.

His family's return to America at the start of August, however, precipitated him into a kind of breakdown. His time with them had left him 'tormented'[59] by a backlog of

3. T. S. Eliot and Henry Eliot in Itchenor, Sussex, summer 1921.

work and correspondence, along with a terrible sense of being a failure, and a renewed inability to cope with what he once called 'the burden of anxiety and fear which presses upon our daily life';[60] he suffered incessant worry and anxiety.[61] Things quickly got so bad that he was advised by a 'nerve specialist' (whom Vivien insisted he saw) to stop work for three months – and the Bank fortunately accepted that he must do so, on full salary, although he believed that what he really needed was 'a specialist in psychological troubles'.[62] By October, he was in the Hotel Albermarle in Margate, instructed to do no work and to see no-one, though Vivien did keep him company for a while; he was only allowed to read for two hours a day.

But it was here that he allowed the poetry to take over again; he wrote the savagely sexual passages of Part III, the opening of which – later cut by Ezra Pound – was in satirical couplets in the style of Pope.[63] In reaction, perhaps, against his family's visit, Eliot was now permitting himself, in his poetry, what he later called the 'breaking down of strong habitual barriers'.[64] His own experience transferred itself directly into the poem, even if obscurely for most readers: 'On Margate Sands. / I can connect / Nothing with nothing.'[65] He also drafted some poems that he believed might fit into the main body of the work. By 19 November, briefly back in London, he probably produced a typed copy of what he thought would be the poem's Part III.

In the writing of the poem so far, Vivien's role had been crucial. She had read and commented on Parts I and II, had been responsible for two lines in Part II ('If you don't like it you can get on with it' and the poignant 'What you get married for if you don't want children?'[66]) and she also had some particular link with the Pope-like couplets about 'Fresca' which started Part III (in 1924 a version of them would appear in print under her pseudonym: I discuss them below). In October 1922 she would describe how the poem 'has become a part of me (or I of it) this last year';[67] in 1936 she would actually sign herself 'Tiresias'.[68] In 'The Waste Land', 'I, Tiresias' – according to Eliot's note – 'although a mere spectator and not indeed a "character", is yet the most important personage in the poem, uniting all the rest'.[69] Vivien (even more than Eliot) was courageous in facing the emotional crises of her life, and her encouragement would have been crucial in Eliot's inclusion in the poem of so much sexual material – remarkable for a poem at that date[70] – and of passages that to knowing contemporaries would have seemed to have come directly out of their own marriage. In 1919, Eliot had written about the 'indestructible barriers between one human being and another';[71] he was now recreating them in his poetry.

Above all, it may well have been Vivien who encouraged him in this poem to write while suppressing his active, rational mind, so far as he could, and in a state of hypnotic unconsciousness. She would later boast happily how she was 'very *hypnotic, always was.* Could be 1st class MEDIUM'.[72] After Eliot had drafted Part III of the poem in Margate, he felt he 'must wait for Vivien's opinion as to whether it is printable',[73] perhaps referring to the Fresca lines, perhaps wondering if it in any way matched her idea of the unconscious, perhaps concerned whether she would object to his version of the 'indestructible barriers' between people appearing in print. Eliot's cousin Abigail would record her own recollection of Eliot and Vivien, many years later, that 'In the beginning he lived through her. Her hand was all over his work.'[74]

But the only line to which she objected came in Part II; at some point in 1922, she asked Eliot to remove 'The ivory men make company between us' from a passage against which she had previously written 'Yes' in the margin of the manuscript. The line may suggest that – perhaps in the act of the pieces being 'taken' – the chessmen make 'company' (a word with a potentially strong sexual meaning[75]) in ways that provoke the players to special awareness.[76] For Vivien it may, after all, have been too intimate a recollection. Eliot removed the line but never forgot it. Some thirty-eight years after last having had access to the manuscript, but after Vivien's death, he restored the line from memory to a text of the poem he was copying out.[77]

This does not mean that Eliot actually pictured Vivien in his poetry, in spite of the assertion by Carole Seymour-Jones that in 'The Waste Land' he showed her 'as a reproachful gorgon, whose hysterical complaints follow him night and day': and this in a section – 'Elegy' – cut 'by the cautious Pound'.[78] The idea of Pound being 'cautious' in what he cut from the poem is as odd as that of a gorgon being 'reproachful' (gorgons have simpler means of getting their way). 'Elegy' is a six stanza 'couplet' poem with no conceivable connection to Vivien, in spite of the link taken for granted by Gordon and

Seymour-Jones:[79] and it has no link with Pound either. Tones of voice, a sensibility, a vulnerability – these were qualities to which Eliot was acutely sensitive in Vivien and wanted to recreate in his poetry. Portraying an actual person was alien to him.

❀

After Margate, with feelings about his marriage spilling out into his poem, Eliot went (via Paris) to Lausanne, to be treated at the clinic of Dr Roger Vittoz, a psychologist who 'saw his method as opposed to psychoanalysis'[80] and who had been recommended by Julian Huxley. Eliot knew that his friend Ottoline Morrell had consulted Vittoz some years earlier, and Russell also knew about him. While stopping in Paris with Vivien for a couple of days en route to Lausanne, Eliot sought out Pound and consulted him about the unfinished poem. Pound was now resident in Paris: he had left England and moved to France at the very end of 1920. It had been a symbolic act, in which he attempted to cut himself free from an England which had (he declared) 'no longer any intellectual *life*';[81] he hated 'the full weight and extent of the British insensitivity to, and irritation with, mental agility in any and every form'[82] and deeply regretted the way that a man like Eliot – for him the most important poet writing in English – 'wastes his time in a bank'.[83]

Pound had been making practical comments and suggestions on Eliot's poems for years,[84] so it was entirely natural for

Eliot to consult him now. Eliot told Scofield Thayer a couple of months later that the poem had *in toto* been 'three times through the sieve by Pound';[85] as we know Eliot consulted Pound on his way back from Lausanne (when he stayed in Paris with Vivien from late December 1921 to mid-January 1922), and then again by post from London, later in January 1922, November 1921 must have been the occasion of Pound's first sieving.[86] But we do not know how Pound first reacted to the poem which he would later influence so much.

Leaving Vivien in a small Parisian hotel, Eliot then went on to Lausanne to consult Vittoz. He had read Vittoz's book *Treatment of Neurasthenia by Means of Brain Control* and had been impressed by what it said about will-power and its lack, '*aboulie*'.[87] Vittoz's technique was to train his patients in techniques for mastering the painful thoughts and anxieties that sapped their will and made everyday life a torture.[88] Eliot believed that he was suffering from 'emotional derangement which has been a lifelong affliction',[89] but – rather than believing anyone could cure it – hoped that Vittoz would help him control it.

And Vittoz did indeed bring him some relief. There were however more deeply rooted causes for Eliot's remoteness and his lack of vitality. He told the kindly American lawyer John Quinn in 1922 about how, whenever he got very tired or worried, 'all the old symptoms' would return: he mentioned the strain 'of trying to suppress a vague but intensely acute horror and apprehension'.[90] Ten years later, he would describe even more unguardedly to a friend 'the void that I find in the middle of all human happiness and all human relations ... I am one whom this sense of void tends to drive towards asceticism or sensuality'.[91] Only 'severe religious discipline' (on the one hand) or 'gross sexual indulgence' (on the other) might alleviate – temporarily – such feelings of emptiness.[92] His sense of void – and how it might be bridgeable – would actually play a huge part in what he was producing as a poet in 1921: in his poem he found ways of voicing the 'horror and apprehension'.

That was one very good reason why he did not want to understand his poetry. His rational mind remained perfectly fine, he insisted, but he underwent some very strange experiences in Lausanne; in 1937 he described how 'he felt at one moment that his brain was going to burst'.[93] He later explained how 'I wasn't even bothering whether I understood what I was saying',[94] and he preferred to believe that the experienced reader 'does not bother about understanding' either.[95] For he was at last engaged in what, three years earlier, he had called 'thinking with our feelings',[96] a state in which he believed that 'the "psychic material" tends to create its own form'.[97] And in the poem he was now writing, his deadly 'sense of void' in all human relations took centre stage, whether he wanted it to or not. One empty relationship succeeds another: the couple in the firelit room, the woman in the pub and her husband, Sweeney and Mrs Porter, Mr Eugenides and his lover, the typist and her lover, the couple in the canoe on the Thames. Eliot would tell his brother Henry – who did not like the poem – 'There is a good deal about it that I do not like myself'.[98] But liking was not the point.

It was in Lausanne that he wrote Part IV (the first section a kind of seaman's yarn about a shipwreck off the New England coast, the rest a reworking of lines from a French poem he had written earlier). In Lausanne, too, the last section (Part V) came out very close to its final state and Eliot felt that it 'justifies the whole';[99] he wrote it, he remembered, 'in a trance – unconsciously'.[100] That does not mean that it came without anxiety: he would tell a friend on 19 December that 'I am trying to finish a poem ... *Je ne sais pas si ça tient*.'[101] But a few years later he would describe how, all the same, 'some forms of illness' could help imaginative writing. He quoted A. E. Housman's remark 'I have seldom ... written poetry unless I was rather out of health' and commented 'I believe I understand that sentence.'[102] During illness, 'A piece of writing meditated, apparently without progress, for months or years, may suddenly take shape and word'.[103] This kind of shaping seems to have happened to Eliot more than once during 1921, especially late in the year; he was articulating the asceticism and the sensuality that his particular sense of void and apprehension provoked. His possession by the poetry in Lausanne felt like the 'haunting' which later he suggested was Coleridge's fate: 'anyone who has ever been visited by the Muse is thenceforth haunted'.[104]

We do not actually know either when he read or when he started to make use of a book by the medieval scholar Jessie Weston, *From Ritual to Romance*, with its account of the Grail Legend and its frequent use of the phrase 'waste land'. But it seems likely that he only realised how useful the book might be while working on Part V of his poem, and that the title 'The Waste Land' – which gives the poem a slightly spurious unity and solemnity – also came much later.[105] In Part V, there is a suggestion of a grail quest, which might lead to the restoration of a barren land. But it is without any kind of object; the 'chapel perilous' described by Weston is empty, the door swings in the wind.

In Part V, relief apparently comes from another and unexpected quarter. First there is a hint of thunder – and thunder might accompany rain – though the land of 'mudcracked houses'[106] seems as dry as ever. But the thunder sounds again (*Da*: the Sanskrit *da* is an Indo-European root which lies behind many languages' word for giving: dare, donner, geben, give): and a voice from the dawn of western civilisation speaks to the inhabitants of the wasteland. The questing hero has obviously got nowhere; individuals remain locked within themselves, while tormenting themselves with the might-have-been: 'each in his prison / Thinking of the key'. Vivien, remembering their meeting and marriage in 1915, would have been especially struck by the lines 'blood shaking my heart / The awful daring of a moment's surrender / Which an age of prudence can never retract'[107] which Eliot brought back from Lausanne. But the end of the poem groups itself around the three Sanskrit words of power and instruction, *Datta*, *Dayadhvam*, *Damyata*, for self control, giving and mercy, and the poem's last word 'shantih' tells us that a religious poem has ended with a word meaning 'peace'.[108]

❀

And yet the Sanskrit is as fragmentary as anything else in the poem: in most ways, rather more so. The Fisher King written into Part I at some point, who might be the sick ruler of the vegetation myth (and who is seen in Part III quietly fishing 'in the dull canal'), in Part V is found fishing again,[109] but seems unable to catch any more than the equivalent of old shopping trolleys of the cultural past (Isaiah, a nursery rhyme, Dante, the *Pervigilium Veneris*, *The Spanish Tragedy*). 'These fragments I have shored against my ruins'[110] says the narrator – but they *are* fragments, and the ruins are only ruins, even though they are still standing.

We do not know if Eliot corresponded with Vivien about the poem while he was in Lausanne: it seems likely. When he returned to Paris around Christmas 1921, he probably showed her what he had now written, but he also showed it again to Pound, and typed up Parts IV and V, so that Pound could give them his full attention.[111] Vivien had been overjoyed at being out of England; but while waiting for Eliot to come back had showed herself strangely uncertain about her feelings for him. 'About Tom – I *don't know* I don't know', she had written to her friend Mary Hutchinson: that may have been because she was on the point of getting a visit from her old friend Scofield Thayer, currently working in Cologne, whom – she wrote on 20 December – 'arrives tomorrow – will stay with me. After that I don't know'.[112] She obviously hoped that Thayer would help her 'know'. Mary Hutchinson was her confidante, but even Mary was not apparently told exactly what happened between Vivien and Thayer before Eliot returned.

Pound now read Eliot's poem and got to work. One of his final acts before leaving England had been to help with the proofs of *The Sacred Wood*; now he attended to an even more important job and – in effect – 'performed the caesarean Operation'[113] on the new poem, not only by querying individual words and lines throughout but by recommending the removal of whole sections that he thought superfluous. He also advised against other passages Eliot was considering including; as a result of Pound's advice, more than 360 lines vanished from the text. The music-hall narrative at the start of Part I went; Part III lost its opening satirical narrative, and was left without a beginning; Part IV lost its opening shipwreck narrative. (It was perhaps odd that Pound did not also suggest removing the congested Elizabethan narrative at the start of Part II.)

And so it was that, probably in Paris, Eliot wrote (on the back of one of the duplicate typescript pages of Part III) what may well have been the last part of the poem to be finished: a new opening for Part III about a land deserted and a river in winter[114] – appropriate for a poem which had now been cut down to focus more sharply on images of dryness, and of sea and river. Only when back in London with Vivien from mid-January, it seems, did Eliot put an epigraph from Conrad on his title-page: the passage from *Heart of Darkness* ending with Kurtz's 'cry that was no more than a breath: "The horror!

the horror!'"[115] But these were probably the only parts of the poem consciously constructed to fit its final form. Midwife Pound had assisted in getting a poem out of the drafts, and had convinced Eliot that the poem was nineteen pages long, and 'now runs from April ... to shantih without break'.[116] His work had been wonderfully helpful, and Eliot was deeply grateful, but it was a little unfortunate that he provoked the removal of the epigraph, which Eliot rightly felt was 'somewhat elucidative'.[117] The reader was thus deprived of an excellent clue to the poem – that when reading it we are constantly reminded of the way we inhabit a world violently alien to us. The poem is best experienced in its hallucinatory, rhythmical, violently dissociating, at times comic and at times horrific display of recollections, images and voices. A sensitive early listener to the poem, who heard it less than six months after it had been finished, was very struck by the way Eliot himself 'sang it & chanted it & rhythmed it. It has great beauty & force of phrase: symmetry; & tensity.'[118]

Eliot felt that it was good ('his best work, he says'[119]) but 1922 became a year when he was once again so concerned with Vivien's health,[120] with his own feelings of despair, with his day job, with attempts to publish the poem in magazines and as a short book, with the usual demands of his literary journalism, and – above all – with very serious attempts to start a literary periodical with him as its editor, that once again there was no way he could write poetry. The friend who heard him reading the new poem aloud in 1922, and who interpreted it as 'Tom's autobiography – a melancholy one',[121] was at least partly wrong, in thinking it simply autobiographical, and in finding it melancholy. In the winter of 1922–23, Eliot rounded on Conrad Aiken 'with that icy fury of which he alone was capable', insisting 'There is nothing melancholy about it!'[122] But he would have known, all too well, the anger and desperation of the personal drama of dispossession which infiltrated the poem as its significant undertone, at a level too deep for ordinary biography to extract. He himself would write, admiringly, about how the Jacobean dramatists, present 'the pattern' of 'the personal drama and struggle, which no biography, however full and intimate, could give us'.[123] It was Vivien who, writing to Eliot's brother Henry in August 1921, had insisted to him: '*be personal*, you must be personal, or else it's no good. Nothing's any good'.[124] That had been one of the hardest lessons Eliot had ever had to confront: it went clean against everything he had been brought up to be and to believe. It had been Vivien who, during their years together, had insisted on it to him.

6

Sweeney at large

After 'The Waste Land', Eliot seems to have written no poetry for another couple of years; again he wondered if the poem's completion had marked the end of his career as a poet. But the Eliot of the early and middle 1920s was nevertheless writing and publishing a good deal; in the autumn of 1922 he had embarked on the considerable responsibility of running a quarterly critical magazine, the *Criterion*, which – although it took up a vast amount of his time – also allowed him to publish his own work at will; and in spite of the fact that, at times, he suffered badly from the time and responsibility it demanded, taking it on 'changed the whole course of his life'.[1]

It was at first sponsored by the aristocrat Viscountess Lilian Rothermere, who had hoped for a literary magazine 'that would have a social éclat among a select audience of writers, critics, and patrons of the arts'.[2] The first numbers are a good deal more intellectual than this (she thought the first one rather dull); they exemplify Eliot's determination that the magazine should live up to the promise of its title, actually proposed by Vivien, in printing the best literature and criticism

– European as well as English – of its age. Accordingly, the first issue not only included 'The Waste Land' but also work by Hermann Hesse, George Saintsbury, Valéry Larbaud ('The "Ulysses" of James Joyce'), Sturge Moore and May Sinclair, while in the next four numbers there would be contributions by Luigi Pirandello, Virginia Woolf, Ezra Pound, W. B. Yeats, E. M Forster and Hugo von Hofmannsthal.

But the need for the magazine to attune itself to its patron's 'craving for the clever, brittle conversation of fashionable society drawing-rooms'[3] meant that by 1924 the *Criterion* was also regularly printing witty, satirical short sketches. It became a monthly in 1926, in an attempt to corner the market in up-to-date contemporary reviews, but the tension between its various constituencies continued until the end of 1927, when Lady Rothermere gave up her sponsorship. The magazine was then rescued by the publishers Faber & Gwyer; and after some months of financial instability it reverted to being a quarterly journal with a cover price of 7/6 (nearly the cost of a full-length novel) as opposed to its starting price of 3/6, back in 1922. It never sold many copies – around 700 is one estimate, and by 1938 the figure was down to 600 – but it carried Faber advertising and was itself an advertisement for the firm. Post Rothermere, it could also become again the rather more dedicated project that Eliot had imagined. By the later 1920s, too, Eliot's own religious commitments made him want a rather different kind of journal. The *Criterion* grew conservative in many ways, more aligned with the theologically right-wing; it began to take itself rather seriously as what has been called 'the institutional consolidation of a revolutionary artistic movement'.[4]

The *Criterion* was however never a source of income for Eliot. Until 1925, his income came mostly from the bank; the more dreadful Vivien's health grew, and the more desperate and demanding she was, the more he felt he had to safeguard his income in order to provide for the future. Friends like Ezra Pound and Virginia Woolf wondered callously why on earth he stayed with Vivien (Pound fantasised in February 1922 about the chances of someone turning up prepared 'to elope, kidnap, or otherwise eliminate Mrs. E.'[5]).

Such a reaction stemmed from ignorance. In spite of knowing both Eliots well from 1915, and being regularly in their company, it took Ezra Pound seven years to find out what was wrong with Vivien.

> Eliot has always been very reserved about his domestic situation, so much so that I thought Mrs. E. had syph; and marvelled that they didn't get a dose of 606.[6] Last time I saw him [Verona, June 1922] I got down to brass tacks. and [*sic*] find that the girl really has a long complication of things, tuberculosis in infancy, *supposed* to have been cured. Symptoms, so far as I now see, point to pituitary trouble ...[7]

That wasn't right either. But Pound was totally – if temporarily – converted to a sympathetic understanding of Vivien's situation, and better understood Eliot's need to have an assured income. During the 1920s there never seemed a question of Eliot's leaving Vivien, even though – by 1925 – he would reckon her state a great deal worse than when he had married her,[8] and believed that her only alternative to living with him would be to live on her own – if she could manage it.[9] In 1922 she had already offered to live separately, 'so she couldn't get on T's nerves, and prevent his working', Pound recalled; she remained 'ready to live by herself it if it will bring T. to write etc. And in general ready to do anything she can to help his work'.[10] Vivien herself confessed to Richard Aldington in July 1922 that 'You know I am ill and an endless drag on him'.[11] But Eliot continued to do what he could for her; country cottages were rented, doctors hired, new drugs tried, all at great expense. Numbers of cures were attempted. In the spring of 1923, the cure they were trying almost starved her to death: she 'wasted away to a skeleton'.[12] She was taking a cocktail of drugs, as she had done for years, to try and control her various addictions and symptoms, and these resulted in some bizarre changes to her appearance; she came out in blotches and spots, and Virginia Woolf became especially aware of her skin: 'very spotty, much powdered', 'so scented, so powdered', 'her powdered spots'.[13] As almost anyone would in her situation, Vivien grew deeply unhappy and agonisingly self-critical; years later Eliot recalled

> The dreadful nights when she would say 'I ought never to have married you' or, 'I am useless and better dead' – and then my disclaimers and her floods of tears ...[14]

He blamed himself for her state. Why had he married her? Had he ever loved her – as opposed to desiring 'gross sexual indulgence'[15] with her? Had he ever listened to her? Had he been impatient and uncaring? Vivien had complained to a friend in 1921 that 'he is often very unkind to me in a way',[16] and Virginia Woolf was of the opinion that 'Tom, though infinitely considerate, is also perfectly detached. His cell, is I'm sure, a very lofty one, but a little chilly.'[17] All he could now do was go on taking care of Vivien. Virginia Woolf saw them at tea in July 1923, soon after Vivien had started visiting friends again:

> Tom. Put brandy in your tea, Vivien.
>> No, no, Tom.
>> Yes. You must Put a tea spoonful of brandy in your tea.
> Vivien. Oh all right – I don't want it.[18]

Some writing she did for the *Criterion* between February 1924 and July 1925 seemed, for a while, to offer her a new lease of life and a significant new occupation. She had 'a very strong feeling that this is a sort of flash in the pan – that it won't go on'[19] – and it didn't. But in all she managed twelve pieces: three book reviews, a poem, four brief stories about women in fashionable society and four 'diary' pieces.[20] Her prose consists of odd little commentaries and quick, vivid sketches, mostly about the experience of single women in society who are *not* having sexual adventures, in spite of comments like 'Not bad for a pick-up'[21] after a man is encountered – and danced with

– at an afternoon party. Vivien described how her pieces were written 'from the point of view of a very interested, & a very *intimate*, outsider'.[22] She was dismissive about what she had done, referring to it as 'this temporary aberration of mine',[23] but Eliot was thoroughly impressed by it and was especially struck by her originality;[24] he commented how one piece seemed 'amazingly brilliant and humorous and horrible, and I have never read anything in the least like it.'[25] How highly he rated her work was demonstrated by the *Criterion* issues of October 1924 and July 1925. In the first he included the story 'Jimmy and the Desperate Woman' by D. H. Lawrence but also 'Thé Dansant' by 'Feiron Morris' and 'Mrs Pilkington' by 'Felix Morrison' (both by Vivien); in the latter he included 'Fragment of an Unpublished Work' by James Joyce (part of what would become *Finnegan's Wake*), the first part of 'The Woman who Rode Away' by D. H. Lawrence and 'Fête Galante' by 'Fanny Marlow'.[26] (Vivien's pieces used either the initials 'F. M.' or a name with those initials.[27])

Eliot also printed her diary sketch 'Letters of the Moment – II' which mentioned in passing (and quoted) a poem about 'Fresca' having breakfast in bed; a poem remarkably similar to a passage cut from Part III of 'The Waste Land' on Pound's advice three-and-a-half years earlier. It is now impossible to say whether the lines might originally have been written by Eliot when Vivien was with him (she had been in Margate at just the right time during the drafting of Part III), whether what she included was an alternative version of Eliot's own work, or whether she was now re-drafting the old poem herself.[28] All three possibilities may of course be true; she knew the passage intimately, she may well have been working from an early draft Eliot still possessed (the original typescripts for 'The Waste Land'[29] had by now been sold to John Quinn, the American collector), and she was also probably making extensive changes of her own. It would, for example, have taken more of an expert on eighteenth-century pronunciation than Vivien probably ever was to know that 'tea' and 'day' – which end her first two lines – were a possible rhyme ('tea' rhymes with 'tray' in Eliot's 1921 typescript). On the other hand, some couplets in Vivien's version seem rather below Eliot's practised standard:

> Or were you in the seats of cheaper price?
> Dorilant sat with me, and I looked nice.

And one line has fourteen syllables, not twelve ('I told him you were there, but I don't think he heard'). The similarities between the two poems are all the same extensive. Eliot's 1921 typescript had contained the lines

> Her hands caress the egg's well-rounded dome,
> She sinks in revery, till the letters come ...
> "My dear, how are you? I'm unwell today,
> And have been, since I saw you at the play ...
> What are you reading? anything that's new?
> I have a clever book by Giraudoux ..."[30]

Vivien's 1924 version ran, in part,

"I'm very well, my dear, and how are you?
I have another book by Giraudoux.
My dear, I missed you last night at the Play;
Were you not there? Or did you slip away? ..."
Her hands caress the egg's well-rounded dome;
As her mind labours till the phrases come.[31]

Perhaps the most significant fact was the way that the Eliots felt mutually responsible for such writing, and enjoyed the fun of mystifying their readers: it was not probably an accident that 'Letters of the Moment – II' was dated '*1st April*'.[32] Later in the piece comes the sentence 'if one had said, "settling a pillow or throwing off a shawl": No, I did not much care for the *Boutique* at all, not at all',[33] with its direct parody of 'Prufrock': 'If one, settling a pillow or throwing off a shawl, / And turning toward the window, should say: / "That is not it at all, / That is not what I meant at all."'[34]

The best joke of all, perhaps, was that although Eliot received nothing for his work on the magazine (he was still a full-time employee of Lloyd's Bank), Vivien could be paid – a reason why 'anonymity is vital'.[35] Cheques for her pseudonymous pieces went 'to a flat in Charing Cross Road and not to the Eliots' home address'.[36] But she was not being paid at the magazine's standard rate. 'Thé Dansant', 7 pages long, is around 2,200 words, so might (at the standard rate of £1 for 500 words) have been expected to earn £4 or even £4.10.0.; 'Jimmy and the Desperate Woman', 28 pages long in the same number, had earned Lawrence £18.[37] Vivien was paid only £1. 10. 0. for 'Thé

Dansant'; she probably earned no more than £10 or £12 in all for her contributions.

Her appearances in the *Criterion* during 1924 and 1925, however, were not simply for the money. They seem to have been the culmination – and the external proof – of a partnership that had been operating for some nine or ten years. It is striking that two of the books which 'F. M.' and 'Feiron Morris' reviewed were by Middleton Murry (savagely) and Virginia Woolf (critically)[38] – and that both were people whom Eliot himself did not want to attack or offend, though it seems extremely likely that the reviews expressed what he thought.

❀

It was in the 1920s, too, that Eliot began trying to develop completely new forms for his own work, and some of the language of anger and blame got involved in his poetry. The Sweeney poems had, in 1917 and 1918, been a step forward in a new direction for him, and in 1920 Virginia Woolf noted that he was planning 'to write a verse play in which the 4 characters of Sweeny act the parts'.[39] He was under no illusions about the problems of doing such a thing; in May of the same year (in a review of Middleton Murry's *Cinnamon and Angelica: A Play*) he had noted that writing a verse play in modern times 'is in fact the most difficult, the most exhausting task that a poet can set himself'.[40]

Sweeney had acquired a walk-on role in 'The Waste Land', alongside Mrs Porter,[41] while sometime early in 1923, Eliot started to draft Sweeney's starring role in a Sweeney play, at this stage called 'Pereira; or, The Marriage of Life and Death, a Dream': in the surviving plot draft he jotted down 'Murder of Mrs Porter'.[42] Eliot told John Quinn in April 1923 that 'the work I have in mind ... is more ambitious than anything I have ever done yet'.[43] By September 1924 he could tell Arnold Bennett that he was 'now centred on dramatic writing. He wanted to write a drama of modern life (furnished flat sort of people) in a rhythmic prose "perhaps with certain things in it accentuated by drum-beats."'[44] But as yet he apparently only had plans. Rather like 'The Waste Land', this poem/play seems also to have stayed 'in mind' for years, and then to have come with a rush.

In 1924, in further homage to the Sweeney characters, he published three short poems as 'Doris's Dream Songs', one of them reworking some discarded 'Waste Land' material, one being part of his new poem 'The Hollow Men', and the third having once have been part of the latter, sharing some of its language.[45] They were prefaces to the final manifestations of the Sweeney character. In an odd way – for all their simplicity and clarity – the Sweeney and Doris poems had always been learned poetry too, written with reference to sources with which most of Eliot's readers would never have thought to link the poetry.

❦

Sweeney Agonistes survives in three fragments.[46] Eliot once commented that he finished it, probably sometime in 1926, in two nights and assisted by 'a bottle of gin',[47] though there seems to be some myth-making in that account; the fragments are heavily revised and extensively different from a surviving early typescript, which may have been the one induced by the gin.[48] The published fragments are in a real mixture of styles. Eliot subtitled the piece 'an Aristophanic melodrama': earlier in 1926, he had referred to 'Aristophanic farce' as a 'relief from the sublime'.[49] There was also a chorus which ended the 'Fragment of an Agon', and – exactly as specified in Francis Cornford's book *The Origin of Attic Comedy*, which Eliot knew – it is 'more or less violently'[50] on the side of Sweeney, following the argument about life and death between him and Doris which comprises the *Agon*.[51] Two of the three fragments appeared in magazines in 1926 and 1927, but had to wait for publication in volume form until 1932, when Eliot chose a significant moment to bring them out.

In key with his attempt in the early twenties to argue that both poetry and drama worked best as varieties of myth – and his characteristically provocative attempt to defend British music-hall as part of a surviving mythic culture[52] – Eliot was now trying to see a way forward for poetry imbued with elements both of myth and of Aristophanic comedy. Sweeney is not simply sensual man, a grown-up version of the growing-up soul of 'Animula' ('selfish, misshapen, lame'[53]). His development into the unfinished dramatic fragments of *Sweeney Agonistes* shows him to be the thing itself: committed to sensuality, enjoying violence, perfectly and unthinkingly sexual, but also highly intelligent: 'sordid, emotional, intense'.[54] In 'Sweeney Erect' he had been 'Slitted below and gashed with eyes',[55] as much a pumpkin mask as a person, slicing his way, razor at the ready, to a position of dominance, but never talking. In the *Agonistes*, even while making scrambled eggs during the performance ('You see this egg / You see this egg')[56] he is always extremely articulate. (In 1933 Eliot would define the 'function of the poet' as that of making 'inarticulate folk articulate'.[57]) Sweeney intones a number of lyrics, the most famous of which are

> I knew a man once did a girl in
> Any man might do a girl in
> Any man has to, needs to, wants to,
> Once in a lifetime, do a girl in.[58]

and

> Birth, and copulation and death.
> That's all, that's all, that's all, that's all,
> Birth, and copulation, and death.[59]

And he explains: 'That's all the facts when you come to brass tacks'.[60]

But it is specifically an 'Agon' in which Sweeney is participating: a formal argument, in which he attempts to convince Doris that – as life is meaningless – life is really the same as death ('Death is life and life is death'). This is one of those moments when we again become aware of the overwhelmingly attractive power of the *other* argument from the one with which Eliot himself (responsible, religious, prose-writing) would have wished to be associated. Eliot would speak in 1933 about

> that at which I have long aimed, in writing poetry; to write poetry which would be essentially poetry, with nothing poetic about it, poetry standing naked in its bare bones ...[61]

That is what he approaches in the 'Fragment of an Agon' making up the second scene of *Sweeney*. All Doris can say, in response to Sweeney, is that she would be bored on the cannibal isle with nothing but birth and copulation and death to occupy her: to which Sweeney responds

> You'd be bored ...
> I've been born, and once is enough.
> You don't remember, but I remember,
> Once is enough.[62]

Who would want re-birth, or life after death, if one 'remembers'? Being born is bad enough, in all conscience. The logical, intelligent attitude (lacking any kind of belief in anything outside himself) is exactly that articulated by Sweeney.

> I gotta use words when I talk to you
> But if you understand or if you don't
> That's nothing to me and nothing to you

We all gotta do what we gotta do ...[63]

That last line – now so deeply part of the culture that it cannot even count as a quotation – must have been new when Eliot wrote it down in the mid-1920s. He either picked it up from his contemporaries or passed it on to them. It perfectly expresses the Sweeney attitude; you have to use words, but it really doesn't matter if anyone understands. You *act*.

Eliot later confessed that, for the *Sweeney* play, he wanted a character 'whose sensibility and intelligence should be on the plane of the most sensitive and intelligent members of the audience', and he believed that such a character should address himself to the audience as much as to 'the other personages in the play'.[64] That role is clearly Sweeney's: we are to take him with the greatest seriousness. The songs at times suggest the music-hall ('Any old tree will do for me / Any old wood is just as good'); elsewhere in the 'Aristophanic melodrama' which the Sweeney material now turned into, a song is accompanied by Swarts as Tambo and Snow as Bones, two traditional Minstrel Show characters, confirming Eliot's suggestion that his poetry, 'in its sources, its emotional springs ... comes from America'[65] (he would publish the second scene in the *Criterion* in January 1927 under the title *Wanna Go Home, Baby?*). He was drawing on the American popular tradition as well as on music-hall and ancient Greek culture, which suggests just how eclectic his search for form now was. The scene includes the parody of part of a 1902 Broadway musical hit song, 'Under the bamboo tree', the last two lines of the original chorus having run

One live as two, two live as one,
Under the bamboo tree.[66]

In Eliot's *Sweeney* drama, these lines turn into

Two live as one
One live as two
Two live as three
Under the bam
Under the boo
Under the bamboo tree.[67]

Eliot's continued liking for such material is demonstrated by the fact that, as late as 1948, he would be heard happily singing 'Under the bamboo tree' at the party which commemorated his winning the Nobel Prize for literature.[68]

The fact that he never finished the Sweeney drama suggests that he realised that it didn't and couldn't really 'work' as a stage piece, but at least it partly satisfied his search for an imaginative way of mixing the popular with the radical, the classical with the utterly contemporary: it offered what Virginia Woolf called 'modernity & poetry locked together'[69] and Eliot knew that it was 'the most *original* thing'[70] he had written. It was a way of starting to write the dramatic poetry that, after 'The Waste Land', he was liberating himself into. As has been said, 'He wanted a drama established upon firm theatrical conventions, not one messily engaged in "realism" – ritual rather than life, actors rather than people.'[71] The fact that alcohol apparently helped so much with its original inscription should not surprise us. Eliot told Elizabeth Bowen in 1932 how 'without alcohol he would never have got into the mood for his poems',[72] and there are a number of reports about how much he was currently drinking, though his self-control meant that he very rarely appeared drunk in public. Virginia Woolf however recorded one occasion, in December 1923, when Eliot's 'eyes were blurred' and he could only just 'stand on his legs' (he apologised to her on the phone for ten minutes the next day).[73] The drinking was of course partly to do with the unhappiness and stress; but at times it would also have been a way of attempting to lower his level of conscious intelligence and awareness, to try and get into something more like a dream state, in which (ideally) he might be able to write what he called 'poetry so transparent that we should not see the poetry, but that which we are meant to see through the poetry'.[74] Such thinking, of course, inhabits the usual paradox that – in his every-day, conscious, cautious, highly controlled self (which we can describe as the banker and editor) – Eliot was almost a different person from the highly emotional, uninhibited and violent being with 'wild hazel eyes',[75] 'a great toad with jewelled eyes',[76] 'the wild eye still',[77] of whom Virginia Woolf was so conscious over the years, and who had also been glimpsed by Colette O'Niel in 1918: 'His eyes were most remarkable. One felt they might spring out on one at any moment – like a cat'.[78] That wilder, more dangerous person is the one who knew what it meant to be a writer, and at times was liberated into language.

It is clear that his marriage to Vivien had been an instinctive attempt to induce that state of mind in him: sexuality may at one stage of his life have seemed to offer as much of a release as alcohol. Life with her had, between 1915 and 1925, for all its terrible problems, offered (for better and for worse) some form of the liberation that Eliot craved: it did something to break down in him his logical, rational self, his fundamental belief in what he once called the artist's role 'in the development and maintenance of the mind'.[79] In his daily self as a banker, he remained almost a parody of his rational and non-poetic self, and people like Pound were deeply shocked that – as a poet – he should have continued in such a way of life. They underrated his profound need not only to do his best to make up to Vivien for the complex mistake involved in having married her (by providing a secure financial future), but to enact – in one part of his life – the self which from upbringing and habit he also needed to be.

It seems likely that – until their problems started to overwhelm their relationship in the mid 1920s, and Eliot also turned to religion – it was life with Vivien which he had also found most liberating, as a person and as a writer. As Sweeney puts it, 'We all gotta do what we gotta do': just as he had *had* to write 'The Waste Land' with her support, against the grain of the person he was and had been brought up to be, so now *Sweeney Agonistes* seems to have been his first – if almost his only – work in his new style. It is simply an enormous pity he did not further develop the vein of writing he pioneered in it; it brought together so many of his strengths as a writer.

❁

It has been argued by Ronald Bush that Eliot's next poem, 'The Hollow Men' of 1925, was not so much a continuation of 'Waste Land' material as another, rather different attempt to write dramatic verse with links to Greek theatre; and this suggestion would be supported by what Eliot had been doing with his Sweeney myth. 'The Hollow Men' was not so much a poem as a collection of lyrics which Eliot began to publish in 1924: all of them very brief, short-lined poems centring enigmatically on phrases like 'death's dream kingdom', and apparently charting a movement into death.[80] Vivien Eliot, who was deeply impressed by the poem ('I think it is amazing, terrible'), would not be the last (though she may have been the first) to see 'The Hollow Men' as 'a fitting & proper follow-on to the Waste Land'.[81] The poem finally came out as a book in November 1925. This put the four previously published poem sections into a new order and added what Bush called a new 'choral ode' (no. V) at the end. It also added an epigraph to the whole poem, which comes from Conrad's *Heart of Darkness* just a few lines after the epigraph which Eliot had originally put in front of 'The Waste Land'. Here, '*Mistah Kurtz – he dead*' reminds its readers how laconically the death of Kurtz is related in Conrad's novel. Kurtz ('All Europe contributed to the making of Kurtz'[82]), supposed to be a man whose experiences have been profound, and whose rhetoric is magnificent, dies in reported speech ineffectively translated.[83] But the

'Hollow Men's status as a series of choruses, which might also be read as meditations on death (and which might in turn be taken independently or together) is thus confirmed.

It was the last section, first published in November 1925, that showed Eliot's eclectic method at its strangest and most compelling. It uses modified nursery rhyme (*'Here we go round the prickly pear'*) and the language of the prayer book along with the same kind of lively chorus as had infiltrated the Sweeney work throughout, to bring the work to its famous and arguably choral conclusion: *'This is the way the world ends / Not with a bang but a whimper.'* The vigorously eclectic style makes it impossible not to relish what logically 'ought' to be extremely unpleasant. It has been suggested that 'The Hollow Men', like *Sweeney Agonistes*, has its chorus return 'from the dead to tell the story of [their] horrible purgation, [their] divestment of the love of created beings'.[84] That seems to be exactly the kind of serious suggestion that might well be the meaning of these peculiar utterances: except that the poetry constantly contradicts such meanings. We find, for example, a reference to 'Trembling with tenderness', but such tenderness is clearly outlawed by the poem: 'Lips that would kiss / Form prayers to broken stone.' Except, of course, that the poem ensures that in turn we can read those two lines as demonstrating what has, tragically, been lost, not what has been gained.

The opposite is also true. The horrid intellectual detachment suggested by lines like 'I see the eyes but not the tears / This is my affliction'[85] in one of the supporting poems to

'The Hollow Men', which Gordon reads as a straightforward confession of the guilt which Eliot felt at not sympathising enough with the pain of others (in particular not being sufficiently sympathetic to Vivien),[86] is neutralised as guilt by the very context the poem gives it – in 'death's dream kingdom'. It is not, after all, a personal or confessional poem; it is a meditation on the last things, even if finally an ironic one.

7

Conversion: what kind of new life?

By the autumn of 1925, Eliot was the most famous young poet of the age, as well as a man of great reputation who, though a complete outsider, had made his way through the London literary world ('conscientious, scrupulous, careful, attentive'[1]) to a position of extraordinary authority. 'The Waste Land' was turning out to be the most influential poem of the decade, as well as the most notorious (one early review had described it as 'so much waste paper', another thought it demonstrated Eliot's own 'indolence of imagination'[2]). Eliot's first collected edition of his poems would be published as *Poems 1909–1925* in November 1925; he had written leading articles in the *Times Literary Supplement*; his prose books *The Sacred Wood* (1920) and *Homage to John Dryden* (1924) were highly regarded; the influence of the *Criterion* was out of all proportion to its sales. His status was confirmed in April 1925 when he was invited to give the prestigious 1925–26 Clark lectures at Trinity College, Cambridge, in spite of being an American 'who lived in London as a banker,

editor and controversial poet with limited academic creden-
tials and no college affiliation'.[3] In the autumn of 1925, too,
he would accept the offer of a directorship in the publishing
house Faber & Gwyer, and was at last able to leave the bank.
We know how he looked at this point in his life: 'very much the
city man. His strong-set aquiline features and his well set-up
figure were observed to advantage in the traditional costume
of bowler hat, black coat and striped trousers ... He carried
a Malacca-handled umbrella which was always neatly rolled'.[4]
To observers of the literary scene, Eliot's progress as the major
poet, critic and literary authority in the English language must
have seemed unstoppable. It had taken him almost exactly ten
years' work to reach that position.

❀

It has also been authoritatively stated that it was during just
these years between 1921 and 1925 that Eliot started a 'new life'
in reaction against the disasters of his marriage: when, after
years of evasion, at last he became a practising homosexual. It
has, for example, been argued that, during the writing of 'The
Waste Land' in Lausanne, Eliot had found himself 'flooded
with "unacceptable homosexual longings"'[5] and that he subsequently had affairs with at least two (named) young men, as
well as devoting himself to the gay sub-culture of London.
I have no particular interest in proving Eliot heterosexual
or homosexual or asexual, but I would like to ensure that
speculation about his life, of whatever kind, should not go

unquestioned, especially when (as in this case) it touches so nearly upon his marriage and his behaviour to Vivien.

The argument for his homosexuality runs as follows.[6] He was a deprived child who was left 'isolated and uncomfortable in his ill-fitting masculinity'.[7] During his twenties – between the years 1908 and 1918 – and as a result of his uncertain sexuality, 'Eliot struggled ... to confess and yet to repress his homosexual feelings: it was a kind of torture'.[8] This part of the argument depends on how we understand his relationship with Jean Verdenal in 1911. At the time of his marriage to Vivien in 1915, it does seem unlikely that Eliot had ever had any sexual or even close emotional ties with any other women, even those he was fond of (like Emily Hale). As was natural for men of his age, background and education, he had spent his formative years with other men; and if he had fallen in love with anyone when young (a common enough experience) it might well have been with another boy or another man. To me, some such half-truth may lie behind his acquaintance Robert Sencourt's belief that Eliot's marriage went wrong because he was worried about being homosexual, and that he got married 'in the hope that he would become "normal"'. Sencourt recalled Eliot telling him this in 1927, and reported the story in 1971 to his editor Frances Lindley, who in turn passed it on to T. S. Matthews.[9] There is thus nothing first-hand about the chain of reporting, and the story was only written down some forty-four years after Eliot talked to Sencourt – who is not an altogether reliable witness about other matters.[10] Nevertheless, before his marriage, what Eliot knew about love may well have been derived from feelings for men. As he remarked in 1933, when in love 'we do not so much see the person' as recognise the presence of something external, 'which sets in motion these new and delightful feelings'.[11]

Those who assume that Eliot was at least in tendency homosexual will expect his marriage to have brought his already problematic sexuality under severe strain. Carole Seymour-Jones has argued that this was why Eliot was happy to engage in what she terms a 'triple ménage'[12] with Vivien and Bertrand Russell when the chance materialised, and that it was his own homosexuality that made Eliot turn to Russell to relieve him of his 'conjugal responsibilities'. Seymour-Jones goes so far as to state that Eliot actually encouraged Russell's seduction of Vivien – 'when he needed Russell's support, Tom had offered Vivien as bait'[13] – because he wanted the money (in the form of debentures) which Russell loaned him, and because Russell brought him introductions to other influential Bloomsbury figures: Eliot 'had knowingly colluded in order to further his career ... and to gain financial advantage'.[14]

She also states that, by 1921, Eliot's 'acute sexual conflict' had become something which 'urgently demanded resolution'.[15] Accordingly, runs her argument, the following year Eliot acted upon his feelings. She states that 'there is little doubt' that during 1922 Eliot 'was, in fact, romantically and sexually involved'[16] with a German boy called Jack. No evidence survives of that relationship beyond what Vivien recalled in a facetious poem, which described how Jack was such a perfect nuisance that Eliot once hit him (no other passions are recorded). Seymour-Jones nevertheless takes it for granted that 'Jack had successors',[17] and names the Hon. Philip Ritchie, on the grounds that, on one occasion, an Oxford 'youth' was observed lying on the floor of Eliot's flat during a party, and that some years later, a friend of Eliot's recalled that Ritchie had on one occasion stayed at Eliot's address. Seymour-Jones offers this as her evidence of Eliot's 'physical relationship with the young men like ... Ritchie with whom he consorted',[18] and goes on to state that Eliot, by the middle 1920s, was encouraging Vivien to lead her own sexual life 'in return for her silence over his homosexual alliances'.[19]

In spite of Seymour-Jones's relentless assertions that these relationships and alliances were taking place – and the conclusions which she draws from her belief that they were – there is not actually a scrap of hard evidence for any such alliances, or any such relationship with Russell.

There is evidence that Eliot sometimes wore make-up in the 1920s. In March 1922, for example, Virginia Woolf recorded how Clive Bell said that Eliot 'uses violet powder to make him look cadaverous',[20] and six months later she herself was 'not sure that he does not paint his lips'.[21] Both Virginia Woolf and Osbert Sitwell believed they had seen 'a dusting of green powder' on his cheeks in 1924;[22] in a sketch by Vivien published in July 1925 a character rather similar to Eliot has a 'heavy, slumbering white face, thickly powdered'.[23] Such suggestions have been taken as proof that Eliot was moving in homosexual circles, and was having problems 'maintaining a mask which had never fitted'.[24] It is all the same striking how much of the available evidence from this period comes from women. If Eliot was wearing makeup, it was not perhaps in order to attract men, but to influence how people of both sexes perceived him. Clive Bell thought that he was wearing make-up to make himself look ill (and thus to elicit sympathy) but it seems rather more likely – as the lip-painting suggests – that he was doing his best to disguise how ill, tired and old he feared he was starting to look. Evidence of his wearing make-up drawn from later in his life – from the 1930s – I will discuss in its proper place.

A final argument has been adopted from the odd case of John Peter, who in 1952 published a piece about 'The Waste Land' in Essays in Criticism which suggested that the narrator had 'fallen completely – perhaps the right word is "irretrievably" – in love'[25] with a young man who had later drowned. The fact that Eliot threatened legal action unless the piece was withdrawn (it was) has been seen as the behaviour of a man trying to protect a guilty secret. Such commentators ignore the fact that an accusation of homosexuality in the early 1950s (when homosexuality was still illegal and perpetrators might be prosecuted) could do considerable damage to an individual in public life. Not to respond to what was apparently an accusation might be seen as tacit and fearful acceptance of what had been said. Eliot proved extremely sensitive to what he thought might have been such a charge. That does not mean that the charge was correct. If anything, it proves the opposite; only the person absolutely sure the charge was groundless would have threatened legal action which might have ended in court.

That much, at least, might have been learned from the case of Oscar Wilde.

❁

The effect of this line of assertion on accounts of Eliot has been considerable. As is revealed by any search of the web, of papers and periodicals, and of books about the period, it is now a matter of common assumption that Eliot was gay, certainly by inclination if not always in practice, that he constantly wrote about gay experience in his poetry, and that he behaved badly in his marriage because of his sexual orientation. To me, the matter is important not because it actually matters whether Eliot was straight or gay, but because unsubstantiated versions of his sexual behaviour make accounts of his poetry and his marriage unreliable: in particular the effect on Eliot of Vivien's unfaithfulness with Russell and her 'ostentatious flirtations'[26] with other men. The fact that Vivien later 'turned outside the marriage for consolation'[27] can – to such biographers – be explained because of Eliot's own sexual exploits: Vivien simply 'emulated her husband'.

At the heart of all the arguments I have seen for Eliot's homosexuality lies a series of fabrications, half-truths and suppositions. He may have been attracted to men when young; he may even have found when he got married that he was not entirely heterosexual, though I suspect that exactly the opposite was the case: that he discovered just how startlingly heterosexual he was. But evidence for his homosexuality does not exist, whereas evidence for his being a troubled hetero-sexual exists in quantity.

❀

Following the lead given by his biographer Lyndall Gordon in 1988, it has become common to see the second half of Eliot's life as his 'New Life' in another sense: one which broke away from his earlier self, and during which he found, in the Christian religion he formally embraced in 1927–28, the satis-faction, consolation and purpose which had been denied to him earlier. In such a reading, the four poems written 1935–42, making up his *Four Quartets*, effectively 'set a crown' upon his 'lifetime's effort'[28] as a poet.

Religious conversion is something that in many cases only slowly takes effect: Eliot would in 1932 describe how 'one is borne gradually, perhaps insensibly over a long period of time'[29] into such a change. After his initial Unitarianism, Eliot as a college student turned against the old faith and for a while was agnostic or positively anti-religious; but after flirtations in the early 1920s with Buddhism and Catholicism, he finally gravitated towards the Church of England. From around 1923 he was undeniably thinking harder about religion than at any time since his childhood. He had begun to correspond with the American convert William Force Stead, and it became clear that he was moving towards a massive change in the way he thought about himself and about the world. To their astonishment, his wife, brother and sister-in-law saw him fall to his knees when he caught sight of the Michelangelo *Pietà* in St Peter's in Rome in 1926. Six years later, he would describe how in conversion 'a kind of crystallisation occurs, in which appears an element of *faith*'.[30] Michelangelo's dead Christ – or living mother – had had a very palpable effect. On 29 June 1927 he was baptised and the following day confirmed.[31] In 1928 he made his first confession; in the same year he publicly declared himself 'anglo-catholic in religion'.[32] In 1929 he would remark that 'only Christianity helps to reconcile me to life, which is otherwise disgusting'.[33] And although his conversion meant that thereafter he lived (he confessed) 'in daily terror of eternity' – Christianity brought him 'the very dark night and the desert'[34] – his faith at least allowed him to view his own concerns and pains in the context of a meaningful universe rather than simply within that of an individual (necessarily failing) life.

His original Unitarian upbringing had not stressed good and evil at all but only the inadequacies of human behaviour; accordingly, it had always implied the possibility of human betterment. He had commented dryly, when he was twenty-five or so, in a talk given to the Philosophical Society of Harvard, that he belonged to a church which apparently believed in 'the Progress of Mankind onward and upward forever. I do not understand what this phrase means'.[35] From the early 1920s, he had found himself wanting to define 'the problem of good and evil'[36] as what was most important in life. But in the later 1920s he wanted to go still further, to describe what had become (to him) a basic fact about the human condition.

Original sin – 'a very real and tremendous thing'[37] he called it in 1934 – meant that all bodily appetites, but in particular sexual appetites separated from moral behaviour, were necessarily sinful. Eliot wanted to use language that could say things like: 'So far as we are human, what we do must be either evil or good'; and 'so far as we do evil or good, we are human.'[38] That sentence comes from an essay on Baudelaire which he wrote in 1930; such language only became available to him following his Christian conversion.

The 1930 Baudelaire essay is actually a very acute guide to the way he was by then thinking about himself. The quoted sentence continues: 'it is better, in a paradoxical way, to do evil than to do nothing: at least, we exist'. It would therefore be better to have (necessarily evil) sexual desires, upon which one acts, than not to have them, or to do nothing about them. Baudelaire is championed as one who was

> at least able to understand that the sexual act as evil is more dignified, less boring, than as the natural, 'life-giving', cheery automatism of the modern world. For Baudelaire, sexual operation is at least something not analogous to Kruschen Salts.[39]

Kruschen salts are a laxative; 'the modern world' sees sex as a kind of pleasurable evacuation. The contempt contained within such an analogy is almost palpable, as Eliot – rather astonishingly – attempts to rescue 'sexual operation' as something not only compelling but also as participation in actual wickedness.

This might suggest a way of reading Eliot's letter to Pound of January 1934, which enclosed a very cheerful little poem. 'About Coarseness', Eliot had written, 'I dont want to boast', but he enclosed some verses advising Pound to settle his scores with his enemies. 'Not once, or twice, shalt thou bugger 'em, in our rough island story' but – Eliot suggested to his old friend – over and over again.[40] Although Carol Seymour-Jones has quoted the lines as evidence of how attractive 'the pleasures of buggery'[41] were to Eliot, such a conclusion ludicrously misunderstands him. In order to encourage Pound to swear 'bugger them' more savagely, Eliot is adopting a national treasure, the late Alfred Lord Tennyson, and his famous lines

> Not once or twice in our rough island-story
> The path of duty was the way to glory ...[42]

Eliot would have known how Tennyson's 'rough' was used in 'rough trade'[43] and – following a quotation from Dante about beatitude – he had inscribed a couple of lines at the start of his 'Lectures on the Metaphysical Poetry of the Seventeenth Century' delivered in Cambridge in 1926:

> I want someone to treat me rough.
> Give me a cabman.
>
> *Popular song*[44]

The poem he sent to Pound in 1934 – although not the kind of poetry he could ever publish – could still be skilful, witty, absolutely to the point, and full of the secular energy of what Eliot cheerfully characterised as the 'dæmonic powers'.[45] He would have been proud of being viewed as the person he admired Tennyson for being a couple of years later: 'the most instinctive rebel against the society in which he was the most perfect conformist'.[46] When asked by a pious friend if his conversion to Christianity meant that he had abandoned poetry, he answered: 'in that "I am absolutely unconverted"'.[47] He might have said the same about his writing of the obscene. He used the obscene very deliberately because to him sexual violence was (in a very precise sense of the word) aboriginal: native to human beings. He found the obscene both funny and natural: obscenity could hardly degrade human beings any further than he believed them already degraded, in consequence of original sin.

❀

One of the things of which we are most ignorant is Vivien's attitude to what her husband was going through in the 1920s. A photograph of her, apparently taken by Eliot himself in 1928 while the Eliots were resident at 57 Chester Terrace, survives to commemorate how she looked – and how she looked at him – in these years: 'awakened, lips parted',[48] in passionate address. We do know that by April 1925 she and Eliot had deeper problems than ever. Vivien had developed an awful 'terror of loneliness',

4. Vivien Eliot at 57 Chester Terrace, London, photograph perhaps by T. S. Eliot, *c.* 1928.

> & now she cant let him, Tom, out of her sight. There he has sat
> mewed in her room these 3 months, poor pale creature, or if he
> has to go out, comes in to find her in a half fainting state.

As he had spent that particular evening out, he knew very well
that 'Tomorrow will be wretched'.[49] But he was in no better
state himself. The *Criterion* for April 1925 had explained how,
because of serious illness, Eliot had been unable to complete
three items intended for the magazine.[50] And Eliot wrote a
letter to Russell about Vivien early in May 1925 – just ten years
after first meeting her – in which he not only stressed again his
conviction that 'living with me has done her so much damage',
but also in the strangest way confided in Russell his need for
the assistance of somebody who understood her: as if Russell –
a man who had briefly been her lover – might be able to help.
Eliot himself found her 'perpetually baffling and deceptive.'
This was a very odd statement from someone who had been
married to Vivien for ten years. Eliot sounds as if he barely
knew Vivien, as if he had hardly begun to cope with living
with her: he could for example never get away from what he
called the 'spell' of Vivien's 'persuasive (even coercive) gift of
argument'. She was like 'a child of 6', 'immensely clever and
precocious'.[51] It is also a peculiarly distancing series of state-
ments about Vivien, and how Eliot still felt unable to understand her. Was *understanding* really what she needed?

At the back of his remarks, perhaps, is the simple confession he drafted ten years later, in his list of 'the essential
moments / That were the times of birth and death and

change': 'Remember also fear, loathing and hate'.[52] Those were the emotions that he and Vivien increasingly felt for each other. Eliot felt so disturbed that he wrote to Leonard Woolf in May 1925 asking him for 'the name of the best M.D. with psychoanalytic knowledge, emphasizing that he wanted this information not for V. [Vivien] but for himself'.[53]

❀

It is hard to escape the conclusion that Eliot's conversion to Anglo-Catholic Christianity had a great deal to do with the years of depression he had suffered, and with the ways in which he needed to deal with his relationship with Vivien. It did not make that relationship easier, not at all, which would even have been part of its appeal. It would effectively rule out any thought he might ever have had of getting a divorce. It would remind him constantly of his obligations: it would bind him to her for ever as a married man. But, oddly, it also meant that understanding her was not something he would ever need to try to do again: he could allow himself to feel a simple distance from her, and at times a horror of her. By December 1925, he had started to believe that Vivien hated him;[54] she was apparently telling him how attracted she was to other men. It is striking that, in March 1928 (while of course remaining married, and still living with Vivien), Eliot should have taken a vow of celibacy. That might suggest that, without a vow, he might have found himself troubled by a desire to sleep with her, or with another woman: something supported by the fact that it took him more than two years to find keeping his vow 'easy'.[55] But in her turn Vivien feared that 'Tom hates the sight of me';[56] and because of his experiences in marriage, like Harry in his play *The Family Reunion*, Eliot was actually developing 'a horror of women as of unclean creatures' as well as a horror of his own sexuality, sensing 'always the filthiness, that lies a little deeper'. (He would later describe Harry's sense of the 'pollution' of a woman's life.[57]) A vow of celibacy would, oddly, have been a way not just of formalising, but of legitimising such feelings. He would eventually be able to define his state in relation to Vivien as that of someone who – married to her – had become 'psychologically partially desexed'.[58] As he continued to have sexual feelings towards her (his vow of celibacy demonstrates that), we can estimate the state of mind of the man who declared, in 1930, that it was 'the knowledge of Good and Evil' that 'distinguishes the relations of man and woman from the copulation of beasts'.[59] He presumably meant that without a framework of moral responsibility (based on a belief in good and evil) sex was simply and inevitably appetite. According to the marriage vows in which he now believed (and doubtless applied retrospectively), he should have been able to promise 'with my body I thee worship'. He was now insisting that such worship would not, could not, be part of his own marriage. A vow of celibacy was a way of declaring his marriage in a kind of limbo, but he would certainly not have felt that it released him from his other vows or from his duty of care.

In that way his conversion helped legitimise what seems

by now to have been a horror of his own – and other people's – sexuality: of the 'personal animal feelings' he referred to in 1927,[60] the '"bewildering minutes" in which we are all very much alike'[61] over which he would agonise in 1933. When defining lust in his poem 'Marina' in 1930, he describes it as suffering 'the ecstasy of the animals'.[62] There seems in fact little difference between sinful desire and 'normal' sexual desire; the 'ecstasy of the animals' suggests that 'normal' sexual desire is *per se* violent and disgusting – though characteristically Eliot was especially interested in those who have to 'suffer' the ecstasy, and therefore need to deal with the consequences, rather than in those who are happily lustful (like Sweeney) or devoid of desires. We should certainly number Eliot among the bewildered sufferers of his own attitude to sex: among those who had painfully to deal with the consequences.

❁

It might be still more accurate to see Eliot in 1927–28 attempting to reverse everything he had 'done and been' for the previous twelve years or so.[63] Just as he had attempted to do when he met and married Vivien, in his conversion he was now attempting to deal with a whole slew of long-standing problems: his love for his mother, his frequent depression, his sexual desires and – now – the problem of his marriage. His determination in 1927–28 was to categorise the body and all its desires as sinful: neither just unpleasant, nor even disgusting, but evil. One effect was to make religious what had previously been a secular or emotional attempt at austerity, and so far as possible to start to leave behind – along with his first marriage – his great poetic period, which had run at its deepest between 1917 and the late 1920s.

Being a poet was never a pleasure to Eliot; he once remarked that, for the poet, 'the shadows lengthen, and the solitude becomes harder to endure' when he realises that he 'may have wasted his time and messed up his life for nothing'[64] – as if waste and mess were inevitable for someone committed to poetry. Eliot himself would comment ruefully in 1933 how 'the poet in a man does tend to spoil everything else',[65] and he would regularly quote a poem by Elizabeth Barrett Browning describing how the god Pan

> sits by the river,
> Making a poet out of a man:
> The true gods sigh for the cost and pain,––
> For the reed which grows nevermore again
> As a reed with the reeds in the river.[66]

He ended up feeling that 'he had paid too high a price to be a poet, that he had suffered too much'.[67] The intense, unthinking, unconscious, but necessary revelation of his feelings, without considering the cost either to himself or to Vivien during his marriage, was what he had in mind. (He once sardonically described Coleridge as 'one of those unhappy persons' who 'if they had not been poets ... might have made something of their lives'.[68]) But in 1929 he would hopefully, if ironically, remark that 'one outgrows and outlives the majority of human passions,'[69] in 1933 he would comment that 'passion ... must always fade out,'[70] and after 1930 he did his best not to write poetry that was personal. He failed, of course, and the revelatory personal writing, the 'sharpening of personal poignancy'[71] in the *Four Quartets*, remains the poetry of his later career that stands out most vividly.

But the *Four Quartets* were also the end of his life as a poet, although he had marvellous skills as a verse-maker, whether demonstrated in *Old Possum's Book of Practical Cats*, or in his occasional verses to friends, or in plays like *The Cocktail Party* (1949). His religious faith increasingly meant that the kind of profoundly questioning self-exploration and self-examination which, in the past, his poetry had demanded of him was now much of the time neither appropriate nor necessary. Just one more big poem lay between him and that desirable state.

8

'Ash-Wednesday' and the ending of a marriage

Like 'The Hollow Men', 'Ash-Wednesday' started as a series of separate poems which came to occupy Eliot after 'The Hollow Men' had reached its final form in November 1925. It came together just like the earlier poem; parts were published separately, finally the whole poem appeared. At one stage a separate short poem (which eventually became part II of the whole) bore the title 'All Aboard for Natchez / Cairo and St Louis' – the conductor's final call on the rail journey to St Louis – as if that were somehow one of the strata from which the poem had sprung.[1] Part II, by now 'Salutation', was first published in December 1927, Part I (as 'Perch' Io Non Spero') in Spring 1928, Part III (as 'Som de l'Escalina') in Autumn 1929, and all six parts as 'Ash-Wednesday', an expensive signed limited edition, on 24 April 1930;[2] but on the dust jacket of the trade edition, published six days later, appeared 'ASH / WEDNES / DAY / SIX POEMS' – as if it were still not quite a single work but a collection.

Just as 'The Hollow Men' had acquired various helpful

epigraphs when published as a single poem, when 'Ash-Wednesday' finally appeared as a book it too came with something new: the dedication 'To My Wife'.[3] This was a fascinating choice, because the poem has usually been read as one of religious devotion (Helen Gardner was sure that 'the theme is penitence'[4]), and nothing suggests that Vivien had been positively affected by her husband's conversion; her only recorded comment was to deride his new-found affiliation as 'monastic'.[5] Eliot would abandon Vivien two and a half years after the publication of 'Ash-Wednesday', while the dedication itself (after surviving the book's second impression) lasted just six years, when it was dropped for ever.[6]

The dedication has been described as 'a puzzling gesture', given Eliot's 'emotional and moral estrangement' from Vivien.[7] Such a conclusion ignores the fact that estrangement could have provoked the dedication, as a kind of reassurance to Vivien that, in spite of Eliot's 1928 vow of celibacy (we know nothing about what she thought of that), she remained 'My Wife'. He had by no means given up on his marriage. As late as 1930, he went abroad with Vivien in order to try (Sencourt said) to 'establish serenity between them', while he told another friend, Ottoline Morrell, about his continuing affection for Vivien.[8]

It is always dangerous to read back motives from later events. Because Eliot left Vivien in 1933, it is easy to interpret all his actions leading up to that moment as reflections of what he intended to do. But Eliot did not make up his mind to leave Vivien until February 1933; and although the idea of doing so must have crossed his mind before, it may well have been as something he knew he could not and would not do. The dedication may have been a public statement for his own benefit as much as for Vivien's: designed to reassure her that he did not intend to leave her, and that he knew himself still married to her.

The poem's first three lines, with their direct reference to Cavalcanti's touching love poem about having no hope of ever returning to his beloved (explicit in the title of the 1928 publication of Section I), might have encouraged Vivien in just such a way of thinking. Cavalcanti had started 'Because I do not hope to return'. Eliot started:

Because I do not hope to turn again
Because I do not hope
Because I do not hope to turn

Each of the three very different propositions is prefaced with a 'because' which would normally lead to a consequence (or even to three different consequences) ... but there is not a consequence in sight. Yet if we read the lines as Vivien Eliot, dedicatee, might have read them, they would have been redolent with consequence. They would have read as part of an ongoing conversation, in which they were as much answers as propositions. They would have told her that although the writer no longer feels any hope of turning to her again, there is (also) a chance that he might do so. Like Cavalcanti, he feels there is no way back ... but the very fact of the poem, of course, shows him reaching out to her.

Some of the odder things about 'Ash-Wednesday' (Gardner thought it 'the most obscure'[9] of Eliot's poems) can actually be understood most easily as Eliot's finding words for his predicament as a married man who has given up sex – sex which once had been 'the one veritable transitory power'.[10] Now he feels dismembered, devoured by those three white leopards and reduced to merely indigestible bits: bodily he is 'forgotten / And would be forgotten' (like the man insisting on having no biography written about him). The place is, after all, 'Where all loves end', and the chirping bones are glad to be scattered: in life 'we did little good to each other',[11] as he and Vivien might sadly have agreed.

'Ash-Wednesday' was the only one of his works which Eliot specifically linked with Vivien. A dedication to a person does not, of course, necessarily mean that the work is *about* that person (Eliot's dedication of *Poems 1909–1925* to 'Henry Ware Eliot / 1843–1919' did not mean that his father was somehow the book's subject), but the 'Ash-Wednesday' dedication seems nonetheless appropriate, in that a poem usually regarded as a proof of Eliot's dedication of himself to his new Christian faith is also necessarily seen in the context of his marriage, of his long farewell to Vivien, and of his original – and still manifest – 'dedication' to her, in spite of everything. It might very well also suggest that, among other things, the poem was a kind of explanation to her of what it was like for him to have moved on, while still remaining her husband, and while still – 'though I do not wish to wish these things'[12] – remaining 'torn on the horn':[13] agonised by sexual desire.

And in an especially daring ambiguity for a man of his faith, Eliot ventured on the striking declaration:

> I renounce the blessèd face
> And renounce the voice
> Because I cannot hope to turn again[14]

Is it the Virgin, Beatrice in paradise, or Vivien who is the object of these lines? Can Eliot really be leaving us in doubt? The blessèd face of the woman he had once loved ... and Vivien's voice, so adept at parody, once so attractive, so enviable ... now seem to find themselves part of a renunciation: reasons for not turning back to her. It was her very appeal as a woman which had to be resisted, as Eliot's vow of celibacy had confirmed. And, what is more, the renunciation itself is constructed as something formally to rejoice over, but is not – by itself – anything desirable. In April 1928, Eliot told William Force Stead he believed that, as a Christian, he required the most severe kind of discipline, in what Ronald Bush summarised as 'a question of compensation'. Nothing, Eliot believed, 'could be too ascetic, too violent'.[15] Like his sexual desires, his poetry also needed to be compensated for, for what it had said over the years, and continued to say: just like his original attraction to Vivien.

Such a formulation is characteristic of 'Ash-Wednesday'. Throughout a thoroughly religious poem, the idea is kept vividly alive of, after all, *not* being religiously oriented. This is one of the deep honesties of the poem. Section III contains some of the most sensual writing that Eliot ever produced; not only descriptions of 'Lilac and brown hair', but of 'a slotted window bellied like the fig's fruit': a 'startlingly graphic description of that female pudenda that roused in him such shame and such desire'.[16] Eliot not only insisted on poetry's right to its own existence almost independent of him, but refused even to think of imposing a moral or spiritual arbiter upon it, or doing anything except to let it take its own course. Poetry refused to be determined by serious or conscious authorial intention; it instinctively undermined the religious seriousness he was at most other times concerned to create. As he said about Yeats, 'unlike many writers, he cared more for poetry than for his own reputation as a poet'.[17] And the way 'Ash-Wednesday' turns away from religion, as much as towards it, is nowhere more true than in the concluding section, where – in some of the most moving lines he ever wrote – Eliot expresses an extraordinarily powerful continuing desire for 'the lost lilac and the lost sea voices': the lilac perhaps recalling 'the memory of a friend [Jean Verdenal] coming across the Luxembourg Gardens in the late afternoon, waving a branch of lilac',[18] the 'sea voices' recalling Eliot's own 'nostalgic longing' for childhood on the coast of New England.[19]

And what is more, he describes how 'the weak spirit' – the newly converted, not yet entirely resolute spirit – is inevitably affected and attracted, in just the old way, by such recollections. It 'quickens to rebel / For the bent golden-rod and the lost sea smell'. It comes alive again, that is, in rebelliously wanting such things back; it 'quickens to recover' them, exactly as – of course – the poetry is, at that very moment, bringing them back to life by recreating them so powerfully. The weak spirit turns out to be weaker than the fervent poetic recollection. Just as the 'lost heart stiffens and rejoices' in what the newly religious spirit is coldly attempting to put behind it, so the possibility of the heart's being 'found' again (both stiffened and rejoicing) is made real in its reasserted desire for the smell and taste of natural things. The sensual and reminiscent self, in the very act of being given up, is not given up. 'This is writing in which anything that is said may be unsaid in the saying.'[20] It is the inability actually to renounce, in a poem about renunciation, which is so impressive. (Eliot would later suggest about Tennyson's 'In Memoriam' was religious not 'because of the quality of its faith, but because of the quality of its doubt.'[21])

So that the narrator's final appeal 'Teach us to care and not to care / Teach us to sit still' is as much a desperate remark about how a marriage might learn to continue as it is about how religious devotion might be fostered. A wife reading this poem would know a good deal more about her husband's religious feelings, but would also know how very conflicted they were by his old needs, his old sexuality, and his nostalgia for childhood. As always in Eliot's major poetry, the intellec-tually, morally and spiritually unacceptable is, in the course of a poem, allowed (indeed energised and liberated) to play its full and awkward part. The poetic discourse is rich, surprising and inclusive, where the speech of a would-be moral narrator or a religious commentator would attempt to be narrow and discriminatory.

❀

It is important to present such considerations in the context created by the tangle of anecdotes and reminiscences which delineate the state of the Eliots' marriage during these final years. There is Vivien suddenly saying to Eliot '"You're the bloodiest snob I ever knew"', for example, and 'shouting and banging the door if anybody failed to speak to her';[22] or Virginia Woolf's description of Vivien as a 'bag of ferrets' around Tom's neck[23] (though since 'clever as a bag of ferrets'[24] was another of Woolf's phrases, she was also paying tribute to Vivien's frightening intelligence). And there is Conrad Aiken's description of an emaciated Vivien ('a scarecrow of a woman with legs like jackstraws, sallow as to face') picking a quarrel with her husband at lunch:

> [Gordon] George said something about pure intellect. Tom, giving his best pontifical frown, said there was no such thing. Vivian [*sic*] at this looked at me, then at Tom, and gave a peacock's laugh. Why what do you mean, she said. You argue with me every night in your life about pure intellect, don't you. – I don't know what you mean, says Tom. – Why don't be absurd – you know perfectly well that *every* night you tell me that there *is* such a thing: and what's more, that *you* have it, and that nobody *else* has it. – To which Tom's lame reply was You don't know what you're saying.[25]

For years Eliot believed that his marriage to Vivien was

something he could not walk away from, in spite of her accusations and attacks, that 'peacock laugh', and his own distancing of himself from her. He continued to care for her, in every sense; Virginia Woolf reproduced his account of how ill Vivien was at the end of April 1929:

> Vivien can't walk. Her legs have gone. But what's the matter? No one knows. And so she lies in bed – can't put a shoe on. And they have difficulties, humiliations, with servants ... Vivien with her foot on a stool, in bed all day; Tom hurrying back lest she abuse him ...[26]

They moved accommodation constantly because Vivien wanted to (five times in six months, according to Virginia Woolf: 'which means I suppose that the worm in Vivien turns and turns, and not a nice worm at that'[27]). Her illnesses, now including bowel trouble, raged on.

But by marrying Vivien, Eliot had made an endless commitment to her, 'for better for worse, for richer for poorer, in sickness and in health, to love and to cherish, till death us do part'.[28] He must by now have expected to carry out his dedicated duty for the rest of his life, even though it meant that, by 1933, he felt as if he had 'seen nothing, nobody, for the last 10 years'.[29] (Another incidental function of his conversion had been formally to state that, in spite of his absolute secular commitment, his deeper loyalties could now lie elsewhere.) 'Ash-Wednesday' is both tender and mournful about sensual attraction, in the same way as it is about the Garden 'Where all loves end'. The poem actually enunciates a plea to the 'Lady of silences': 'Terminate torment / Of love unsatisfied / The greater torment / Of love satisfied'.[30] Love (or at least sex) had perhaps once been satisfied, if never happily so. But that was now the worst of it, not the best of it, and the once utterly compelling person had become someone whom Eliot – in spite of his continuing affection – was agonised by.

❀

To describe the state of his marriage as it was by the early 1930s, he used the phrase 'a Dostoevsky novel written by Middleton Murry'.[31] His contempt for Murry's writing ('torrid taste-lessness and hypocritical insensibility'[32]) demonstrates just how savage a description this was of the state in which he found himself: he had always believed Murry 'the victim of emotion'[33] and his writing deeply damaged accordingly. If we couple that insight with the loving and loathing and murdering of the typical Dostoevsky novel, then the entanglements and madnesses of the Eliot marriage are very vividly and horridly suggested. The writer Hope Mirrlees remembered encounters with Vivien in the early 1930s:

> Supposing you would say to her, 'Oh, will you have some more cake?' she'd say, 'What's that? What do you mean? What do you say that for?' She was terrifying. At the end of an hour I was abso-lutely exhausted, sucked dry. And I said to myself: Poor Tom, this is enough! But she was his muse all the same.[34]

Together with the drugs she had always taken, Vivien was now using paraldehyde (smelling strongly of ether) as a massaging gel,[35] which led more than one person to suspect she was drinking ether ('she smells'); she was also suffering from depression and paranoia, and her hold on reality was fragile. Many people beside Hope Mirrlees experienced her frightened, angry, desperate questions, Virginia Woolf at least twice: in November 1930, for example, 'seeing insults if I say China or India or do you like more water?'[36] Vivien would respond:

> Does your dog do that to frighten me? Have you visitors? Yes we have moved again. Tell me, Mrs Woolf, why do we move so often? Is it accident?[37]

Virginia was also unwise enough to ask her – when they were having Monks House honey for tea – 'Have you any bees? (& as I say it, I know I am awaking suspicion).' The reply she got was the characteristically acerbic response of the disturbed person, 'suspiciously, cryptically, taking hidden meanings': 'Not bees. Hornets. But where? Under the bed.' Vivien's paranoia grew more and more evident, as when she accused Virginia Woolf of having 'made a signal that they should go.'[38] And on another occasion: 'Oh but why didn't they tell me Adrian Stephen was your brother. Why? Why! Nobody mentioned it. They kept it from me.'[39] 'Where is my bag? Where – where ...' A lady offered her a cigarette at a tea party in 1932, only to find Vivien telling her that she '*never* accepted anything from strangers.'[40]

As Hope Mirrlees suggested, Vivien in the early 1930s was utterly exhausting – 'And so on, until worn out with half an hour of it, we gladly see them go' wrote another hostess. At times she was thoroughly disturbing. Ottoline Morrell was at the Eliot's flat in November 1930 when Vivien spoke to Eliot 'as if he was a dog',[41] and Geoffrey Grigson recalled how, while Eliot was 'gravely and courteously' answering Grigson's questions, Vivien kept on asking Eliot 'Why? Why? Why?'[42] Robert Sencourt described how 'One friend saw her take off the stones of a necklace, throw them on to the floor and pretend they were animals which Tom must drive back into their stall.'[43] Edith Sitwell told the story of meeting Vivien in London and greeting her, only to hear Vivien say: 'No, no, you don't know me. You have mistaken me *again* for that *terrible* woman who is so like me ... She is always getting me into trouble.'[44] Virginia Woolf put it with unerring, horrid accuracy when she described Vivien as 'insane, yet sane to the point of insanity'.[45] Vivien had the unforgiving tendency of the miserably depressed and disturbed person to be able to hurt others easily, and to hurt herself even worse. To sum her up – as has recently been attempted – as 'no doubt ... a difficult woman, who would have tried anyone's patience'[46] is utterly inadequate.

The Eliots' social existence by the early thirties had thus been reduced to a combination of polite visiting (disrupted by Vivien's confused and confusing outbursts) and a great deal of living at home about which we know very little but which must have been loud and at least verbally violent, when it wasn't horribly silent (in 1928, Vivien would tell a friend how Eliot 'is *so* reserved and peculiar, and one cannot get him to speak'[47]). There were also stories that Eliot was drinking heavily: Ottoline Morrell, a teetotaller, remembered how she 'often found it unbearable to be near him'[48] and Virginia Woolf noted how 'Tom drinks'[49] while Vivien accused him of various crimes. The combination of day-time work at Fabers and the evening and night-time editing of the *Criterion* would have meant that Eliot must have gone on working ferociously hard while at home – as well as doing a great deal of caring for Vivien. Just the occasional visit to them by a friend gives us an insight. Elizabeth Bowen remembered the atmosphere in 1932 of 'two highly nervous people shut up together in grinding proximity.'[50]

One of their last appearances in public together, as it turned out, was a visit to the Woolfs at Rodmell on 2 September 1932. A photograph taken on the occasion shows Vivien as a terrifyingly shrunken wraith of a figure, fully bearing out Hope Mirrlees's description of her as giving the impression

of absolute terror, of a person who's seen a hideous, a goblin ghost, and who was always seeing a goblin in front of her. Her face was all drawn and white, with wild, frightened, angry eyes.

Virginia Woolf, less sympathetically, described how 'On a wild wet day she dresses in white satin, and exudes ether from a dirty pocket handkerchief. Also she has whims and fancies all the time – some amorous, some pornographic.'[51] Virginia

5. T. S. Eliot, Virginia Woolf and Vivien Eliot at Rodmell, Sussex, photograph by Leonard Woolf, 2 September 1932.

found herself in 'a sudden amorous embrace'. Meanwhile, 'Tom, poor man, all battened down as usual, prim, grey' was 'making his kind jokes' with Vivien.[52] But she became 'increasingly distraught as the afternoon wore on, changing her mind every second, and flying from one extreme to the other':[53] 'trailing about the garden – never settling – seizing the wheel of their car – suddenly telling Tom to drive – all of which he bears with great patience'.[54] Virginia noted Eliot's tenderness, while unworthily imagining how much he must be looking forward to 'his 7 months of freedom': he was (momentous occasion) on the point of going to the USA for the winter of 1932 and spring of 1933, to lecture and teach. It would be his first return to his home country since 1915. Interestingly, in the spring of 1932 he had drawn up a document for Vivien in which he solemnly undertook to return to her; she must have been desperately scared of losing him.

On 17 September 1932 – shortly before his forty-fourth birthday – Eliot went with Vivien and her brother Maurice to Southampton, to join his boat. He and Vivien walked on the deck together for a while, and then she returned to Maurice on shore. And Eliot sailed away. He would only see her twice more in his life.

❀

He had prepared for a salary-less year by publishing all he could. In September 1932 a volume of his *Selected Essays* had been published (over 6000 copies in the UK and the US together);

but it cannot have been an accident that, in December 1932, with his Sweeney fragments coming out as the volume *Sweeney Agonistes* (Eliot, of course, was out of the country, though he had corrected the proofs before leaving) there should have appeared on the title page the startling remark by St John of the Cross he had first selected in 1926: '*Hence the soul cannot be possessed of the divine union, until it has divested itself of the love of created beings.*'[55] There is very little in *Sweeney* about love, though there is a good deal about sex ('Birth, and copulation, and death'). But the epigraph confirms how Eliot was able to conceive of divesting himself of any traces of sexual and loving feeling as part of his religious duty. To divest himself of the last traces of loving Vivien (and also to free her from his own past sexual attraction to her) would among other things be a religious act. He would not have made a decision to leave her on the strength of such a quotation, but it is telling that he should have had it re-published at such a moment. It doubtless contributed to the kind of moral and intellectual confirmation which he needed, to be convinced of the horrible rightness of what he was now doing.

❀

It seems certain, however, that he only finally decided to leave Vivien while actually in America. He later used lines from Shakespeare's *Julius Caesar* – 'Like a phantasma, or a hideous dream' – to describe the nightmare period between the first idea of an action, and actually taking it;[56] in February 1933 he posted a letter to his solicitor instructing him to prepare a Deed of Separation, and enclosing a letter to be given personally to Vivien. What finally brought him to the decision we do not now know and may never know: it is quite likely that he did not know himself. The death of his mother in 1929 may, in one way, have emotionally liberated him into abandoning the second woman in his life: his conversion had certainly played its part. Another reason would have been the fact that he knew very well that he could do nothing for Vivien except look after her, weather the resulting storm, and try to protect her, for which he would have gone on getting ferociously attacked. It may have struck him that, by constantly helping her through the problems of her life, and to some extent shielding her, he was not actually helping her. At some stage before going to the USA he had talked through his dilemma with Vivien's brother Maurice, and with his own spiritual counsellor, Father Francis Underhill, and both seem to have advised him to separate from her. But actually initiating the process of leaving Vivien was still a terrible step. Scott Fitzgerald, who saw him within a few days of his writing to his solicitors in February 1933, described him as 'very broken and sad + shrunk inside'.[57]

Feeling as he did about her, and about women in general, however, he had decided that it was no good going on. He made this very clear in mid-March 1933 when he wrote explaining himself to Ottoline Morrell. By then he had taken his final decision about Vivien: he wanted 'never to see her again'. He did not think that it could be good for her to continue living with a man who finds her 'morally ... unpleasant' and to whom she was 'physically indifferent'.[58] He found her 'unpleasant' not (as has been suggested) because of her affair with Russell,[59] but because she was 'unpleasant as woman': morally unclean. Vivien in her turn was also 'physically indifferent' to him: she no longer wished to sleep with him. (Interestingly, it is *her* indifference to him he mentions: his silence about his own feelings confirms his need for a vow of chastity.) He probably also felt that he was damaging her, by being so different from her and (behind the dutiful care) having always been so coldly critical of her, so detached and judgmental; and in particular by having taken his own road away from her, emotionally and spiritually, over the last few years.

But it is striking how he makes no reference in his letter to Ottoline either to Vivien's attacks on him or to his own feelings of agonised responsibility. He may well have felt that the mortification Vivien had already inflicted on him (and what she was doubtless going to inflict in the future) was appropriate, given his own growing moral distance from her.

❦

His turbulent state of mind in America affected the work he did. He gave a number of lecture series, the most famous (or notorious) of which, the Page-Barbour lectures of 10–12 May 1933 at the University of Virginia, written very fast at the end of an exhausting year's lecturing and teaching, would be published in 1934 as *After Strange Gods: A Primer of Modern Heresy*. Eliot later gave the impression that he only published the book because, by the terms of the lecture contract, the lectures had to go into print; but a second impression of the book was ordered before the book was finally taken off the market, never to appear again, and he had, anyway, been planning a book on 'Modern Heresy' for some years; he had first mentioned it in 1928.[60]

In his lectures in Virginia – his poem 'Virginia' contains the striking line 'Iron thoughts came with me' – he took his chance to attack a number of writers: most notoriously, D. H. Lawrence.[61] He had once admired Lawrence, in 1922 having praised him not only as 'the most interesting novelist in England'[62] but as the only one – apart from Joyce – whom he cared to read,[63] and he had published Lawrence's fiction in *The Criterion*. In 1927, however, he stated that when Lawrence's characters make love, they lose all 'the habits, refinements and graces which several centuries have elaborated in order to make love bearable'.[64] The very idea of *Lady Chatterley's Lover* (published in 1928), which insisted on sexuality as a necessary component of marriage, irritated Eliot, although he confessed to never having read it;[65] but he proceeded during the next few years to do Lawrence all the damage he could. In 1930, he wrote to the *Athenaeum* protesting that a letter from E. M. Forster mourning Lawrence's death was meaningless when it called Lawrence 'the greatest imaginative novelist of our generation'.[66] Later that year, Eliot denounced those who dared think of the sexual act as 'natural, "life-giving"'[67] and in 1931 – in a savage book-review in the *Criterion* – he imagined what Lawrence would have been like as a teacher at Cambridge: "'rotten and rotting others'".[68] When lecturing to undergraduates at Harvard in the early spring of 1933, he criticised the 'sentimentality' of *Sons and Lovers* and called it 'devoid of the moral sense, an evil book';[69] while in his May 1933 lectures in Virginia, he would refer to Lawrence as a 'very sick man indeed', deeply amoral, driven by 'a distinct sexual morbidity'. He called him incapable of 'what we ordinarily call thinking', and his books remarkable for 'the absence of any moral or social sense'.[70] In 1934, he had Lawrence in mind when creating the drunken, rebellious, blustering and boorish third tempter in *Murder in the Cathedral*;[71] in 1935, discussing writers who might be pernicious in their influence, he singled out Lawrence.[72] The fact that Lawrence was from the working class also prejudiced Eliot against him. The 'hereditary transmission of culture within a culture',[73] as Eliot understood it, depended upon regulated class divisions, and he could conceive of Lawrence's mother's working-class Congregationalism as no more than 'vague hymn-singing pietism'.[74]

He later expressed some regrets about his long campaign against Lawrence[75] and – as an exemplary piece of penitence – made himself available among the crowds of witnesses prepared to take the stand for the defence in 1960 at the prosecution of the Penguin edition of *Lady Chatterley's Lover* at the Old Bailey.[76] But between 1927 and 1939 he had been perfectly serious in his denunciations. Lawrence, to Eliot, was terribly like Vivien: a believer in emotion for its own sake, one who demanded '*be personal*',[77] a proclaimer of the importance of the inner voice,[78] a rebel against (or – even worse – an ignoramus ignoring) the conception of a traditional, religiously based culture which Eliot was now determined to define as the only possible hope for his adopted country. Lawrence's insistence on instinct, on the body, on women's desires, on thwarted sexuality as a reason for ending a marriage, were things Eliot rejected savagely[79] – even though, in the end, he would confess that it had been he rather than Lawrence who had been 'very sick in soul' when he wrote the kind of material which appeared in *After Strange Gods*.[80]

9

Torment and
Four Quartets

What remained was his return to England, and the problem of Vivien. It is perfectly possible to believe that Eliot was thinking entirely of the Christian redemption when, in 'Little Gidding', written in 1941–2, he would pose the question 'Who then devised the torment?' and supplied the answer 'Love.'[1] In his poetry, however, the deepest concerns of his own life had always had a habit of surfacing, in ways that he very well understood, though may not always have enjoyed. In 1932 or 1933, he might easily have given the answer 'Love' to the question of what had gone wrong in his own life: first in his relationship with his mother, subsequently in his getting married to Vivien, later still in the torment he had endured towards the end of his marriage, and then finally in his own conscience after walking out on the marriage.

Eliot used the word 'torment' sparingly in his writing, but always with great precision. I quoted above his lines in 'Ash-Wednesday' about the torments 'Of love unsatisfied' and 'Of love satisfied'.[2] Writing to Paul Elmer More in 1930, he had explained how 'there were certain decisions which instigated a life of torment';[3] in 'The Dry Salvages' he would write specifically about the word (I shall discuss this below).[4] In each case he was thinking about his own marriage: what had happened within it and what had happened because of it. As he well knew, Vivien was – in her own way – as tormented as he was. And of course he also believed that, in this mortal life, 'everything is irrevocable, / The past unredeemable'.[5] As F. R. Leavis pointed out, the word 'unredeemable' suggests something 'to be expiated'.[6]

❀

Attempts have been made to rescue Eliot from his emotional and moral impasse in the early 1930s by offering him Emily Hale as a means of escape; he had travelled to see her at least twice while he had been in America. In her initial biography of Eliot, Lyndall Gordon went so far as to proclaim that it was Emily who had been responsible for 'the sudden emotional fertility that came to Eliot between 1927 and 1930 ... an unlooked-for blessing after years of hollowness'; and she stated that, in 'Ash-Wednesday', 'Emily replaced Vivienne as Eliot's muse'.[7] My analysis of those years shows no such 'emotional fertility' and my reading of 'Ash-Wednesday' does not support any such conclusion. Everything we know for certain about Emily Hale suggests that not only did she *not* perform such a role – she herself remarked, with great honesty, that 'there is *mighty little* of me in any poetry!'[8] – but that for the Eliot who was trying to make a new life from 1927 onwards, a new woman in his life would not have been a godsend but actually a terrible hindrance. 'Love satisfied' – if somehow it could ever have been achieved, and there is not the least sign that it might – would have been a still 'greater torment' than love unsatisfied. It may have been coincidence, but it may not, that when Eliot went to California to see Emily at the turn of the year 1932–33, he presented her with an inscribed copy of his recently published *Sweeney Agonistes*,[9] with its terrifying epigraph about the soul's need to divest itself of human love.

For if – still worse – Emily Hale had gone on believing in his early love (as she seems to have done), and Eliot, back in the USA in the winter of 1932, found himself unable to offer any real response to her (as it seems he was unable), that would have been reason for still further remorse. Rather than being assured of 'his relationship with Emily Hale renewed',[10] as has been claimed, he would have come back to England in the summer of 1933 knowing that, whatever happened, a future with Emily Hale was not going to be the answer to his problems: problems that – back in 1915 – he had hoped Vivien was going to resolve.

⚜

The story of the remainder of Eliot's marriage is shattering, whether extensively or briefly told. Vivien had been in an increasingly miserable state while he was away; in March 1933 she had told Ottoline Morrell that she 'had taken only two or three baths since Tom had left'.[11] By the time Eliot got back from the USA late in June 1933, he had ensured that Vivien had received his letter informing her that he would not be returning to her. He had planned well in advance what he would have to do:[12] go to ground, lodge with friends and – to Vivien's considerable distress – give her no hint of where he was. In July 1933, he saw her for the first time since his return when they attended the offices of his lawyers for a formal meeting: 'he sat near me & I held his hand, but he never looked at me.'[13] Eliot would have had many reasons for not looking at Vivien, but not desiring to be in any way attracted – or distracted – would certainly have been one of them.

He had made it plain to Vivien that their marriage had ended 'irrevocably';[14] but for some time after his return from North America, he had to remain in hiding so that she could not contact him. She spent months doing her best to do so (Virginia Woolf described her as 'poor V... running amok all over London'[15]), and her confused state was rendered still more confused by the way Eliot constantly seemed to disappear – from his office at Fabers whenever she called, for example (he would be informed that she had arrived and would slip out of the building). She also tried – but failed – 'to waylay him on the stairs'. She expressed herself constantly baffled as to why he never returned 'home' to her. He lived with various friends in country cottages, took flats briefly, lodged in a boarding house, and pursued an evasive existence; very few people knew his address. Even good friends like the Woolfs had, to begin with, only a vague notion that the Eliots had finally parted. Nevertheless – away from Vivien for the first time since 1915 – Eliot relished his freedom. When Virginia Woolf finally saw him, in September 1933, she thought he looked '10 years younger'[16] and observed a 'bubbling up of life' in him: 'At 46 he wants to live, to love'.[17]

For a while he lodged in a flat in Great Ormond Street occupied by a group of homosexual friends (the novelist, lawyer and financier Clifford Kitchin, the book-collector Richard Jennings, and the financier Ken Ritchie); some thirty years later Kitchin told a friend that Eliot would go out in the evening wearing 'a bit of slap'[18] – 'rouged and lipsticked, with eyeshadow'. Such lodgings would have been an ideal place for a man on the run, and it is extremely unlikely that Eliot was living any kind of gay existence, though he may well have gone on trying to look young. Kitchin was happy to welcome a publisher into his ménage, and equally happy many years later to claim as gay his (by then distinguished) lodger.

The agony Vivien sustained – and continued to endure – was that of a woman convinced that her husband had somehow been delayed or deceived or betrayed, not that of a woman who had been left by her husband. She could never bring herself to believe what he had written to her and then told her, and what was so appallingly obvious to everyone else: that he had left her. Nothing is more revealing of what had become, by the early 1930s, her catastrophically unbalanced emotional state than this desperate, long-drawn-out period of self-deception. She went on for the next three years, at least, appealing to Eliot to come back, believing at times that he really wished to return to her but was somehow being prevented from doing so. She put a wreath of flowers around 'Toms photo by Elliot Fry' and told some people at least 'that he was drowned';[19] she also tried to let him know that she was leaving the door open between 10.30 and 11.00 every night: 'Here is your home & here is your *protection. Which you need*', she wrote to him.[20] It is of course illuminating that she saw *him* as the endangered person. As Eliot had told his mother in 1918, 'Vivien worries a great deal about me';[21] one of her old marital roles had been to take care of him emotionally and to guard him against depression, as when she had signed the contract with him that restricted his reading and writing. Sometime around 1917 she had actually remarked to her friend Brigit Patmore: 'If anything happens to me, will you look after Tom?'[22]

Although, following the death of her father in 1927, she had acquired some money of her own (an allowance from the Haigh-Wood Estate), Eliot had now also settled into paying her £260 a year maintenance. But there are indications that she found it impossible to survive on her income; she lived extravagantly and at times recklessly,[23] and by her own account, by 1934 she was at times 'a helpless and unspeakable wreck of drugs, fear and self-paralysis'.[24] It was a desperate time for her, obsessed as she was by her hope that Eliot might at any moment come back to her. In its own very different way it was humiliating for Eliot too, forced to live without a home, away from his books and papers, hidden by friends, driven to take lodgings with his parish priest, and to be protected by loyal secretaries whenever Vivien attempted to waylay him: but in all such ways constantly being reminded of her, of what a state of distress she was in, and of what he had done: and, exactly as he had been before he had left her, feeling quite unable to protest about what she did or said about him. He told a friend many years later how afraid he was 'of the dreadfully untrue things'[25] she was saying, and how he feared that his friends might believe her. Interestingly, he was strongly resistant to the idea that Vivien might be insane. 'He wont admit the excuse of insanity for her – thinks she puts it on; tries to take herself in; for this reason, mystifies Eth Bowen.'[26] (Elizabeth Bowen was a sympathetic friend to Vivien, and spent hours listening to her.) It was a very hard line to take; but even if Vivien had not been insane before the summer of 1933, she seems to have come very close to it afterwards.

A court order – and a raid by court-appointed bailiffs – allowed Eliot to recover books from the old flat in December 1934, after Vivien had repeatedly refused to give them up; and another raid recovered some more of his possessions in July 1935. He also very much wanted to get back the Eliot family silver and photographs, but – again – Vivien refused to co-operate unless Eliot promised to see her: and the silver was lodged in a bank vault where he could not get at it. In such a situation, he could obviously have taken even stronger legal action against her, but he declined to do so. Vivien went on believing that Eliot wished to return to her: 'poor little loyal Tom' she called him in July 1935,[27] shortly after one of the bailiffs' raids, for which she clearly had no thought of blaming him. When *Murder in the Cathedral* started its run in London in 1935, she regularly went to see performances, and she also went to see *Sweeney Agonistes* on several occasions when it was staged at the Westminster Theatre in September 1935. She had already joined the British Union of Fascists ('wears a black shirt, believes in Mussolini'[28]); now she started attending church services and was also working to develop her musical talents.

By luck, trickery and bland deception Eliot managed to go on avoiding her for nearly two and a half years, until on 18 November 1935 she finally confronted him, just before a public lecture he was preparing to give at a book fair in London. At the door she greeted him 'Oh *Tom.*' He took her hand, loudly pronounced 'how do you *do?*' and walked quickly past her. After the lecture she went up to see him; she had brought their dog Polly, and the dog of course recognised Eliot, racing across the floor to greet him. Eliot signed the books Vivien had brought for him to sign, but when she asked 'Will you come back with me?' he answered 'I cannot talk to you now' and left as quickly as he could.[29] Vivien's precarious mental state can be judged from her own version of the encounter, in which she declared that 'my husband has now found me … When I say found, I mean he claimed me in public'.[30] In fact they would never see each other again.

Vivien's refusal to help him by letting him have his possessions, along with her attempts to track him down and confront him, were things Eliot would also have accepted as what was owed him. No man can escape the Furies, he knew very well.

Back in 1926, preparing for the first publication of *Sweeney Agonistes* and fearing what was going to happen – in fact, what had already started to happen – he had prefixed the play with Orestes' final speech from *The Libation Bearers*: 'You don't see them, you don't – but *I* see them: they are hunting me down, I must move on'.[31] For Harry, pursued by the Furies in his 1939 play *The Family Reunion*, Eliot wrote the lines

> ... I thought I might escape from one life to another.
> And it may be all one life, with no escape.[32]

Harry has – it seems – pushed his wife off the deck of an ocean liner, and as well as seeing his Furies out of the corner of his eye, dreams them too: 'inside too, in the nightly panic / Of dreaming dissolution.'[33] Back in 1919, Eliot had written how 'a dream restores / The always inconvenient dead'.[34] He was now subjected to all kinds of recollection, dream, reminder and panic.

The situation continued for years, with Vivien's behaviour being at times both alarming and foolish, although at other times perfectly normal. Virginia Woolf, a loyal friend of Eliot's, recorded how on 31 December 1933 she had had 'a remarkable letter ... from Vivienne Haigh Eliot' (as Vivien was now calling herself) about the fact that 'Tom refuses to come back to her'; she wrote 'sensibly – rather severely, and with some dignity, poor woman, believing, she says, that I respect marriage'.[35] In 1936, Vivien was devoting herself to her musical studies, and aiming to become a singer. But in July 1938 she was found wandering the streets of London 'in a deplorable condition', too afraid to go anywhere, and apparently now believing that Eliot had been beheaded.[36] Eliot was out of London at the time. At the behest of her brother Maurice, two doctors examined her, and she was eventually committed to a mental asylum, Northumberland House in Northwick Park, North London, with the assistance of two individuals who have never been named; her brother Maurice was one, the lawyer and family friend Jack Hutchinson may well have been the other. To Maurice's annoyance, Eliot refused to sign any committal order.[37] He did not believe that Vivien was mad, and so could not have agreed to her committal on the grounds that she was. But he was also not going to be the one who actually turned the key in the door confining her, any more than he would institute legal proceedings against her in person, however much he may have wished for his own sake – and for hers – that she might be institutionalised.

In the late twentieth century, it became accepted as fact that Vivien had in reality been perfectly sane all along, and that her committal had been an outrageous act of masculine bigotry. This interpretation of events was provoked by an interview her brother Maurice had with the writer Michael Hastings in March 1980, in which he declared that, when he had last seen his sister (in 1946) she had been 'as sane as I was':[38] 'She was never a lunatic. I'm as sure as the day I was born.'[39] A few visits to an asylum (Maurice only visited Vivien very rarely) are not enough to make such a judgement convincing: and Maurice had also clearly forgotten (if indeed he ever knew) the dreadful highs and lows of her behaviour between 1933 and 1938. With a carefully regulated drugs regime, Vivien may very well have been stable most of the time in Northumberland House. But by the middle 1930s, when she would apparently save up her prescription drugs and take them all in one dose together, at times she was obviously incapable of taking care of herself, as well as being subjected to massive delusions. She would, for example, tell a friend about Eliot in the late 1930s: 'I *trust* the man ... He has some very strong reasons. You do not argue with God, or question his ways.'[40] Such evidence speaks volumes against the single comment about her sanity made by Maurice; and if her own family were not prepared to take her in, and they were not, it is hard to see what future she could have had at that date which was non-institutional.

Carole Seymour-Jones has also asserted that Vivien was committed in order to stop her spending recklessly, and because Eliot had 'pressing' motives 'for locking his wife up: gagging Vivienne would put a stop to her innuendos about his private life and prevent her attendance at his plays.'[41] The absurdity of such proffered reasons (what harm did such attendance do him? and for the moment he had no plays on stage) is matched only by the malice of the accusation. There is no evidence for any such motives on Eliot's part, and throughout he had been careful to take no part in something in which – anyway – he did not believe. He had left Vivien, and although the thought of her being at last properly cared for might have brought him a kind of relief, at every stage he had felt and would continue to feel horribly guilty, even if at times 'a little resentful of all the past waste & exaction'.[42] He would now have to live with the knowledge of her enduring existence in the asylum. 'I can never forget anything', he would tell E. W. F. Tomlin,[43] and he characterised Harry's reaction to his lost wife in *The Family Reunion* as one in which 'He still wants to *forget*, and that is the way forbidden' (adding, grimly, 'It is not I who have forbidden it, I see it as Law'[44]). He did not visit Vivien – 'the doctors had told him he mustn't',[45] his second wife recalled – but it is hard to see what the point of such a visit might have been. To torment Vivien all over again, to torment himself still further? He kept in touch with what was happening to her via his solicitors.

※

But when it comes to what he may really have felt now, about his life, as usual we have to turn to his poetry. There had been another period of drought after 'Ash-Wednesday', broken only by the ironic, witty and politically subversive fragments of 'Coriolan' (the writing of a man deeply sceptical of totalitarian politics). In North America in 1933, he had drafted the poems eventually published as 'New Hampshire', 'Virginia' and 'Cape Ann', the last a hymn to the birds of 'this land'.[46] There were other poems he classified as 'minor' too, including 'nonsense verses' in August 1933.[47]

But it was not until he wrote 'Burnt Norton' in 1935, and it turned into the first of a sequence of four poems that would crystallize as *Four Quartets*, that he really dug deep again. It took a long time before he did anything else along similar lines; in 1939 he actually told Bonamy Dobrée that 'he was abandoning the writing of poems because ... he did not want to repeat himself'.[48] He also gave up editing the *Criterion* and allowed it to fold; he believed it had outstayed its welcome as a periodical. In 1940, however, he started on the poem 'East Coker'; and, in 1941, he would write most movingly in his poem 'The Dry Salvages' about how 'the moments of agony' in a life are, in fact, not moments at all, but permanent – 'With such permanence as time has'.[49] That is, sufficiently permanent. In these, some of the most powerful lines of the poem, 'unqualified' torment seems to have been a description of what he had found himself committed to during the subsequent years of his life; though it was characteristic of him that it should have been in the emotional 'actuality' of a poem that he found a way of talking about it – and thus not just preserving it as a testament to his feelings but addressing himself, awkwardly and uncomfortably, to what was at the bottom of his emotional mind, and finally letting it out. 'One doesn't know quite what it is that one wants to get off the chest until one's got it off'.[50] It was at just this time, too, that he quoted Yeats's famous lines 'You think it horrible that lust and rage / Should dance attendance upon my old age', and commented: 'To what honest man, old enough, can these sentiments be entirely alien?' What made them special was their particular 'clarity, honesty and vigour'.[51] That is revealing about Eliot in several ways: of his old demand for 'clarity, honesty and vigour', and as a confirmation that 'lust and rage' were still powerful forces within him; but, too, of his acceptance that writing them into poetry made such things, inevitably, a personal confession. He was very aware that Tennyson's famous poem 'In Memoriam' had been a constant re-creation of that poet's feelings for Arthur Hallam, so that nothing in it – its religious anxiety, its struggles for faith, its attempt to capture the dilemma of the mid nineteenth century – turned out as impressive as the feeling of emotional impasse it creates. Eliot himself had been very clear about this in his own 1936 essay on 'In Memoriam' when he called the poem 'the concentrated diary of a man confessing himself'.[52] In just the same way, nothing in Eliot's last four major (and primarily religious) poems *Four Quartets* is now so compelling as their equivalent confession of the guilt and remorse he experienced because of his marriage and how he had ended it.

❀

This is not to say that the poems are 'about' Vivien. They are not; and 'Burnt Norton' in particular avoids the subject of Vivien with especial care. The poems are focused upon a life in which experiences of the transcendental arise suddenly, surprisingly, at times blessedly out of experiences of the everyday. The everyday, nevertheless, remains so profoundly grim that the moments of revelation are no more than relieving moments.

'Burnt Norton' seems to have been provoked by a visit which Eliot had paid in September 1934 with Emily Hale to the gardens of the (burned) house of that name in Gloucestershire, with its rose-garden and dry garden pools. The visit – which might well have aroused in both of them ideas of 'What might have been' – instead impels the poem's narrator back to thoughts of the 'passage which we did not take / Towards the door we never opened / Into the rose-garden'.[53] A period before Eliot was married is thus suggested – together with the gloomy fact that nothing actually came of it. Reawakening thoughts of what had *not* happened are described as 'Disturbing the dust on a bowl of rose-leaves'.[54] Dried leaves, not dried petals, are in the bowl: it is not love which comes to mind but the sheer passage of time – the leaves have not been touched for years. An apparent moment of revelation comes with a vision of water suddenly filling the dried pools (shades of 'The Waste Land'), but it does not come as a life-changing or life-affirming moment. It comes, instead, as a grim reminder that 'human kind / Cannot bear very much reality'.[55] The present is where you are, and you are stuck in it and with it; and most of the time all you can do is try to live with it and through it. 'You do not know what hope is, until you have lost it.'[56]

It is a deeply depressing work about a life actually lived: for 'that which is only living / Can only die.'[57] Feelings about 'What might have been' are pure speculation; past and future point to one end only, 'which is always present'.[58] All that the narrator can or might look forward to is 'The inner freedom from the practical desire', when he will stop wanting to love or to be loved humanly, when sexuality ('partial ecstasy' is the poem's term for it) will no longer be a burden.[59] Paradoxically, the deepest desire one can hope for is to be 'undesiring', a very special 'form of limitation' for human beings. The poem attempts to distinguish between 'desire' (which 'is movement / Not in itself desirable') and 'love', which may be of the divine, and 'is itself unmoving'.[60] Emily Hale may have been a participant at the start of these reflections, but Vivien remains the deep subject. Freedom from her, and from the feelings (both desire and disgust) that in the past she had aroused, is profoundly to be desired, though the 'form of limitation' which such freedom would entail is very clear – and would also have excluded Emily Hale.

'East Coker', written in 1940, takes the reader to the village in Somerset from which the Eliot family originally came, and which Eliot had visited in 1937.[61] It recreates an immemorial rustic life, making an implicit and constant contrast with everyday life in 1940. And yet 'dark dark dark. They all go into the dark': 'And we all go with them, into the silent funeral'.[62] All those years when the Eliots had lived and worked in East Coker, they were simply contributing themselves 'to the earth / Which is already flesh, fur and faeces'.[63] As Sweeney has known for years, 'Birth, copulation and death' are the only fate. Confronted with such a future, all the narrator can advise is: 'wait without hope / For hope would be hope of the wrong thing; wait without love / For love would be love of the wrong thing.'[64] And that is how one spends one's life: in 'the waiting'. One lives forward only 'by a way wherein there is no ecstasy'.[65] Again, 'ecstasy' as humans know it is sexual; and, as such, inimical to a life of dedication and faith.

In common with the other three poems, the fifth section of

'East Coker' turns to the matter of writing poetry, and makes it sound an especially hopeless business: 'every attempt' is 'a different kind of failure'. But 'For us, there is only the trying'.[66] What the subject of this ideal poetry might be, or why it has to be written, is never clear. Like most writers, Eliot found himself simply subject to 'the obligation to express'.[67] But it is clear that his obligation was, again and again, to express remorse, lost love, guilt, nostalgia (John Hayward called 'East Coker' 'poignantly self-revealing'[68]). The poetry Eliot was now writing would ideally not be about 'the intense moment / Isolated, with no before or after' (which is how human love is ordinarily conceived and felt, and as which it is mourned) but would exemplify 'a lifetime burning in every moment', in which the burning might perhaps signify religious fulfil-ment, although 'burning' inevitably also implies pain leading to guilt: one of the consequences of a lifetime of damage.[69] But then 'East Coker' offers a startling version of love: 'Love is most nearly itself / When here and now cease to matter'.[70] For most people in love, the 'here and now' of each other are of the very essence of feeling. But Eliot's new poetry insists that such love is to be given up in favour of a non-human love which has nothing to do either with the sexual or with the everyday.

In 'The Dry Salvages', the poem of 1941 which Eliot origi-nally thought might complete a trilogy, although he is specifi-cally concerned with the 'point of intersection of the timeless / With time',[71] time itself constantly intrudes. The guilt, the sense of pain and loss, go on and on: 'Time is no healer'.[72] It would be nice to assert (as the poem tries to) that 'Right action is freedom / From past and future also'.[73] That would be wonderful, but freedom from those years, from that life, that responsibility, that guilt – all turn out quite impossible. 'For most of us, this is the aim / Never here to be realised'.[74] The poem states that 'the moments of agony … are likewise permanent' but it adds, remorselessly, that 'We appreciate this better / In the agony of others, nearly experienced, / Involving ourselves, than in our own.'[75] Eliot never came nearer to identifying his own later married experience, so 'involving' of himself, so 'nearly experienced'. 'People change, and smile: but the agony abides. / Time the destroyer is time the preserver.'[76] All that awful expenditure of feeling is just water under the bridge, one might say: but the water is constantly there, the memory indelibly preserved. We are 'only undefeated' because 'we have gone on trying'.[77] But all we actually have to look forward to (in life and time) is our own death, while we consider how our physical bodies will nourish 'the life of significant soil'.[78]

Eighteen months after visiting Burnt Norton, Eliot had been taken to the Cambridgeshire hamlet of Little Gidding, which now became a quintessentially English location for the poem which ended the sequence. 'Little Gidding' nevertheless took a long time to write (it was only finished in 1942); a long *terza rima* section in imitation of Dante, which gave Eliot enormous trouble, ends with a profoundly disturbing listing of the 'gifts reserved for age' concluding with the 'rending pain of re-enactment / Of all that you have done, and been', and the 'awareness / Of things ill done and done to others' harm / Which once you took for exercise of virtue.'[79] Such writing suggests a remarkable, concentration not only upon human folly and personal guilt, but on 'the association of "enact" – to take the part of oneself on a stage for oneself as the audience'.[80]

But Eliot also launched on a deep analysis of his own role as a husband in his description of 'three conditions which often look alike':

> Attachment to self and to things and to persons, detachment
> From self and from things and from persons; and, growing
>   between them, indifference
> Which resembles the others as death resembles life ...[81]

The reference to Eliot's own marriage, and how it had come to an end, is clear, as in the touching reference to the loved ones now lost: 'See, now they vanish, / The faces and places, with the self which, as it could, loved them ...'[82] The loving had become impossibly hard: the self, as it could, loved; but not always, and not freely, and never enough; and from the perspective Eliot was now adopting, such love would, anyway, always have been (as 'East Coker' put it) 'love of the wrong thing'.[83] 'Little Gidding' itself speaks of the longed-for liberation, 'Of love beyond desire'.[84] That was the only kind of longing which the poetry was now prepared to admit; and in that way, too, the poetry had set out in a new and different direction from the one which Eliot's own life had taken.

In these ways, at least, Eliot's poetry in *Four Quartets* remains vivid in offering a series of accounts of the continuing after-shocks of his marriage and of what he believed he might have done to Emily Hale too. As he had realised, 'acute personal reminiscence' – 'never to be explicated, of course' – was something simply necessary in his poetry, to give 'power from well below the surface'.[85] In a sense these passages are the successors to the poetry Vivien had been responsible for helping him to write between 1916 and 1930.

❀

All the same, even this poetry in the *Four Quartets* always tends to be 'about' Eliot's experiences: it very rarely takes us into any kind of 're-enactment' of those experiences. Whereas 'The Waste Land' and some of his other earlier poems had been written so as 'to render the nerve endings of a sensibility',[86] that was not how he was now writing. One of the causes of his conversion had been a deep concern with the need for some kind of stabilisation of culture and society, and he was now much more aware than he had been of the social function of poetry: its responsibility to 'purify the dialect of the tribe'.[87] He was interested a good deal more in its accessibility, and in what it could usefully say to its readers. Partly as a result, the language of *Four Quartets* is at times prosy, at other times diffuse. Such writing comes nowhere near the experiments with raw 'psychic material' which he had made between 1916 and 1930, and which had necessitated such innovations in both language and form. Experimental poetry always needed to struggle to create its own poetic form,[88] as 'Gerontion' and 'The Waste Land' had struggled; even the unfinished *Sweeney*

Agonistes had started to find its own peculiar shape. The form adopted in the *Four Quartets*, following the model of 'Burnt Norton', was in each case the same: a poem of five sections, organised in the same way in each poem, with (in general) slack rhythms and roughly iambic lines. Behind such poetry lay no such equivalent desire to find the matching and appropriate shape for what was forcing itself into the mind. Instead, there was a poetic version of a structure Eliot had observed in a piece of music he was very fond of, Beethoven's A minor string quartet Op. 132.[89]

In such poetry, too, feelings themselves are for the most part simply not allowed; they are part of the 'Sense and notion' which the religious point of view demands should be 'put off'.[90] Only at moments – as in 'The Dry Salvages' – is the expression more than description or statement. This was of course to some extent deliberate: a reaction to the kind of poetry Eliot now believed he should be writing. But Eliot's famous detachment – or should it be called indifference? – was now for the first time actually getting into and controlling his poetry, rather than being by-passed or undercut by it. One critic put it rather savagely: 'The same impulses that thickened Eliot's verse also led him to adopt a form that would not let him face his demons honestly.'[91] That, of course, is only a way of putting it; his very writing of poetry was a sign that at least the demons were still being summoned up.[92]

The poems are full of wonderful things – like the creation of the short-lived winters' day at the start of 'Little Gidding', with the 'brief sun' flaming 'the ice, on pond and ditches';[93]

and there are deep and moving insights into how we consider history. But it tells its own story that Eliot chose to end the sequence of four poems with a triumphant bringing together in 'Little Gidding' of two symbols, the fire and the rose – symbols suggesting pain and love – and at the very end presenting them as, potentially, inextricably entwined ('The fire and the rose are one').[94] The ringing conclusion has understandably been challenged as 'mere statement – statement so insistent as fairly to be called emphatic assertion'.[95] The subjects of pain, suffering and love had always deeply concerned Eliot, but such a way of writing about them has very little to do with actual experiences of pain or suffering or love; for example the pain, suffering and love which had been linked and intertwined in his own life since 1915. The poetry climaxes, instead, with a series of beautifully organised verbal patterns. What Eliot admired about Paul Valéry's poetry was the way it ensured that 'not our feelings, but the pattern which we may make of our feelings, is the centre of value'.[96] What tends to happen in his own later poetry is that the feelings of life are evaded or ignored by the patterns, and that the patterns become 'the centre of value'. Robert Lowell, who knew him well, would say – with some irony, but a great deal of insight – that after the *Four Quartets* Eliot had become 'such a good man ... that he doesn't need to write poetry any more'.[97] It was as if Eliot's writing of poetry had only been 'necessary' to the discontented and unhappy man: the one who desperately needed to turn 'his personal and private agonies into something rich and strange'.[98]

10

Eminence and theatre

So it goes. Not many poets in full possession of their faculties bring their poetic careers to an end at the age of fifty-three. But that was what Eliot did after completing 'Little Gidding' in 1942: *Four Quartets* crowned his 'lifetime's effort' by concluding it. Ironically, this was just at the start of the time when he would be most honoured as a poet and writer. He was awarded the British Order of Merit in January 1948 and the Nobel Prize in December 1948; he became a Chevalier Officier de la Legion d'Honneur in 1951, was given the German Orden Pour le Mérite in 1951 and the Hansischer Goethe-Preis in 1955, and by 1960 had acquired honorary degrees from the Oxford, Cambridge, Harvard, Yale, Princeton and Columbia. But he would write just four very brief 'occasional' poems during the whole of the rest of the 1940s,[1] and two short poems between 1954 and 1958.[2] And those – together with a number of tiny *jeux d'esprit* – were his poetic output for the twenty-two years between the completion of 'Little Gidding' and his death in January 1965.

He was, however, still a very busy man and a superbly professional publisher. Since the late 1920s he had naturally been interested in building up the poetry list at Fabers ('he was made the chief interviewer of poets'[3]) and commented in 1955 that his ambition had been to make the phrase 'Faber poetry' a by-word. He certainly succeeded: Faber published Ezra Pound, W. H. Auden, Stephen Spender, Louis MacNeice, Cecil Day-Lewis, W. S. Graham, Robert Lowell, later on Ted Hughes and Sylvia Plath. A colleague recalled that 'Because he refused to over-estimate his own enthusiasms, his judgements, within the firm, were more and more respected'.[4] Eliot spent a vast amount of time on publishing in general too: he had originally been taken on by the firm because of his business expertise, and he played his full part as a member of the team. He was, too, 'our best blurb-writer ... They are torture to write. Eliot wrote thousands of them'.[5] The same colleague remembered that, when unsolicited manuscripts were distributed, 'He had more manuscripts to read than anybody else, and the odd thing was, he really read them';[6] a friend observed how 'he had always studied work submitted to him with generous attention, and his reactions, positive or negative, had no less weight for being usually brief'.[7] What was perhaps most remarkable was his attitude towards prospective authors. 'He treated them all, including the less promising, as fellow-artists in the craft, while they looked up to him as a master who might also help them to publication'.[8] Eliot was adviser for more than one generation of young writers, an encourager and a conscience for many, offering not only emotional but at times financial support for those more needy than himself. He lived a strict but extraordinarily generous life – so far as others were concerned. To himself he was never so forgiving.

By the late 1940s, he was mostly going to Faber and Faber in the afternoons, and keeping his mornings clear for writing. Every day he would stand at a kind of lectern in his room and type for a couple of hours at least. But it was not poetry which concerned him. As well as the dramas, there were lectures to prepare, on Christianity, culture and literature; he was more and more in demand as a public speaker, and many of the essays that now got into print had started out as lectures. He would bring out a second edition of his *Selected Essays* in 1951 and another volume of criticism, *On Poetry and Poets*, in 1957. His writings about culture had moved him to an extremely conservative position, to an extent that belied the experience of his own early years. In 1948, he would for example argue his changed attitude towards the role of the family, insisting that it remained the 'primary channel of transmission of culture': 'no man wholly escapes from the kind, or wholly surpasses the degree, of culture which he acquired from his early environment.'[9] Such a conviction runs clean counter to the way he had been thinking, feeling and writing during the years between 1914 and 1930, when he had been above all concerned to escape the cultural influence of his 'elders'.

❧

Yet by the 1940s he was neither simply conservative nor even political in the usual sense. He enjoyed believing in tradition, hierarchical order, authority; in social, European, moral and religious conformity; and for those reasons his social criticism (for example) attacked material progress and 'the values arising in a mechanised, commercialised, urbanised way of life' with as much energy as a D. H. Lawrence would have shown, though for none of the same reasons. What is striking is the extent to which Eliot (like the writer and philosopher T. E. Hulme, whom he thoroughly admired and to some extent had modelled himself upon[10]) enjoyed taking up an extreme, polemical and at times absurdly idealistic stance, as when in 1933 he had argued against 'a spirit of excessive tolerance' in society and had stressed the ideals of a 'unity of religious background' and of a population which, in the ideal kind of society he had in mind, should be 'homogeneous'. This was the fantasy that led him on to pronounce in 1933 that 'reasons of race and religion combine to make any large number of free-thinking Jews undesirable'.[11] This is by no means the simple anti-Semitism it has sometimes been claimed to be, nor even 'objectionable because it is badly written',[12] but inspired by a savage if truly academic intolerance of free-thinking, which also took it casually for granted that no-one cared very much about what happened to Jews. Eliot doubtless hoped his light touch would make such formulations acceptable, but his playfulness now seems cursed with a very heavy hand.[13]

None of the ideas of social change Eliot was promoting, to create a homogeneous society, could actually have been brought about by any conceivable kind of public or private action: neither by government, nor by war, nor even by ethnic cleansing or holocaust (removing all free-thinkers would be impossible). They were the speculative ideals of a mind which remained primarily philosophical and which – like a certain kind of academic philosopher – very much enjoyed carrying arguments to their logical, shocking conclusion, however unfeeling or – in this case – anti-Semitic they might be. Eliot remained confident that 'in one's prose reflexions one may be legitimately occupied with ideals',[14] and along the way he took pleasure in being politely and at times extremely offensive to all kinds of people he did not like. The reason he would refuse to withdraw such a statement, even after 1945, would not be because he remained fundamentally anti-Semitic, but because he continued to think the same about free-thinkers. So how could (and why should) he withdraw?

This was the kind of speculative role he had assumed in his capacity as an outsider. He enjoyed the poses which his foreignness allowed him, while positioning himself at the heart of the established church and the literary establishment. The photograph taken of him about 1932 by the London portrait photographers Elliot and Fry exemplified this person.[15] He wears the pin-stripe trousers of the City man; his perfectly equal white cuffs and breast-pocket handkerchief, his necktie rich and modest, his pose with one arm resting on what looks like a briefcase, his marble profile, all position him as a pillar of the perfectly dressed establishment. (He kept a copy of this photograph in his flat.) And yet he is clearly posed (by the photographers) and a poem like 'Difficulties of a Statesman' demonstrates the degree to which he also occupied an ironic

6. T. S. Eliot, London, photography by Elliott and Fry, *c.* 1932.

and subversive pose: the Coriolanus figure in the poem finds himself in a world where 'A commission is appointed / To confer with a Volscian commission / About perpetual peace'.[16] I suspect that Eliot's most extravagant formulations about society sprang from the same kind of playfulness – Virginia Woolf called it his 'humorous sardonic gift'[17] – which informed his letter to the *Times* about Stilton cheese and had once provoked him to write his 'Bolo' poems (though not his Sweeney poems). The real point was their provocativeness, the way in which a serious and utterly respectable establishment figure enjoyed playing the role of the outsider as well as that of the child insisting that the emperor's new clothes (or peace plans) did not and never could exist.

❦

Living with unhappiness and guilt, however, takes its toll. Eliot's early middle age, before he separated from Vivien, had been characterised by illness, depression, and what seemed to many like premature ageing. His old, haunting sense of 'the void' that he found in 'all human relations' was not changed – indeed, in many ways it would have been made still more profound – by his conversion to Christianity. In 1930, at the age of only forty-one, he had written, in a line that seems wholly personal, 'Why should the agéd eagle stretch its wings?'[18] In his mid-forties, too, he would write his compelling 'Lines for an Old man'. Such a way of expressing exhaustion and a consciousness of failure was one that became habitual the older he grew: early in 1935, a friend observed how 'He seemed to have got so little joy or satisfaction out of being Tom'.[19] In 'Little Gidding', at the age of fifty-three, he would sardonically number those 'gifts reserved for age': 'First, the cold friction of expiring sense / Without enchantment ...' As late as 1954, at the age of sixty-five, in his late 'Ariel' poem 'The Cultivation of Christmas Trees', he would write about what was characteristic of 'later experience':

the bored habituation, the fatigue, the tedium,
The awareness of death, the consciousness of failure ...[20]

And he would entitle his last play (and last poetic work) *The Elder Statesman*. Such writing, of course, in part exploited one of the poses or faces Eliot enjoyed assuming, while remaining at the level of statement: it actually gave very little away. Virginia Woolf was conscious of exactly this mask, and of what it apparently depended on, when she described his appearance in February 1940:

Tom's great yellow bronze mask all draped upon an iron framework. An inhibited, nerve drawn; dropped face – as if hung on a scaffold of heavy private brooding; & thought. A very serious face.[21]

❀

But of all the kinds of writing Eliot was doing in these years after he had finished writing poetry, it was his plays that made and retained him a public name. He actually wrote more verse in the period 1938–1958 than in his entire life before – he called it poetry 'on a very thin diet'.[22] His plays might have been the major creative work of his last period.

In the early autumn of 1933, he had been approached with a request for a church pageant designed to raise money for forty-five churches in north London; he was asked by the man who hoped to produce it, E. Martin Browne. The job meant that Eliot had to start writing again, and in 1934 he had dutifully produced *The Rock* (he would preserve its choruses in his *Collected Poems*, but not the rest of the text). The following year, 1935, he had written the moral, historical play *Murder in the Cathedral* for the Canterbury Festival, again to be directed by Browne, and it had a West End run afterwards; Eliot found himself being encouraged to write more such work. He did not want to reproduce either kind of play again; he had actually hoped to write something more like *Sweeney Agonistes* when he started to write plays. But his next play – though again Greek in origin – was very different; in 1936, soon after completing 'Burnt Norton', he started writing *The Family Reunion*. The play concerned the return of a haunted young man to the family he has not seen for many years; his wife has recently died (he feels that he may have killed her). In many ways it drew upon events and feelings in Eliot's own life, both his marriage and his relationship with his American family; it took him a considerable time to write and revise it. Not until May 1939 (inauspicious moment) was it produced in London, with Browne directing. It lasted only five weeks.

But Eliot was thrilled to have broken into the theatre, even with only a minor success. After the war he embarked on a play in which he was less personally involved, *The Cocktail Party*. This was a great success at the Edinburgh Festival in 1949, again directed by Browne, and transferred to London's West End, where it ran both successfully and profitably. Buoyed up by this success, Eliot produced another play fairly quickly, *The Confidential Clerk*, which was again premiered at the Edinburgh Festival in 1953 and again transferred to London (though not with the runaway success of *The Cocktail Party*). Eliot embarked upon his final play, *The Elder Statesman*, in the mid-1950s; it was staged in 1958.

❁

The problems with Eliot's plays can be stated very simply. Although Eliot worked with enormous care at the verse of the plays, to get it as near conventional speech as he could, his new, slackly-rhythmed verse was still verse, and never speech. As a result, an awful artificiality constantly overwhelms the stage action, in spite of some touching lines and moments. Most of the time, the plays now seem irreversibly of their period, in exactly the way that Eliot's poetry does not. His characters also always tend to make speeches rather than talk to each other. 'Not *dialogue*, then, but serial monologue', it has been claimed, and Virginia Woolf would have agreed: 'not a dramatist. A monologist'[23] was her reaction to the author of *The Family Reunion*. When faced with criticism of the speech-making characters he had invented, Eliot 'put up no defence except to say "you mustn't want to know too much about people". It was the point of view of a man who on the one hand seemed 'to know so much about people', and yet didn't very much like them.[24] He would have said that if you were to look too hard at human beings, what you would find would be quite appalling. In his plays, therefore, Eliot allowed himself to depict human behaviour in perfectly articulated constructions, everything fitting wittily and neatly into place in the pattern. The resulting superficiality of the lives with which the plays were concerned sits very oddly with the deep accounts Eliot proffers of how it might be possible to live better.

For each of the plays (including *Murder in the Cathedral* but ignoring *The Rock*) is at bottom concerned with a profoundly important spiritual event or series of events – an awakening, a realisation, a revelation – which overtakes or is chosen by one or more of the central characters. The last four of the plays situate these events in the context of polite English society as realised in the standard conventions of early twentieth-century drama. The plays occupy the spaces of drawing-rooms, libraries, a consulting room, a business room, a terrace; their characters include Sir Claude, Lady Elizabeth, Lord Claverton, Lord Monchensey and Dowager Duchess Lady Monchensey; subsidiary characters in the grand houses include a parlour maid, a chauffeur, a nurse-secretary; a comic police sergeant appears in *The Family Reunion*. Into these stereotypical dramatic worlds of house guests and cocktail parties, themselves almost a parody of the characters and settings of British drama of the period, Eliot seeks to introduce his profound spiritual action: a man feeling that the Eumenides are hunting him down, a Harley Street consultant playing the role of spiritual Guardian for a number of the other characters (including a young woman finding out how she will die), a man discovering the identity of his real father, a business man dying at the very moment of liberation from the haunting ghosts of his past. The contrast between the profound spiritual underlying action and the stereotypical dramatic speech-making is total.

Eliot clearly enjoyed the contrast – for one thing, it would playfully have exemplified his conception of the violent intersection of the concerns of the timeless moment with events occurring in time – but for playgoers the effect is often of being on two quite different levels simultaneously. The dramatic action of *The Cocktail Party* depends on there being a kind of wise psychologist (Sir Henry Harcourt-Reilly) who combines his professional role with that of priest and magus, to send people on their way helped or healed or (occasionally) doomed: but doomed only in a 'triumphant'[25] higher cause. Without such a figure to impart wisdom, the play could not work: no-one else in such a world as the play depicts would ever be capable of Reilly's kinds of insight. Not many of the audience, having learned in *The Cocktail Party* that a young woman has died after being crucified near an ant-hill, will concentrate on the next few trivial speeches; but they will quickly cotton on to the idea that Celia was a saint or martyr, and will be happy to hear how an anecdote of an extreme life can be contrasted with the play's central account of how most people manage to live with themselves and each other. And most of the time, anyway, Reilly's 'wisdom' is of no deeper a kind than what can be absorbed by a West End theatre audience out for an evening's entertainment, and happy to enjoy a frisson of seriousness. He states at the end of *The Cocktail Party*, for example, that 'Only by acceptance / Of the past will you alter its meaning.'[26] The cracker-barrel quality of the thought is demonstrated by the fact that its own author never paid any attention to it, and went on suffering profoundly from what had happened in his own past.

Eliot strongly believed that he should be doing something in the public or popular domain to advance his Christian convictions; drama was his chosen medium, and he worked immensely hard. Theatre and performance had always intrigued him, with the fascination they offered of an alternative to the life of study and introspection to which he had found himself committed. In one sense, he was lucky: the unrealities of British drama during the period of his particular dramatic flowering, 1938–1958, allowed his plays a brief lease of life before the revolutions in British theatre of the middle 1950s (Beckett, Brecht, *Look Back in Anger*, the Royal Court) would kill stone dead, for a generation at least, theatre such as his. His penultimate play, *The Confidential Clerk,* would be staged in the August of the same year as *Waiting for Godot* had first been performed (in January); European theatre would never be the same again. His last play, *The Elder Statesman,* reaching the stage only in 1958, already appeared something of a throwback.

❀

For most of this period Eliot remained solitary. He lived with a number of clergymen in the house of the Rev. Eric Cheetham in Cromwell Road, Kensington, for some years. It was a tough life: even in the middle of February 1940, their landlady would only provide her lodgers with one jug of hot water apiece, and Eliot was obliged to take his baths at Faber & Faber.[27] But in 1946 his disabled friend the scholar and bibliophile John Hayward invited him to share a flat at 19 Carlyle Mansions in Chelsea ('I wanted to take him away from the sort of life he was living with all those parsons'[28]). Hayward was confined to a wheelchair, but was extrovert, theatrical and vituperative in a way quite different from Eliot: a witty, sarcastic, clever man, who lived his own desperately diminished life in his own utterly undiminished way. For Eliot to move in with him had, probably quite deliberately, been a way of entering the world of another suffering person he could do something to look after (he wheeled Hayward out in his chair on Saturday afternoons and would accompany him to restaurants and on visits to friends), though it was also to enjoy the witty, at times obscene talk of such a companion. Such a way of life, though, was also an act of remorse; whereas Hayward's rooms were comfortably and elegantly furnished, Eliot chose to live in complete, withdrawn simplicity. His rooms were ostentatiously bare and a large crucifix dominated the bedroom. He had instructed himself in 1939: 'To rest in our own suffering / Is evasion of suffering. We must learn to suffer more.'[29] Most of the time between the late 1930s and 1956 he took care to teach himself that lesson, catching the bus to attend mass at 6.30 every morning in St Stephen's church in Gloucester Road, memorising passages from the Bible, saying the rosary every night, keeping the fasts. During Lent he denied himself gin and also limited how often he played his favourite game of patience.[30] It was a settled, hard-working, dedicated life, if also clearly an impoverished one: 'emotion takes to itself the emotionless / Years of living among the breakage', as he put it in 'The Dry Salvages'. In the 1930s, Virginia Woolf had believed him 'all wrapt up' in 'self torture, doubt, conceit, desire for warmth & intimacy';[31] now, both Hayward and Eliot's old friend Mary Trevelyan felt that they were, in some sense, bound to care for and watch over a man whose loneliness and unhappiness suggested a breakage of some fundamental kind, and who (able-bodied and utterly successful although he was) seemed to need their care even more than they (single and vulnerable people) needed his. A brilliant photograph by John Gay from 1948 shows Eliot in his habitual three-piece suit (dark tie, shining waistcoat buttons) standing in a room full of books; he supports himself with his right hand on a pile of books, his enormous left hand (complete with signet ring on the little finger) has its thumb casually hooked into his waistcoat pocket. So why is the photograph so unlike the superbly posed

7. T. S. Eliot, London, photograph by John Gay, 1948.

and respectable Elliot and Fry photograph to which Vivien had been so attached? Because it shows a man who, although his eyes are focused forwards, is apparently looking away from the camera, whose pose looks deeply uneasy, whose hand (if six inches higher) might have been saying 'how ill's all here, about my heart'. He appears apprehensive, not welcoming; his respectability seems insufficient to protect him.

❀

Harry's role in *The Family Reunion*, in apparently pushing his wife off the deck of an ocean liner, had been rather more spectacular than the role Eliot had played in Vivien's confinement to Northumberland House. But on 22 January 1947 Vivien Eliot died, apparently rather suddenly; she was only fifty-nine. On hearing the news, Eliot reportedly 'buried his face in his hands, crying "Oh God! Oh God!"'[32] He still felt himself to be, in some way, responsible for her situation and the disasters of her life, and now she was dead. After such responsibility and knowledge, what forgiveness was possible? As he had written bleakly, back in 1933: 'There was no way out. There never is.'[33] And he also believed in the absoluteness, the indivisibility of marriage. 'Through his tears he said to Hayward, "I've not a single second of happiness to look back on, and that makes it worse."'[34] He and Maurice went together to Vivien's funeral, in Pinner. His friends knew that, later in life, he could not bear even to mention Vivien's name; they assumed that remorse was the reason.

❀

In 1949 and then again in 1950, Mary Trevelyan in effect proposed to Eliot. She had been a dinner-companion and correspondent of his for years, he visited her regularly, and she had frequently accompanied him on official occasions. On the second occasion when she asked him, he explained to her by letter that his past affection for another woman 'rendered any new relationship impossible for him'. It has been stated confidently but unconvincingly that he was referring to his love for Emily Hale. Mary Trevelyan's account, as paraphrased by Lyndall Gordon, runs as follows:

> he said that he had been in love with someone else for a great many years, and that it would be too simple to say that love had faded ... He had never wanted to marry anyone but this one woman.[35]

In 1914, as I suggested, he may well have been in love with Emily Hale, but in 1915 he had been violently attracted to Vivien. It was only as a kind of fantasy that he had thereafter kept the memory of Emily Hale fresh as that of an ideal, untroubled loving partner. His re-acquaintance with her in the 1930s and 1940s, although he cared very much for her and may well have felt thoroughly guilty about what had happened to her because of her devotion to him, did not lead to any reawakening of his original feelings, though for her clearly a good deal was awoken. According to her American friends and Eliot's own family, she 'felt herself to be unofficially "engaged" to him', and Eliot's English friends found themselves meeting her in his company. But Ottoline Morrell – although warned by Eliot that 'it may not be immediately obvious' that Emily was 'quite an exceptional person' – met someone loudly determined to get her own way and reacted violently against her as 'that *awful* American woman Miss Hale. She is like a sergeant major, quite intolerable'.[36]

❀

My own reading of the situation is that Eliot, following his years of quiet and touching devotion to a youthful Emily whom he never saw, but with whom he again corresponding from the late 1920s, felt a deep obligation to see her when he was in America 1932–33. He continued to see her and to accompany her on her subsequent visits to England, and maintained a caring friendship – but one that (by being caring) actually excluded any kind of emotional commitment on his side. He had been too seared (and touched) by what had happened with Vivien; he was revolted by the thought of the sex he had once given himself up to; his horror of (and his attraction to) women was unchanged. What he felt obliged to do for Emily was 'give her to understand that, if Vivien were to die (but in no other circumstances), he would marry her'. That, at least, was what his sister-in-law Theresa understood his commitment to be, and she was miserable about it. She remembered occasions when Emily and Eliot had '"got across" each other in conversation', so that, after Emily had left, Eliot would convey 'the very real exasperation he felt'. And Eliot's brother Henry was savage: 'Tom has made one mistake, and if he marries Emily he will make another'.[37]

To confirm this, when Vivien died in 1947, and Eliot was at last in a position to do something about what (in Emily's mind) had always been their 'mutual affection', he did absolutely nothing. Instead, she found herself in 'a strange impasse'. His love for her, Eliot explained to her – all we have is her account – was 'not in the way usual to men less gifted i.e. with complete love through a married relationship'. Emily found this, she confessed, an 'abnormal reaction', but there was nothing she could do about it.[38] And that was how things now continued.

But by telling Mary Trevelyan about his 'past affection for another woman', Eliot was doing his very best to let her down lightly too. Apparently allowing her into the profoundest secret of his life was just the kind of gesture of confidence which he knew she would most deeply value, and which would also have successfully kept her at a distance. He did not want to marry anybody now, though in the now distant past it had certainly occurred to him that he might have married Emily. But his original love for Emily had, in complex ways, faded; and what might have been a love for Mary had never even started. He remarked despairingly to Theresa: 'I want someone to love me for myself, not because I am T. S. Eliot.'[39] That, of course, was how Vivien had once loved him.

In spite of everything, his marriage to Vivien ('He had never wanted to marry anyone but this one woman') had made a loving or desiring relationship with anyone else appear absolutely impossible. Thinking of his marriage to Vivien, and the awful daring of his decision to commit himself to her, to England and to poetry, Eliot very well knew that, without her, he would never have written 'another line of poetry'.[40] No wonder that in later life he tried to undermine the significance of the poetry which he had written in consequence – attempting, for example, to dismiss 'The Waste Land' as simply 'the relief of a personal and wholly insignificant grouse against life', as 'just a piece of rhythmical grumbling'.[41] Its grumbling (like the rumble of its unsatisfied thunder) had been profoundly serious, but later in life – so far as possible – he went through the motions of disowning it, as he came to disown so much.[42] His friends in the 1930s had known him as 'Elephant' and 'Possum'. Growing adept at pretence, secrecy and disguise, he forgot very little but grew to conceal almost everything, in a state of profound defensiveness.[43] When the critic Edmund Wilson had met him in New York in 1933, he had been impressed by the extent to which Eliot appeared 'such a completely artificial, or, rather, self-invented character'; Virginia Woolf had been struck in the summer of 1933 by his 'jaunty uneasy manner' in his letters and by how full they were of 'artifice & quips & querks. A defence ...'[44]

The mask he finally and cunningly chose to adopt – authoritarian, intellectual, pious, witty, detached and kindly – was that of the man he had actually reverted to being, at least in part.[45] It was the mask of the man who had finally and successfully escaped from the most awful experiences of his life, which he always linked with his first marriage. Those were not experiences he wished to repeat.

11

My daughter

I n 1933, Eliot had asked himself why – given all that we have experienced – 'do certain images recur, charged with emotion, rather than others?'[1] A recurring image in his poetry between 1918 and 1942 had been that of children in a garden or an orchard. The image had occasionally been linked with the smell of thyme or the sound of a waterfall; the children themselves always remaining hidden, their presence revealed only by their voices or their laughter.[2] The image may originally have been provoked by Frances Hodgson Burnett's 1911 novel *The Secret Garden*,[3] but it also had its origins in the circumstances of Eliot's childhood. The garden of the family house in St Louis had been bounded by a brick wall, on the far side of which was the girls' school founded by Eliot's grandfather, the Mary Institute, its schoolyard shaded by 'a huge ailanthus tree';[4] the children there were regularly heard, hardly ever seen, 'always on the other side of the wall'.[5]

Eliot noted that such images 'charged with emotion' derive, for an author, 'from the whole of his sensitive life since early childhood' and that they 'come to represent the depths of feeling into which we cannot peer'. But, first in 1918 and then decisively in 1930, for reasons we can only guess at, he started not just to peer into but to 'apprehend' these longed-for, lost, energetic presences and hints in an orchard or garden which in 1935 he would specifically call 'our first world'. The children made their initial appearance in 'Ode on Independence Day, July 4th 1918': 'Children singing in the orchard'.[6] They next appeared, much more mysteriously, in 'Marina', Eliot's great poem of 1930,[7] and surfaced again in 1933, in 'New Hampshire': 'Children's voices in the orchard / Between the blossom- and the fruit-time'.[8] But in his writing between 1935 and 1942, their presence became inescapable. Whatever else 'Burnt Norton' does, in its brief exploration of the dilemmas of a relationship never embarked upon, the narrator suddenly becomes aware of children: 'the leaves were full of children, / Hidden excitedly, containing laughter ...' And later, 'There rises the hidden laughter / Of children in the foliage.'[9] The children in 'Burnt Norton' are potential, not real, but they are also objects of intense regret. In *The Family Reunion*, in 'the rose garden' there are 'tiny voices' to be heard;[10] in 'East Coker' we hear 'The laughter in the garden'.[11] And in 'Little Gidding', almost at the end of the poem,

> ... the children in the apple-tree
> Not known, because not looked for
> But heard, half-heard, in the stillness
> Between two waves of the sea.[12]

Eliot was very conscious of the link he was making back to his earlier poems: he would tell John Hayward how 'the children in the appletree' linked 'New Hampshire and Burnt Norton'.[13] Even in 'The Dry Salvages', though no children are mentioned, the 'wild thyme' of 'East Coker' and 'the waterfall' of 'Little Gidding' are both present.[14]

The hidden children always hint at untrammelled excitement and a peculiar delight. They are 'Not known, because not looked for', but are nonetheless presences of whom the poems' narrators are almost unconsciously aware. They clearly have something to do with Eliot's longing for the children he had never had, and his profound nostalgia for his own childhood, but they also suggest a longing for irresponsibility and confidence of a kind that had haunted him all his adult life, growing up as he had done, 'Irresolute and selfish ... / Unable to fare forward or retreat', in some significant ways 'warped or stunted'. The hidden laughter of the children is like 'an intuition of ... uncontrollable resurgent energy'.[15] Such liberated energy, irresponsibility and confidence were things that all Eliot's joking, even his writing for children, even his playful obscene ballads, could only gesture towards. One can see perhaps a glimpse of such confidence in photographs of him as a young man out sailing.

❦

Any man's writing about children when he has none himself is likely to be revealing. As early as Part II of 'The Waste Land', written in the spring of 1921, Eliot had – in collaboration with

Vivien – drawn attention to precisely this fact about their marriage. It was she who first wrote into the manuscript of the poem the single line 'What you get married for if you don't want children?'[16] which he adopted verbatim. The trouble was that he *did* want them but almost certainly did not dare have them – or want to have them – with Vivien, 'for their own guarded reasons'.[17] In 1914, when he had once spelled out what he imagined a conventional life back in North America would have led to, he had automatically included not only 'get married' but 'have a family'.[18] In June 1927, he would explain to Bertrand Russell – who now had two young children, and to whom Eliot was returning the war debentures Russell had given him and Vivien in 1915 – how deeply he was touched by the fact that Russell now had heirs: 'I have, and shall have, none.'[19] Words that sound both determined and deeply regretful. And in 1939 he would tell John Hayward how, for years, he had felt 'acutely the desire for progeny' and how much he had suffered from being childless.[20]

With Eliot's final decision in the early spring of 1933 to abandon Vivien, there had come just a moment, a flicker of another potential life. Almost twenty years after leaving America, Eliot had gone to revisit the places he had known as a young man, and he had seen all his surviving family. Could there now be a new beginning of some kind? Foremost of all the old acquaintance he went to see was Emily Hale: he actually travelled all the way to California to see her at Christmas 1932.

'New Hampshire', a result of his visit to that state in June 1933 – where he met Emily Hale once again – suggests a profound and deeply depressing awareness that it was no longer the spring of his life which he had any chance of sharing. In fact, sharing it with another person felt quite impossible:

> Twenty years and the spring is over;
> Today grieves, to-morrow grieves ...[21]

But in that poem, too, the voices of the unseen children – 'charged with emotion' – are clearly heard, immediately suggesting not only the children Eliot had never had with Vivien, but also the children he might have had with Emily all of whom were now also being grieved over. And the children have their usual, clear-voiced link with ease and naturalness and irresponsibility; with the period before things seemed to have gone so wrong with Eliot's life; the period before whatever it was that was now 'doing the damage'.[22]

❀

Nostalgia for children and for kinds of lost freedom and irresponsibility are reflected in Eliot's writing in another way too. On his return to England in 1933, he had found himself having to camp in the houses of various friends, and was very grateful over the next few years to accept their hospitality and to share holidays with them. As a result, the Morley children, the Faber children and the Roberts children saw a good deal of him.[23] It was for them that he had started to write nonsense verse in August 1933. It was a genre he had always enjoyed ('Bolo' and Columbo' show that) but this kind was a great deal more innocuous: it was about cats. The nonsense book reached the world in general in 1939 as *Old Possum's Book of Practical Cats*, and eventually proceeded to world-wide acclaim as the musical *Cats*. The successful playfulness of Eliot's poems, like the wonderful incidental verse in his letters,[24] owes a great deal to the mastery of language and rhythm which informed his more serious work. Just when you think he will never be able to top his first two rhymes for 'Macavity: the Mystery Cat' – 'gravity' and 'depravity' – he comes up with 'There never was a Cat of such deceitfulness and suavity.' Like all the best nonsense verse, it takes itself with great seriousness and proceeds with unvarying logic and charm: Macavity 'always has an alibi, and one or two to spare ...'[25] Such writing is not actually for children. It is the writing of an adult who knows what children are like, but who always writes as an adult, to the ideally responsive child within his own playful imagination.

All this makes the more striking the apprehension of those invisible children in Eliot's 1930 poem 'Marina', which had drawn upon the Shakespearean play *Pericles* and its search for a lost daughter. In 'Marina', the narrator retraces a journey of imagination into what feels like his own childhood; so that the search for the daughter feels like an attempt to recover his own childhood, as he explores where things had gone wrong (he instances the puritanical teaching about deadly sins) and what might still be recoverable (he recalls Cape Ann and the annual June to September holidays). The fact that Eliot's mother had died the previous year may originally have encouraged such an exploration.

What the narrator manages to recover is an image of childhood like the battered hull of an old boat – something made 'unknowing, half conscious, unknown, my own' – which feels as if it offers a way of going back and reclaiming the life (awakened, full of hope and newness) which he feels has always belonged to him, which he has always wanted but has never had. To recover such a self would be a way of getting past the horribly adult 'me' and 'my' who have dominated his life. His hope now is to 'live in a world of time beyond *me*'; he wants to abandon his normal language 'for that unspoken'.[26] And now, as if voyaging back to childhood in his newly recovered boat, through the granite islands off Cape Ann, he ends with the words 'My daughter'. For Pericles, Marina was a literal daughter who could be recovered. For the poem's narrator, however, 'she' conveys a still vivid sense of his own life before everything went wrong (before the Herculean children of the epigraph were killed,[27] as it were): an apprehension of the irresponsible, untroubled being he was once and somewhere, somehow, still is: the daughter also being the child he never had, and has always so much regretted.

❀

In a quite astonishing way, this experience – so touchingly

developed in 'Marina' in 1930 – managed to describe what Eliot would actually experience twenty-five years later: it was as if he knew exactly what he had always wanted, even though he had grown to believe he would now never have it. By the time he reached his sixties, he was a confirmed bachelor, who had lived primarily in the company of men for twenty years; he shared Hayward's flat for very nearly eleven years. But a girl of twenty-two called Valerie Fletcher came to work at Faber and Faber in August 1949,[28] with the fervent desire of working for the great man whose poetry she had read and loved, and which she avidly collected. She eventually became his personal secretary but remained reserved and impelled by a strong sense of duty: after five years Eliot still felt that he hardly knew her. But increasingly she protected him from a world greedy for access to the great public figure; in that way she assisted him in being the private person behind the public man. She became, in effect, a marvellous, careful daughter: she came to know what he needed before he did himself. In Lyndall Gordon's words, she grew to be 'a disciple with the absolute dedication of an ideal heir'.[29] Because of her youth, too, it was as if she came from far back in Eliot's own life, as if she belonged to a time before things had gone so terribly wrong, and might therefore be able to assist him back into full possession of his own past. And above all she offered him something he was profoundly nostalgic for: she knew how 'deep in him there was a need for family life'.[30]

He had given himself nearly ten solitary years since Vivien's death in January 1947. He now gave himself permission to go further; in 1956 he asked Valerie to marry him. He was sixty-seven years old, thirty-eight years older than her, old enough to be her father. But on 10 January 1957 (thus almost exactly ten years after the death of Vivien), at 6.15 a.m. in St Barnabas church in Addison Road, Kensington,[31] they married, and Eliot executed another of those peculiar *volte faces* with his past of which the first had been his marriage to Vivien in June 1915, and the others had been abandoning academe, converting to Christianity, and leaving Vivien. He only told Hayward that he was getting married just before doing so – 'I thought you'd be so cross' he told his friend[32] – while other friends found out by letter or gossip. Mary Trevelyan and Emily Hale, both of whom he had assured that he would not be marrying again, and who believed themselves his most intimate female friends, found themselves largely excluded from the new life he started to build himself with Valerie.

He had given himself a decade of penitence and (it must be said) mourning for the woman who had been so important to him, who had changed the whole current of his life, and who had come to represent such a dreadful wrong turning for him. Valerie would change him too, but the one thing she could not do was reawaken his desire to write poetry. That belonged to his youth, his first marriage, his emotional and sexual awakening with Vivien, his subsequent agonies, and then to his years of compulsive re-enactment of all that he had done, and been, and felt.[33]

But – now as old as his own father had become, and having given himself this permission to marry – he found himself going much further; he gave himself permission to relax and to be a child again. In some words attributed to Pablo Picasso, 'one starts to get young again at the age of sixty', even if Picasso is supposed grimly to have concluded 'and by then it is too late'.[34] But it was not too late for Eliot. Valerie recalled, fifteen years later, that 'Somehow there was a good deal of little boy in him that had never been released'.[35] She also suggested that 'There was a human love he needed to complete his life, someone who loved him for himself'.[36] His marriage brought him, Eliot told Pound in 1961, a happiness he associated only with his own distant childhood, which (together with his newly married state) he now declared to have been the only two periods of his life when he had been unalloyedly happy.[37] After the violent opening-up of himself which occurred during his first marriage, after subsequent decades of restraint, care, strictness, withdrawal and penitence, of abjuring the flesh and refining the spirit –

a lifetime's death in love,
Ardour and selflessness and self-surrender[38]

– he now allowed himself to trust and love another human being. He held his wife's hand in public and seems to have smiled more than ever before, as he experienced what Robert Lowell called 'the surprise reward of a joyfull [*sic*] marriage'.[39] It may have felt only natural to try and exclude all the friends and features of his old life from it, though by now it was habitual to him to cut himself off from what (and from whomever) he no longer felt he wanted. The new life was quite real but it was also a fragile creation, and Eliot must have been deeply uncertain about how long he might be able to enjoy it; he was only in his sixties but had increasingly been ill, with heart and chest problems (he had had a stroke in the early 1950s): he suffered from asthma, emphysema and bronchitis.

He dedicated his 1957 volume of literary essays *On Poetry and Poets* 'To VALERIE';[40] and for her he wrote a poem, his first in four years, though also his last. But it was a poem for publication, a kind of proof of his feelings; and he called it (of all things) 'A Dedication to my Wife', thus finally renouncing the other 'blessèd face', the one to whom he had dedicated 'Ash-Wednesday' in 1930. In such a poem he was consciously setting the record straight, in ways that even Valerie Eliot may not quite have appreciated; he consciously re-worked a number of old concerns. The severe demands made on language in the *Four Quartets* – 'Words strain, / Crack and sometimes break, under the burden' so that 'one has only learnt to get the better of words / For the thing one no longer has to say'[41] – are abandoned in favour of a language of love which declares that it prefers a 'babble'[42] of sounds (words intuitive and uncon-sidered) which conceal no burden of meaning and require no attempt at understanding.

And other words stand out too. In 'Ash-Wednesday', Eliot had written how 'the weak spirit quickens to rebel / For the bent golden-rod and the lost sea smell'[43] – but in the earlier poem, the senses had given up as irrecoverable the sensations by which they had been so aroused. In 'A Dedication to my

Wife', happiness simply and directly 'quickens'[44] his senses: the things once believed bent and lost are now immediately apprehensible. In *The Cocktail Party* he had sourly referred to the 'leaping vanity' of passion: here he describes its 'leaping delight'.[45]

Even more strikingly, although sex is once more fore-grounded in Eliot's poetry, it is with neither the old violence nor the old pained distaste: only with relaxed happiness. No longer is a knowledge of Good and Evil necessary to rescue sexuality from 'the copulation of the beasts';[46] and whereas, between 1911 and 1921, he had written fastidiously of 'female smells in shuttered rooms', of the 'strong rank feline smell' of 'Grishkin in a drawing room' and of Fresca's 'good old hearty female stench',[47] now, happily and deliberately, he chose to stress lovers whose bodies 'smell of each other'.[48] The inquiring nose is just as sensitive, but comes now not only *without* the distaste, but with an un-self-conscious delight in the senses of a kind which Eliot had never previously shown – had never felt like showing – before.

He and Valerie would have nearly eight years together. His various chest and breathing complaints, especially in winter, easily prostrated him, or confined him to staying indoors (or even in hospital); winters spent abroad in sun and warmth helped, although they also bored him. Valerie was able to assist him enormously with his final play, *The Elder Statesman*, staged in 1958, which describes how an elderly public figure at last realises his love for his daughter – a daughter who is simultaneously falling in love with the man of her own choice.

At the end of the play, the two young lovers talk about their love. Charles says:

> I love you to the limits of speech, and beyond.
> It's strange that words are so inadequate.
> Yet, like the asthmatic struggling for breath,
> So the lover must struggle for words.[49]

The daughter who hears these words from her lover then wishes to speak to her elderly father: but he has died while the words were being spoken. In the last Chapter, I suggested the general weakness of Eliot's plays, and although this scene is touching on a sentimental level, there is an odd discrepancy between the vivid image of 'the asthmatic struggling for breath' (something Eliot knew very well), and the smooth complacency of 'to the limits of speech, and beyond'. But the difference in the case of Eliot's own life was that the elderly public man was now loved, was told so by his young wife (not daughter), did not need many words to articulate his response, and felt that he had miraculously moved into a new life.

Eliot published his last critical piece, a pamphlet about George Herbert, in 1962; two years later, he agreed that his old PhD thesis for Harvard would be allowed to see the light of day (though characteristically he enjoyed complaining that he did not now understand a word of it[50]). He prepared a final book of essays, *To Criticise the Critic and other writings*, but did not live to see its publication. He had been growing increasingly frail, needed sticks to hold himself upright, and – after a series of illnesses from which, more than once, Valerie had helped bring him back from the brink of death – he finally died, highly distinguished and deeply loved, on 4 January 1965. Within twenty years, he was once more famous all over the world: the musical *Cats* of 1981 by Andrew Lloyd-Webber took its libretto from his 1939 book *Old Possum's Book of Practical Cats*, and helped to make T. S. Eliot posthumously a public figure famous as few other English poets have ever been (by 2008 the piece had been enjoyed by more than 50 million people[51]).

❀

His memorial service took place in Westminster Abbey in February 1965. Ezra Pound, at the age of seventy-nine, and having hardly spoken for years, came to London for it. He had done more than anyone else to launch Eliot's career as a published poet between 1914 and 1918; in 1921–22 he had been *il miglior fabbro* who had helped his friend make 'The Waste Land'; but it was Eliot who had been awarded the Nobel prize, while in 1948 Pound had been incarcerated in a mental hospital. He and Eliot were the last of the giants of European modernism, the generation of Conrad, Yeats and Joyce, of Lawrence and Woolf. Pound would not however say anything: 'He's done with talking'.[52] He died in 1972, but only after the 'Waste Land' manuscript itself had been rediscovered and Pound had taken the opportunity to offer the words: 'The more we know of Eliot, the better.'[53]

Somewhat to the bewilderment of the villagers, Eliot's ashes were taken to East Coker, the village from which his own ancestors had originally departed for the New World. The words 'in my beginning is my end', from 'East Coker', are on his memorial stone. Other lines – for example, 'At the source of the longest river / The voice of the hidden waterfall / And the children in the apple-tree', from the end of 'Little Gidding' – would have more richly celebrated a life begun beside the Missouri and the Mississippi, and into which instinctive 'delight'[54] and extraordinary happiness had returned during his final years.

Afterword

In 1931, Eliot had insisted that poetry was great which had a 'significant, consistent, and developing personality' behind it, something that unified it and made it coherent. He praised the Elizabethan and Jacobean dramatists for providing 'the undertone' of the writer's 'personal drama and struggle'[1] in their work; it was the consistency, the coherence of the written work and the writer's personal emotion which impressed him. In the obituary of Virginia Woolf which he wrote ten years later, although he remarked (with the confidence which is one of the unhappy certainties of the biographer) 'No one can be understood',[2] he again stressed the necessary 'unity' of a writer: the way in which 'both – and coherently – the mind in the masterpiece and the man of daily business, pleasure and anxiety'[3] come across to us.

Only a month or so after writing the Woolf obituary, he described in 'Little Gidding' how – from his point of view – every poem was an 'epitaph':[4] an inscription on the tombstone of the experience it commemorated. The poem was not the experience: it was a memorial to something now dead and buried. The poetic 'epitaphs' of his writing lifetime had however succeeded in bringing back to life the actualities of his own life and experience; they commemorated the extraordinary coherence between Eliot's own 'personal drama and struggle' and the poetry that he wrote. I have attempted in this biography – in ways to which I hope he would not only have objected – to reveal the disturbing and at times terrifying openness to moral, verbal, emotional and sexual 'actuality' which had, for so long, made him such a terribly unhappy and vulnerable individual, but which also helped him be such a very great poet.

Sources, acknowledgements and abbreviations

More than previous biographers, I have drawn on the memories of Virginia Woolf, who had a complex relationship with Eliot, but who saw him with more insight than many of her contemporaries. I am also grateful to T. S. Matthews, Peter Ackroyd and Lyndall Gordon, the three principal previous biographers of T. S. Eliot, and to Carol Seymour-Jones, the biographer of Vivien Eliot, though my approach to Eliot for this relatively short book is significantly different from those adopted in previous books. I could not have written this book without Lawrence Rainey's attempts at the dating of Eliot's early poetry and prose, or without Ronald Schuchard's work in elucidating various problems of Eliot's life and writing.

References to Eliot's plays, his early poetry and to *Old Possum's Book of Practical Cats* have been taken from *The Complete Poems and Plays* (1969); all other references to his poetry are taken from *Inventions of the March Hare* and *Collected Poems* (1962). Geoffrey Hartman kindly gave me permission to quote from his 2007 memoir. I am grateful to

Harcourt Brace for permission to quote from the diaries and letters of Virginia Woolf.

Anne Serafin and Jim O'Hare not only read my drafts (including the ending, which they helped me shape) but took me to view the Dry Salvages and the Eliot house at Eastern Point, Gloucester. David Ellis and Peter Preston both read the penultimate draft and gave me moral and practical support. John Turner, as ever, read drafts of parts of this book and commented helpfully. Betsy Fox encouraged me to talk for hours. Frau Fischer at the Universitätsbibliothek in Duisburg assisted an Englishman in distress. Jim McCue was extremely helpful to an unknown man at the next table. Michael Rumpf loaned me his copy of Eliot's poems in August 2007 and thus provoked the whole project.

Abbreviations
A. Works by Eliot

ASG	*After Strange Gods* (1934)
CP	*Collected Poems 1909–1962* (1963)
CPP	*The Complete Poems and Plays* (1969)
ICS	*The Idea of a Christian Society* (1939)
IMH	*Inventions of the March Hare: Poems 1909– 1917*, ed. Christopher Ricks (1996)
L, i.	*The Letters of T. S. Eliot*, vol. I: *1898–1922*, ed. Valerie Eliot (1988)
NTDC	*Notes Towards the Definition of Culture* (1948)

OPP	*On Poetry and Poets* (1957)
SP	*Selected Prose*, ed. John Hayward (1953)
TCTC	*To Criticise the Critic* (1965)
UPUC	*The Use of Poetry and the Use of Criticism* (1933)
VMP	*The Varieties of Metaphysical Poetry*, ed. Ronald Schuchard (1993)
WLF	*The Waste Land: A Facsimile and Transcript of the Original Drafts*, ed. Valerie Eliot (1971)

B. Other works

[*place of publication* London *unless otherwise noted*]

Ackroyd	Peter Ackroyd, *T. S. Eliot* (1984)
Bush	Ronald Bush, *T. S. Eliot: Character and Style* (New York, 1983)
Gallup	Donald Gallup, *T. S. Eliot: A Bibliography* (New York, 1969)
Gardner	Helen Gardner, *The Composition of Four Quartets* (1978)
Gordon	Lyndall Gordon, *T. S. Eliot: An Imperfect Life* (New York, 1998)
Jain	Manju Jain, *T. S. Eliot and American Philosophy: the Harvard Years* (Cambridge, 1992)
Julius	Anthony Julius, *T. S. Eliot, anti-Semitism, and literary form*, New Edition (2003)
Matthews	T. S. Matthews, *Great Tom* (New York, 1974)

Raine	Craig Raine, *T. S. Eliot* (Oxford, 2006)
Schuchard	Ronald Schuchard, *Eliot's Dark Angel* (1996)
Sencourt	Robert Sencourt, *T. S. Eliot: A Memoir* (1971)
Seymour-Jones	Caroline Seymour-Jones, *Painted Shadow: A Life of Vivienne Eliot* (2001)
Soldo	John Joseph Daniel Soldo, *The Tempering of T. S. Eliot, 1885–1915*, Ph. D. thesis (Harvard University, 1972)
Woolf, *Diary*	*The Diaries of Virginia Woolf*, ed. Anne Olivier Bell, 5 vols. (1977–84)
Woolf, *Letters*	*The Letters of Virginia Woolf*, ed. Nigel Nicolson and Joanne Trautmann, 6 vols. (1975–80)

C. Individuals

BR	Bertrand Russell
EH	Emily Hale
EP	Ezra Pound
JH	John Hayward
OM	Ottoline Morrell
TSE	Thomas Stearns Eliot
ValE	Valerie Eliot
VivE	Vivien Eliot
VW	Virginia Woolf

Notes

Introduction

1. It is a matter for celebration that, over the next few years, four more volumes of TSE's letters and a multi-volume edition of his poetry will be published by Faber and Faber, and seven volumes of his prose by Faber and Faber (jointly with John Hopkins Press). TSE's reputation will certainly change and probably develop. I am however less sure what will happen to estimation of his life, given its current standing.

2. *Tom and Viv* (1994), directed by Brian Gilbert, with William Dafoe, Miranda Richardson and Rosemary Harris: 'biopic' dating from 1951.

3. E.g., 'the sexual failure that had undoubtedly occurred' (Seymour-Jones 113); 'the sexual failure, if such it was' (Ackroyd 66); 'sexual failure ... his marriage's failure' (Donald J. Childs, *T. S. Eliot: Mystic, Son and Lover*, 1997, pp. 145–6); 'his marriage was associated with sexual failures' (Gordon 120); John Xiros Cooper also states that their sexual relationship 'could not have been a satisfying one' (*The Cambridge Introduction to T. S. Eliot*, Cambridge, 2006, p. 5).

4. Gabrielle McIntire, *Modernism, Memory, and Desire: T. S. Eliot and Virginia Woolf* (Cambridge, 2008), p. 219 n.

45; Seymour-Jones refers to 'the strength' of TSE's 'own homosexual desires' (365).

5. E.g. Bernard Sharratt's biographical summary in 'Eliot, Postmodernism, and after', *The Cambridge Companion to T. S. Eliot*, ed. A. David Moody (Cambridge, 1994), takes it for granted that 'Eliot was in love with Emily Hale' (p. 224); Schuchard dates the 'rekindling of his love for Emily Hale' to 'no later than September 1923' (153–4); John Xiros Cooper declares that 'With one woman [Vivien] out of his life, another one [Emily] soon took her place' (*The Cambridge Introduction to T. S. Eliot*, p. 16).

6. See Julius 235 n. 109. A citation of TSE now seems obligatory in any discussion of anti-Semitism; see e.g. Christopher Hitchens, 'Nightmare Watch', *Times Literary Supplement* (21 November 2008) and his passing reference to 'the nastier moments that one may encounter in the study of T. S. Eliot' (p. 13).

7. His first surviving independent work – written when he was around seven years old – was a short work of biography: 'GEORGE / WASHINGTON / A Life. / by / Thos. S. Eliot, S. A. / Editor of the "FIRESIDE". / 1st Ed.' It may have been short – less than two sides – but it was written not only with an editor's *savoir-faire* (the 'Fireside' was the magazine TSE wrote out by hand for the Eliot household) but with a grasp of biographical essentials: 'And then he died, of corse.' See the facsimile reproduced in *T. S. Eliot: A Symposium*,

ed. Richard Marsh and Tambimuttu (1948), facing p. 84, and Soldo 203–12.

8. 'Tradition and the Individual Talent', *SE* 17–18, where he also insisted that 'Impressions and experiences which are important for the man may take no place in the poetry' (*SE* 20).

9. See TSE to Alfred Kreymbourg (3 May 1925), Alderman Library, University of Virginia at Charlottesville.

10. VW, *Diary* (20 September 1920), ii. 68.

11. TSE to JH (18 February 1938): Seymour-Jones 577.

12. Jewel Spears Brooker, 'Eliot Studies', *The Cambridge Companion to T. S. Eliot*, ed. Moody, p. 242.

13. 'Charles Whibley', *SE* 494.

14. VivE at times early and late called herself 'Vivienne', but 'Vivien' was her normal signature until 1922; it was also the name by which TSE knew her.

15. VivE to EP (?1925), Beinecke Library, Yale.

16. 'Conclusion', *UPUC* 145.

17. 'Turnbull Lecture III', *VMP* 289.

18. *ASG* 28.

19. 'Shakespeare and the Stoicism of Seneca', *SE* 127.

20. Geoffrey Hartman, *A Scholar's Tale: Intellectual Journey of a Displaced Child of Europe* (New York, 2007), p. 84.

21. 'Shakespeare and the Stoicism of Seneca', *SE* 137.

22. Philip Mairet, 'Memories of T. S. E.', *T. S. Eliot: A Symposium for His Seventieth Birthday*, ed. Nevil Braybrooke (1958), pp. 42, 40.

23. See Maud Ellmann, *The Poetics of Impersonality: T. S. Eliot and Ezra Pound* (Brighton, 1987) for a full discussion.

24. VW, *Diary* (14 September 1925), iii. 41: 'Obliquities' apparently in the sense of *OED* 4. (noted there as *Obs.*): 'Deviations from directness in action, conduct, or speech; ways or methods that are not direct or straightforward' ... VW, *Diary* (2 September 1933), iv. 177.

Chapter 1

1. Cf. *CP* 203.

2. The planting of trees around the property, and extensive building on the plot to seaward, have deprived the house of its original view (visible in period photographs, e.g. *L*, i. Illustration 17A).

3. Soldo 173.

4. See e.g. 'Animula', *CP* 113.

5. *CP* 104.

6. 'Little Gidding', first draft (7 July 1941): Gardner 228.

7. Although Samuel de Champlain (1567–1635) charted the New England coast in 1607, and marked the rocks as a single outcrop, he did not name them, and TSE's belief that the three rocks' name derived from the French ('presumably *les trois sauvages*' – *CP* 205) was incorrect. On a map of 1785 (Beinecke Library, Yale) they are simply named the 'Salvage Rocks' ('salvage'

being a common English spelling of 'savage' in the
17th and 18th centuries) while the appellation 'Dry'
dates only from the mid 19th century, when French
(or German) influence on the name would have been
extremely unlikely. Unlike the 'Little Salvages', a mile
offshore and submerged twice a day, the tops of the 'Big
Salvages' (the 'Dry') remain clear of the water in most
weathers and states of tide. They lie at approximately 42
deg 40' 20" N., 70 deg 34' 06" W., surrounded by swift
currents, with the waters about them at times only three
fathom deep. TSE wrote in 1964 to a relation who had
pointed out to him his error about the French origin of
the name: 'I imagine that it was to my brother [Henry]
that I owe that explanation of the title, and I seem
to remember that the rocks were known to the local
fishermen as the "Dry Salvages". But I myself can give
no further explanation and it may be that mine owes
more to my own imagination than to any explanation
that I heard' (see Samuel Eliot Morison, 'The Dry
Salvages and the Thacher Shipwreck', *The American
Neptune*, xxv, 1965, 233–247).

8. Soldo 161.
9. *CP* 205; Bush 217.
10. *CP* 205.
11. 'American Literature and the American Language',
    TCTC 45.
12. TSE, 'Gentlemen and Seamen', *Harvard Advocate*,
    lxxxvii (25 May 1909), 115; see Soldo 25–6, Jain 22.

13. Cf. the phrase first used in 1859 by Oliver Wendell Holmes (in *Elsie V.* i.): 'The Brahmin caste of New England'.

14. TSE in 1928, quoted by Leonard Unger, 'T. S. Eliot', *T. S. Eliot: Critical Assessments*, ed. Clarke, i. 39.

15. TSE, 'Preface' to Edgar Ansel Mowrer, *This American World* (1928), p. xiii.

16. TSE, 'Preface' to Mowrer, *This American World*, pp. xiii-xiv.

17. *ASG* 20.

18. Quoted by Sir Herbert Read in 'T. S. E. – A Memoir', *Sewanee Review*, lxxiv (1966), 35; quoted J. Margolis, *T. S. Eliot's Intellectual Development* (Chicago and London, 1973), p. 18.

19. *L*, i. 318.

20. Matthews 126.

21. Gordon 533; the friend was Hope Mirrlees.

22. There had been a child (Theodore or Theodora) born in 1887 who had died immediately.

23. See e.g. *VMP* 213 n. 21. His 'Three Poems' in the *Criterion*, iii. no. 10 (January 1925), 170–1, appeared under the name 'Thomas Eliot', in spite of being announced as by 'T. S. Eliot' on the magazine's cover.

24. See TSE to Marquis W. Childs, *St Louis Post-Dispatch* (16 February 1964): Soldo 144.

25. See e.g. *L*, i. Illustration 10C.

26. Ackroyd 16.

27. *VMP* 234.

28. See *L*, i. Illustration 15.

29. 'Introduction', *UPUC* 33.

30. Jain 262 n. 42.

31. *CP* 113.

32. *L*, i. 364.

33. *L*, i. 364–5.

34. See Matthews 12–13 and *L*, i. 364.

35. William Turner Levy and Victor Scherle, *Affectionately, T. S. Eliot* (New York, 1968), p. 135.

36. *CP* 113.

37. 'American Literature and the American Language', *TCTC* 44.

38. Levy and Scherle, *Affectionately, T. S. Eliot*, p. 54.

39. Gordon 18.

40. *CP* 113.

41. Lyndall Gordon, *Eliot's New Life* (Oxford, 1988), p. 273. Gordon 535 removes the phrase and substitutes 'fury, and hatred'.

42. TSE remarked in 1953 that this tradition led to his later 'uncomfortable and very inconvenient obligation to serve upon committees' ('American Literature and the American Language', *TCTC* 44).

43. Matthews 4.

44. VW, *Diary* (10 September 1933), iv. 179.

45. Gordon 20.

46. Ronald Bush, entry on T. S. Eliot, *Oxford Dictionary of National Biography* (2004), xviii. 73.

47. EP to William Carlos Williams (11 September 1920): *The Letters of Ezra Pound, 1907–1941*, ed. D. D. Paige (1951), p. 223.

48. 'American Literature and the American Language', *TCTC* 48.

49. Patmore 89.

50. VW, *Diary* (5 December 1920), ii. 77.

51. VW, *Diary* (17 August 1937), v. 108.

52. VW, *Diary* (25 May 1940), v. 287.

53. Matthews 11. It can hardly have been a coincidence that TSE would quote the Eliot family motto 'Tacuit et fecit' (roughly translated: 'he shut up and got on with it') when he dedicated *The Sacred Wood* to his silent, hard-working father in 1920.

54. 'Matthew Arnold', *UPUC* 119.

55. Victoria Glendinning, *Elizabeth Bowen: Portrait of a Writer* (1977), p. 80.

56. See 'A Commentary', *Criterion*, xiii. no. 52 (April 1934), 117.

57. *L*, i. 6.

58. Neither Ackroyd nor Gordon devotes much space to the subject, while Matthews ignores it almost completely.

59. See *L*, i. 5–12.

60. He grew to be five feet eleven inches tall.

61. See *L*, i. 12.

62. *L*, i. 349.

63. *L*, i. 351.

64. *L*, i. 273.
65. Henry Ware Eliot to Thomas Lamb Eliot (7 March 1914): Soldo 62.
66. See e.g. 'A Fable for Feasters' (*CPP* 587–9) and a poem to his sister Charlotte, *L*, i. 4–5.
67. See e.g. his imitation of seventeenth century poetry – in particular Ben Jonson – in 'If time and space' / 'If space and time' (*CPP* 590–1).
68. 'Suite Clownesque', *IMH* 35.
69. *L*, i. 13.
70. Charlotte Eliot, *Savonarola* (1926), p. 75.
71. *L*, i. 131.
72. *L*, i. 267. It was a fond childhood memory, cf. TSE to his mother (3 October 1917), recalling times 'usually beginning with the "little Tailor" and the firelight on the ceiling' (*L*, i. 198–9). The song may have been a version of the ballad widely known in England and the USA, sometimes called 'The Three Rogues':

The miller he stole corn
And the weaver he stole yarn
And the little tailor he stole broadcloth
For to keep these three rogues warm.

The miller he drowned in his dam,
And the weaver he hung on his yarn;
And the devil put his foot on the little tailor
With the broadcloth under his arm.

> With the broadcloth under his arm.
> With the broadcloth under his arm.
> And the devil put his foot on the little tailor
> With the broadcloth under his arm.

73. Patmore 90.

74. See *L*, i. 408.

75. I only came across the analysis of the poem in Craig Raine, *T. S. Eliot* (Oxford, 2006), pp. 2–5, after writing my own account; we both stress the poem's neglected importance.

76. Soldo 124–5; TSE's remarks appear on p. 64 of the Contemporary Literature lecture typescript at Harvard University. The lectures were given on the course English 26 at Harvard in the spring of 1933; the reading of modern literature which TSE did for the course assisted him with the lectures he gave in Virginia in May (see *ASG* 35). TSE would again recommend *Fantasia of the Unconscious* in his Virginia lectures: 'As a criticism of the modern world ... a book to keep at hand and re-read' (*ASG* 60).

77. D. H. Lawrence, *Psychoanalysis and the Unconscious and Fantasia of the Unconscious*, ed. Bruce Steele (Cambridge, 2004), 149:34, 37–8, 150:2–3.

78. See pp. 171–3.

Chapter 2

1. Quoted Bush 5.
2. Matthews 25.
3. Matthews 23; 'sibylline' meaning 'oracular, occult, mysterious'.
4. See *VMP* 213 n. 21.
5. *IMH* 325–6.
6. *IMH* 13.
7. Ibid.
8. 'Critical [Note]', *The Collected Poems of Harold Monro* (1933), p. xv. 'Viscid' is a word normally used about fluids or soft substances: 'Having a glutinous or gluey character; sticky, adhesive' (*OED*).
9. See *IMH* xi-xviii.
10. *L*, i. 13.
11. TSE interview with Donald Hall, *Paris Review*, no. 21 (Spring-Summer 1959), pp. 47–70; reprinted *T. S. Eliot: Critical Assessments*, ed. Graham Clarke, Volume I (1990), i. 79.
12. Seymour-Jones 53.
13. Ibid.
14. The dedication to the 1917 *Prufrock* volume was 'To Jean Verdenal / 1889–1915'. In 1919, for *Ara Vos Prec*, TSE removed the dedication but inserted the epigraph: '*Or puoi la quantitate / Comprender dell' amor ch'a te mi scalda, / Quando dismento nostra vanitate, / Trattando l'ombre come cosa salda*' (ll. 133–6 of Canto XXI of Dante's *Purgatorio*) meaning 'Now can you

understand the quality of love that warms me towards you, so that I forget our vanity, and treat the shadows like the solid thing.' *Poems 1920* was dedicated 'To Jean Verdenal / 1889–1915', without an epigraph. In 1925, for *Poems 1909–1925*, TSE inserted the dedication in the 'Prufrock' section, it now running: '*For Jean Verdenal, 1889–1915 / mort aux Dardanelles / Or puoi la quantitate / Comprender dell' amor ch'a te mi scalda, / Quando dismento nostra vanitate, / Trattando l'ombre come cosa salda*'. Gabrielle McIntire assumes that the Prufrock *poem* is dedicated to Verdenal, and on that basis constructs a reading of the poem 'as a homoerotic elegy and "epitaph"' for Verdenal, but I find unconvincing her arguments for 'a homoerotic subtext to the poem': see *Modernism, Memory, and Desire: T. S. Eliot and Virginia Woolf* (Cambridge, 2008), pp. 83–5.

15. See 'A Commentary', *Criterion*, xiii. no. 52 (April 1934), 452.

16. See *L*, i. 20–1, 22–4, 27, 28–31, 32–4, 35, 35–6.

17. 'A Commentary', *Criterion*, xiii. no. 52 (April 1934), 452.

18. '[Preludes]', *IMH* 335.

19. *CP* 36.

20. Edmund Wilson counted six notably different poses: the Anglican clergyman, the formidable professor, Dr. Johnson, the genteel Bostonian, the Christian, the oracle. See Matthews 118–19.

21. *IMH* 330.

22. Ibid.

23. 'Clark Lecture VIII', *VMP* 209.

24. *CP* 17.

25. *CP* 13, 14, 15, 16.

26. *CP* 17.

27. *IMH* 318–19.

28. *L*, i. 59.

29. Gordon ix, 76–7.

30. Seymour-Jones 53.

31. Seymour-Jones 365.

32. Seymour-Jones 365–6.

33. McIntire, *Modernism, Memory, and Desire*: she argues that 'sodomy, masturbation, miscegenation, scatological rituals, and rape' are 'the *modus operandi* of imperial conquest' (pp. 10–11).

34. Peter du Sautoy, *T. S. Eliot: Essays from the* Southern Review, ed. Olney, p. 76 .

35. Cf. his remark of 1933: 'the indecent that is funny may be the legitimate source of innocent merriment' (*ASG* 51) – a phrase from *The Mikado* (1885) by Gilbert and Sullivan: 'My object all sublime / I shall achieve in time – / To let the punishment fit the crime – / The punishment fit the crime; / And make each prisoner pent / Unwillingly represent / A source of innocent merriment! / Of innocent merriment.'

36. *IMH* 314. While TSE may have written out (or more likely revised) the verses ascribed to him in *IMH*, there was a tradition of both 'Tinker' and 'Christopher

Columbo' ballads. See e.g. *Bawdy Ballads*, ed. Ed Cray (1978), pp. 9–11, 114–15.

37. *L*, i. 126, where the first line actually runs 'K.B.b.b.b.k.' and copies exactly another verse earlier in the letter.

38. *The Annotated Waste Land with Eliot's Contemporary Prose*, ed. Lawrence Rainey, Second Edition (New Haven and London, 2006), p. 167.

39. Schuchard 239 n. 43.

40. *L*, i. xxi.

41. Jain 59 and 269 n. 84; TSE made the comment in a speech on 4 December 1949.

42. Bradley (1846–1924) was a philosopher whose view combined monism (the claim that reality is one, that there are no real separate things) with absolute idealism (the claim that reality consists solely of idea or experience); TSE's thesis was entitled *Knowledge and Experience in the Thought of F. H. Bradley*.

43. *L*, i. 58.

44. *CP* 33.

45. Short forms: 'rec' = received, 'act = 'account'.

46. *L*, i. 37. The 'P' presumably stands for 'Pater'.

47. EP to H. L. Mencken (3 October 1914): *Pound / Ford: The Story of a Literary Friendship*, ed. Brita Lindberg-Seyersted (1982), p. 23.

48. *L*, i. 94.

49. See Roy Foster, *W. B. Yeats: A Life*, ii. (Oxford, 2003), 41 and 681 n. 113.

50. *L*, i. 77, 92.

51. EP to Ford Madox Ford (7 September 1920): *Pound / Ford*, ed. Lindberg-Seyersted, p. 41.

52. *L*, i. 58–9.

53. TSE would be appropriately guarded in his anonymous pamphlet *Ezra Pound, his Metric and his Poetry* (New York, 1918).

54. *L*, i. 126.

55. Gordon 119; see TSE to Polly Tandy (9 September 1946).

56. VW, *Diary* (10 September 1933), iv. 179.

57. *L*, i. 88.

58. *L*, i. 88.

59. *L*, i. 97.

60. It was set up in type as a galley proof but never published; see *WLF* 90–7, 129.

61. *WLF* 97.

Chapter 3

1. Seymour-Jones 533

2. Patmore 84–5.

3. *L*, i. 97.

4. Seymour-Jones 480.

5. TSE to BR (May 1925): *The Autobiography of Bertrand Russell* (1968), ii. 174.

6. Matthews 83. Matthews gives no source for his remark.

7. BR was there, of course; TSE might also have gone to Cambridge to see George Santayana (1863–1952),

philosopher and critic, who had taught him at Harvard (Santayana was in Cambridge at the end of March 1915 – *L*, i. 94).

8. *L*, i. xvii.

9. Ford Madox Ford, *The Good Soldier*, ed. Martin Stannard (Norton Critical Edition, 1995), pp. 79–80. Ford once used the passage for the dedication of a copy of the book: see cited edition, p. 80, n. 2.

10. TSE's comment dates from a July 1915 letter to his father (*L*, i. 110–11), written to be opened in the event of his death (e.g. if his boat were torpedoed on its way to the USA), which asked that VivE benefit from his life insurance.

11. Aldous Huxley to OM (21 June 1917): *Ottoline at Garsington: Memoirs of Lady Ottoline Morrell 1915–1918* (1974), ed. R. Gathorne Hardy, p. 207.

12. Miranda Seymour, *Ottoline Morrell: Life on the Grand Scale* (1992), p. 244; 'ultra' meaning not just 'extremely' but 'going beyond, surpassing, or transcending the limits of' (*OED*).

13. Aldous Huxley to Julian Huxley (28 June 1918): *Letters of Aldous Huxley*, ed. Grover Smith (1969), p. 156.

14. See *L*, i. 115 n. 3. See Monk 439–46, 449–50 for a discussion of the way BR convinced himself that it would actually be good for the Eliots if VivE were to fall in love with him.

15. Cyril Connolly, 'Revolutionary Out of Missouri', *Sunday Times*, 10 January 1965, p. 38.

16. He was describing Eric Gill (Levy and Scherle, *Affectionately, T. S. Eliot*, p. 65).
17. 'Little Gidding', first draft (7 July 1941): Gardner 228.
18. 'First Debate between the Body and Soul', *IMH* 64.
19. 'Prufrock's Pervigilium', *IMH* 43.
20. *CP* 26.
21. 'Paysage Triste', *IMH* 52.
22. *L*, i. 22 (French original). The English version at *L*, i. 24 is misleading in several respects; I offer a more accurate translation.
23. *L*, i. 75.
24. TSE would later declare himself 'upper-middle through and through' (Hermione Lee, *Virginia Woolf*, 1996, p. 452).
25. Seymour-Jones states (without providing appropriate evidence) that VivE's mother did her best to prevent her daughter marrying (14–15). All that is clear is that Rose Haigh-Wood was fearful of her daughter's overt sexuality (not an unusual reaction) and had disapproved of her previous relationship (also not unusual).
26. This was the conclusion reached by the essayist and critic Logan Pearsall Smith (1865–1946) – incidentally BR's brother-in-law – and passed on to the writer Cyril Connolly; see Matthews 43. Given that TSE on at least two occasions, to different people, named himself as the person primarily responsible for VivE's awful health – see his letters of 1922 to EP (*L*, i. 598), of 1925 to BR (*The Autobiography of Bertrand Russell*, ii. 174) and

p. 31 below – it seems possible that what had overtaken VivE 'at some point' might have been the fear of (or more likely an actual) pregnancy. Any such event in 1915 might have provoked a marriage, and have led TSE to travel to the USA without VivE in July; it might have resulted in a miscarriage, even in the abortion which VivE's brother Maurice recalled (see Seymour Jones 635 n. 72) which in turn might have led to TSE's sudden return in August 1915. If the reason for TSE's feeling of responsibility occurred later, then a marital rape, a miscarriage or even an abortion – perhaps resulting from VivE's brief affair with BR, and occurring on 4 July 1918 – might on the one hand have led to the 'Ode on Independence Day' in *Ara Vos Prec* (*IMH* 383) and on the other to VivE's not having children. If TSE had at any stage insisted on sex, or on an abortion, then he might have felt subsequently responsible for VivE's inability to have children and resulting state of health. I have nb seen no supporting evidence of any of these occurrences, and doubt if any such exists; I offer only a series of 'might's.

27. Dante, *The Inferno*, Canto V, ll. 132 ('ma solo un punto fu quel che ci vinse'). See 'Tradition and the Individual Talent' (*SE* 19) and 'Dante' (*SE* 245–6), which quotes the passage and translates it.

28. *L*, i. xvii.

29. Jane Austen, *Mansfield Park*, chap. 1, about Frances Ward, the mother of the heroine Fanny.

30. EP to John Quinn (4–5 July 1922): *The Selected Letters of Ezra Pound to John Quinn 1915–1924*, ed. Timothy Materer (Durham and London, 1991), p. 210.
31. *L*, i. 90.
32. BR to OM (July 1915): Monk 434.
33. Matthews 42 and ValE in *WLF* ix both omit the fact. Lyndall Gordon, in her account of the early months of the marriage (Gordon 118–132) refers only to a USA 'visit ... cut short' because of VivE's illness (133), while Ackroyd, who mentions the fact that TSE went back to 'confront his parents', simply says that 'he left America after a visit of about three weeks' (65).
34. See TSE to J. H. Woods (16 August [1915]).
35. *L*, i. 139.
36. Jain 34–5.
37. *L*, i. 598.
38. TSE to BR (May 1925): *The Autobiography of Bertrand Russell*, ii. 174.
39. *L*, i. 157.
40. VivE to Scofield Thayer (2 August 1915): Seymour-Jones 92.
41. TSE to E. Martin Browne (19 March 1938): E. Martin Browne, *The Making of T. S. Eliot's Plays* (Cambridge, 1969), p. 108.
42. BR to OM (19 November 1915): Monk 444.
43. BR to OM (10 November 1915): Monk 444.
44. TSE to BR (21 April 1925), *The Autobiography of Bertrand Russell*, ii. 173.

45. 'Thomas Middleton', *SE* 163.

46. TSE to OM (14 March 1933), UT: Schuchard 179.

47. *L*, i. 136.

48. *L*, i. 137.

49. *L*, i. 136.

50. *L*, i. 266.

51. Seymour-Jones 541; in 1936, VivE was still recalling 'when Tom and I were first married'.

52. See her letter to EP (*L*, i. 532–3).

53. See Seymour-Jones 428–9; some of the information came from TSE's sister-in-law Theresa, who interviewed VivE's doctor in 1926.

54. Michael Hastings, *Tom and Viv* (Penguin Books, 1985); see e.g. *L*, i. xvi-xvii. See too the review of Raine, *T. S. Eliot*, by Tom Paulin, which states that the TSE 'marriage is graphically described in *Painted Shadow* by Carole Seymour-Jones, a work Raine fails to engage with ... The effect of this omission is to bury Eliot's life even more deeply' (*The Observer*, 7 January 2007).

55. Seymour-Jones 113–15.

56. Matthews 44; Ackroyd 66; Seymour-Jones 113. The idea apparently originated with Edmund Wilson.

57. TSE to JH (29 November 1939): Seymour-Jones 449.

58. In 1937 he would declare that – 'owing to Church Law' – contraceptives should not be used by Anglo-Catholics like himself; see VW, *Diary* (18 March 1937), v. 71.

59. VW, *Diary* (16 February 1940), v. 268.

60. BR to OM (September 1915): Monk 440.

61. Patmore 89.

62. BR to OM (10 November 1915): Monk 444.

63. John Xiros Cooper, e.g., assumes that her 'psychological ailments' were present from the start of her marriage to TSE (*The Cambridge Introduction to T. S. Eliot*, p. 5) and that by 1918 her 'mental state' was 'increasingly fragile' (p. 8).

64. Henry Eliot to Charlotte Eliot (30 October 1921): Seymour-Jones 277.

65. *L*, i. 598.

66. VW, *Diary* (29 April 1925), iii. 15.

67. BR to OM (10 November 1915): Monk 444.

68. Seymour, *Ottoline Morrell*, p. 314.

69. Patmore 90.

70. 'Baudelaire', *SE* 423.

71. *CP* 25.

72. *L*, i. 544.

73. Frank Morley in 'The Mysterious Mr Eliot', BBC TV (3 January 1971): Seymour-Jones 480. See too Hope Mirrlees below.

74. Theresa Eliot to Peter du Sautoy (*c.* 1951): *T. S. Eliot: Essays from the* Southern Review, ed. James Olney (Oxford, 1988), p. 78.

75. Matthews 48.

76. Copy at UT; see *The T. S. Eliot Collection of the University of Texas at Austin*, compiled by Alexander Sackton (Austin, 1975), p. 15.

77. See e.g. the table in *IMH* xxxviii-xlii.

78. *L*, i. 126.

79. VW, *Diary* (26 September 1937), v. 112.

80. *L*, i. 288.

81. *L*, i. 544.

82. VW, *Diary* (19 December 1937), v. 193.

83. 'Conclusion', *UPUC* 155.

84. 'A Talk on Dante', *SP* 101.

85. *CP* 34.

86. *CP* 134.

87. *L*, i. xvii. He told ValE how 'The years of "The Waste Land" were a terrible nightmare to him' (Interview with Timothy Wilson, *Observer*, 20 February 1972, p. 21).

88. BR to OM (?7–8 September 1915): Monk 440.

89. *Ottoline at Garsington*, ed. Gathorne Hardy, p. 101.

90. Ibid., p. 120.

91. BR to OM (July 1915): Monk 434.

92. *L*, i. 140.

93. See, e.g., her comments to Mary Hutchinson in 1919 (*L*, i. 334).

94. *L*, i. 301.

95. Schuchard 250 n. 8.

96. *Ottoline at Garsington*, ed. Gathorne Hardy, p. 120.

97. *L*, i. xvi-vii.

98. *L*, i. xvii.

99. EH gave TSE's letters to her to the Houghton Library in Harvard in 1956, but put an embargo on his letters being read for fifty years after the death of either TSE

or herself, depending upon which of them was the longer-lived. The letters will remain sealed until 12 October 2019. TSE saw to it that her letters to him were destroyed before he died.

100. See *L*, i. 69–70.

101. *L*, i. 305.

102. Seymour-Jones 454.

103. Gordon 696.

104. Gordon 421.

105. Gordon 431.

106. E.g. Gordon, *Eliot's New Life*, pp. 14–15.

107. Schuchard 154, drawing on Gordon 205.

108. VW, *Letters* (26 November 1935), v. 446.

109. See E. W. F. Tomlin, *T. S. Eliot: A Friendship* (1988), pp. 218–19.

110. 'Turnbull Lecture III', *VMP* 288–9.

111. '" ... Sieti raccomandato il mio Tesoro, / nel qual io vivo ancora, e più non cheggio." / Poi si rivolse ...' (Dante, *The Inferno*, Canto XV, ll. 119–121).

112. *L*, i. 273.

Chapter 4

1. VW, *Diary* (20 September 1920), ii. 68.

2. *L*, i. 217.

3. *L*, i. 224.

4. See *WLF* 104–7. Either TSE's acquaintance with aspidistras was so limited that he was unable to spell

them – 'aspidestra' is a spelling *OED* recognises only under 'Illiterate forms' which 'were formerly frequent' (the last cited from the *Westminster Gazette* in 1899) – or he had made a typing error.

5. TSE wrote fifteen reviews for the latter (the last in July 1918), two for the former.

6. 'Airs of Palestine, No. 2', *IMH* 85; the editor was J. A. Spender (1862–1942).

7. JMM saw it in 1919 (*L*, i. 345), rewritten to apply to the editor J. C. Squire (1884–1958).

8. See *IMH* 283, note on Title.

9. The first five quatrain poems were 'Airs of Palestine, No. 2', 'The Hippopotamus', 'A Cooking Egg', 'Whispers of Immortality' and 'Mr Eliot's Sunday Morning Service', and these may well have been the poems VivE meant; the other three came from perhaps a year later – 'Sweeney Among the Nightingales', 'Sweeney Erect', 'Burbank with a Baedeker; Bleistein with a Cigar'.

10. The USA did indeed enter the war against Germany on 6 April 1917.

11. *L*, i. 161.

12. *L*, i. 164.

13. *L*, i. 178.

14. *L*, i. 164.

15. VW, *Diary* (15 November 1918), i. 219.

16. *L*, i. 178.

17. Quoted Bush 4; the address by TSE to the class of 1933 was 'taken down in shorthand without the speaker's

knowledge and printed without correction' and appeared in the *Milton Graduates Bulletin* (Gallup C344).

18. 'Observations' in the sense of 'an act of observing scientifically' as well as 'a remark in speech or writing in reference to something'. Its contents were: The Love Song of J. Alfred Prufrock – Portrait of a Lady – Preludes I-IV – Rhapsody on a Windy Night – Morning at the Window – The Boston Evening Transcript – Aunt Helen – Cousin Nancy – Mr Apollinax – Hysteria – Conversation galante – La figlia che piange.

19. A. David Moody, *Ezra Pound: Poet* (Oxford, 2007), p. 331.

20. Aldous Huxley to Juliette Baillot (11 December 1917): *Letters of Aldous Huxley*, ed. Smith, p. 140.

21. See Monk 511 n. 2. I agree with Monk that – although the only occasion when we know she 'spent the night' with BR was at the end of October 1917 – they may have had sexual relations for a little while before this: probably after her arrival at Senhurst Farm on 17 October (Monk 510). Schuchard believes that Monk demonstrates how 'the affair lasted from the summer of 1915 to 1919, with sexual intimacy commencing by 1916, if not earlier' (Schuchard 91). That is precisely what Monk does *not* demonstrate.

22. Schuchard 91. I do not however agree with Schuchard's assumption that TSE's remark to OM (14 March 1933)

– that BR had 'done Evil, without being big enough or conscious enough to Be evil' – was a reference to the affair (Schuchard 179). It is a great deal more likely to refer to BR's attacks on Christianity. If TSE had genuinely believed that BR had wickedly seduced VivE and wrecked her life, then he would have paid him the compliment of believing him evil.

23. *CP* 41.
24. VW, *Diary* (22 March 1921), ii. 103.
25. 'Beyle and Balzac' [1919], quoted *VMP* 208 n. 3.
26. *CP* 176.
27. Incomplete, carbon copy draft of *The Cocktail Party* (Browne, *The Making of T. S. Eliot's Plays*, p. 193).
28. See TSE's note on Bradley in 'The Waste Land', *CP* 86.
29. 'Tradition and the Individual Talent', *SE* 17.
30. 'Tradition and the Individual Talent', *SE* 14.
31. 'Introduction', *UPUC* 33.
32. For details see Schuchard 39–44.
33. 'Tradition and the Individual Talent', *SE* 16.
34. Patmore 90.
35. *L*, i. 202.
36. *L*, i. 156.
37. *L*, i. 224.
38. *L*, i. 311. In 1950, the poem 'To T. S. Eliot' attacking TSE for anti-Semitism was read aloud by Emanuel Litvinoff at the Poetry Society in London, while TSE was in the audience. Danny Abse, who was there, heard TSE – with 'his head down' – muttering 'a good poem, it's a

very good poem' and assumed that he was 'generously' paying tribute to Litvinoff (Julius 217–18). It seems to me a good deal more likely that TSE was referring not to the Litvinoff poem but to his own.

39. *CP* 42.

40. Raine, *T. S. Eliot*, pp. 168–70. The lines are anti-Semitic, and Raine's argument is full of holes; there is e.g. not a scrap of evidence that the most virulently anti-Semitic passage in the poem shows 'Bleistein as seen by Burbank' (169). We could only imagine it might be read in such a way if we were to accept Raine's assertion 'It has to be' (169).

41. See *WLF* 118–19 and Raine, *T. S. Eliot,* pp. 170–2.

42. Julius 333.

43. E.g. Ronald Schuchard and Denis Donoghue; see Julius 334–5, 312.

44. See Julius 5.

45. I.e. the whole argument about Rachel *née* Rabinovitch depends on (a) the assumption that the poem is in a tight relationship with Arnold's poem 'Rachel', and I don't think that that can be shown; (b) our acceptance of Julius's assertions that TSE's Rachel is 'a fantasy of feminine evil; she is a whore; she is bestial; she is a literary, Jewish daughter of a Jewish father; she denies her Jewishness by repudiating her surname (which Eliot restores)' (Julius 304). The first of those assertions is untrue; the second is untrue; the third is untrue; the

fourth is partly true, but hardly carries much weight; the fifth is absurd.

46. Randall Jarrell, 'Fifty Years of American Poetry', *The Third Book of Criticism* (New York, 1969), p. 314. TSE adopted and occasionally demonstrated anti-Semitic attitudes until the extent of Nazi attempts to eradicate Jews between 1933 and 1945 became clear. He then made some attempts to clarify his own position as one who was *not* an anti-Semite; he would also describe anti-Semitism as 'a heresy' (Julius 205). He arranged for the lower-case 'jew' in his *CP* to be corrected to upper-case 'Jew' (*CP* 39, 43) which allowed Julius to demonstrate how determined he was to find TSE anti-Semitic, no matter what TSE did: 'we may conclude that he used the lower-case *j* to diminish Jews; he used upper-case initials to mock their suffering' (Julius 169). TSE was however clear (see Julius 204–5) that he did not wish to retract his 1934 remark about a large number of free-thinking Jews being undesirable (*ASG* 20: see p. 199 and note 13.

47. *CP* 59.

48. Spoof advertisement in the *Fireside* c. 1898; see Soldo 211–12.

49. 'I have two close friends whose names are Sweeney', he recalled in 1956 (Levy and Scherle, *Affectionately, T. S. Eliot*, p. 81). EP had 'Sweeney Among the Nightingales' and 'Mr Eliot's Sunday Morning Service' in his hands by 24 May 1918; see *Pound / The Little Review: The*

Letters of Ezra Pound to Margaret Anderson, ed. Thomas
L. Friedman and Melvin J. Scott (New York, 1989),
p. 224.

50. *CP* 58.

51. Nevill Coghill in *T. S. Eliot: A Symposium*, ed. Marsh
and Tambimuttu, p. 86.

52. I.e. 'an ex-pugilist with some such moniker as Steve
O'Donnell', Conrad Aiken, 'King Bolo and Others',
T. S. Eliot: A Symposium, ed. Marsh and Tambimuttu,
p. 21.

53. 'Books of the Quarter', Feiron Morris [review of *Mr.
Bennett and Mrs. Brown* by VW], *Criterion*, iii. no. 10
(January 1925), 328.

54. *CP* 44. 'Cropped out' may take a basic meaning from
OED 10.c. ('to come out, appear, or disclose itself'),
with overtones of 'outcrops' (things just sticking out),
but also suggests an array of teeth equipped to do the
job of chewing or tearing *outside* rather than inside
the 'crop' or throat used by birds for the first stage of
preparing food to be digested.

55. VW, *Diary* (3 August 1922), ii. 187.

56. *CP* 45.

57. The phrase seems first to have been used by Mary
Braddon (1835–1915) in *Birds of Prey* (1867): 'Georgy's
suspicions were too vague for refutation; but they were
nevertheless sufficient ground for all the alternations
of temper – from stolid sulkiness to peevish whining,

from murmured lamentations to loud hysterics – to which the female temperament is liable.'

58. Ralph Waldo Emerson, *Essays 1st and 2nd Series* (1906), p. 56.

59. Schuchard assumes that Doris is helpless because laughing at Sweeney sharpening his razor on his leg (93): but 'the epileptic' is observed from Sweeney's point of view, not from ours as readers.

60. *CP* 45.

61. *CP* 45. The closest Emerson got to the quotation TSE offers was in 'Self-Reliance': 'Every true man is a cause, a country, and an age ... An institution is the lengthened shadow of one man; as, the Reformation, of Luther; Quakerism, of Fox; Methodism, of Wesley; Abolition, of Clarkson. Scipio, Milton called "the height of Rome"; and all history resolves itself very easily into the biography of a few stout and earnest persons' (*Essays 1st and 2nd Series*, p. 39).

62. *Athenaeum* (25 April 1919), p. 237; quoted Schuchard 93.

63. *ASG* 26.

64. *L*, i. 608. Yeats, of course, would later become famous for poetry highlighting the physically comic and grotesque, but TSE was either being ironic or was mistaken; in 1920, Yeats apparently told John Quinn that he disliked TSE's writing (Foster, *W. B. Yeats*, ii. 681 n. 113).

65. Gordon 153. In the first version of her book, Gordon was more dismissive, describing them as 'a digression', not 'something of a digression' (*Eliot's Early Years* (Oxford, 1977), p. 91).

66. 'Clark Lecture V', *VMP* 148.

67. TSE knew e.g. Francis M. Cornford's book *The Origin of Attic Comedy* (1914); see Chapter 6 notes 50–51.

68. *CP* 36, 64, 99.

69. *CP* 59.

70. 'Ode to a Nightingale', ll. 63–4.

71. *CP* 60. 'Siftings' would normally be the result of a process of clearing or cleaning from impurities; the word was supplied by EP, replacing TSE's original 'droppings' (*IMH* 381–2).

72. VW, *Diary* (20 September 1920), ii. 67–8.

73. Ibid, 68.

74. *CP* 59. Julius states that – because of those two lines – the poem is an 'anti-Semitic literary work' (5) and that the man in brown at the window (because his mouth shows golden) 'is Jewish' (81). It borders on anti-Semitism to assume that only Jews have gold fillings.

75. TSE to VW (3 February 1938): Lee, *Virginia Woolf*, p. 452.

76. See *L*, i. 505, where EP wonders if Bolo 'wont unhinge his [Joyce's] somewhat sabbatarian mind' and advises TSE against dispatching any such poems.

77. *CP* 151.

78. See Christopher Ricks, *T. S. Eliot and Prejudice* (1988), pp. 204–7.
79. *L*, i. 259.
80. *L*, i. 247, 254.
81. *L*, i. 245.
82. *L*, i. 261.
83. *L*, i. 266.
84. *L*, i. 274.
85. *WLF* xxviii.
86. *L*, i. 285.
87. *L*, i. 276.
88. Schuchard 200.
89. *L*, i. 280.
90. 'Philip Massinger', *SE* 209: '*eingeschaltet*' in this context probably means 'incorporated', but TSE may be playing with the very modern meaning of 'turned on, illuminated' (when he had last been in Germany in 1914, the word was just becoming the normal verb for turning on a light switch).
91. TSE, 'On Poetry', Address in Concord, Mass. (3 June 1947): Soldo 130.
92. Gardner 14, quoting an interview TSE gave in 1958.
93. *Paris Review* interview with TSE by Donald Hall, reprinted in *T. S. Eliot: Critical Assessments*, i. 80.

Chapter 5

1. *L*, i. 320.

2. *L*, i. 344.

3. Moody, *Ezra Pound*, p. 398.

4. *L*, i. 408, 419, 451.

5. 'Conclusion', *UPUC* 144.

6. *Paris Review* interview with TSE by Donald Hall, reprinted in *T. S. Eliot: Critical Assessments*, i. 77.

7. 'The Three Voices of Poetry', *OPP* 101.

8. 'Rudyard Kipling', *OPP* 237.

9. Terry Eagleton, 'Raine's Sterile Thunder', *Prospect Magazine*, no. 112, 12 March 2007.

10. 'Henry James', *Selected Prose of T. S. Eliot*, ed. Frank Kermode (Oxford, 1975), p. 152.

11. 'A Sceptical Patrician', *Athenaeum* (23 May 1919), p. 362.

12. 'In Memoriam', *SE* 336.

13. 'Critical [Note]', *The Collected Poems of Harold Monro*, p. xiii.

14. 'The "Pensées" of Pascal', *SE* 408.

15. 'Literature and the Modern World', *American Prefaces*, i (November 1935), 20: Schuchard 120.

16. Canto XXIX [1930], *The Cantos of Ezra Pound*, 4th Collected Edition (1987), p. 145.

17. See TSE to William Force Stead (9 August 1930): Schuchard 120.

18. See Schuchard 123–4.

19. *CPP* 330.

20. *CP* 199.

21. *CP* 201.

22. 'Conclusion', *UPUC* 151.

23. VW, 'Modern Fiction' (1925), *The Essays of Virginia Woolf*, iv. 1925–1928, ed. Andrew McNellie (1981), 160.
24. *L*, i. 301.
25. *CP* 64, 65.
26. *CP* 64, 65.
27. *CP* 65, 64, 63, 65.
28. *CP* 63.
29. See 'The Metaphysical Poets': 'In the seventeenth century a dissociation of sensibility set in' (*SE* 288).
30. Eagleton, 'Raine's Sterile Thunder', *Prospect Magazine*, 12 March 2007.
31. 'Conclusion', *UPUC* 151. Philip Le Brun pointed out as long ago as 1967 ('T. S. Eliot and Henri Bergson', *Review of English Studies*, New Series, xviii. no. 71, August 1967, 276) that the idea has similarities with the remark by Henri Bergson that the object of art 'is to put to sleep the active or rather resistant powers of our personality' (*Time and Free Will*, p. 114).
32. Eagleton, 'Raine's Sterile Thunder', *Prospect Magazine*, 12 March 2007.
33. 'John Ford', *SE* 203.
34. 'Clark Lecture V', *VMP* 154.
35. John Berger, 'A Master of Pitilessness', *Hold Everything Dear* (Verso, 2007), p. 87.
36. 'Shakespeare and the Stoicism of Seneca', *SE* 137.
37. *CP* 63.
38. 'Clark Lecture VIII', *VMP* 220.
39. 'Clark Lecture VII', *VMP* 186.

40. Ackroyd 117.
41. *CP* 66, 67.
42. *WLF* 13.
43. *WLF* 127; *L*, i. 497. She had apparently been with them since 1916: see *L*, i. 412.
44. *WLF* 11, 13.
45. VW, *Diary* (7 June 1921), ii. 125.
46. *WLF* 5, 11; the quotation comes from Dickens' *Our Mutual Friend* (1865), in which Sloppy is 'a beautiful reader of a newspaper' aloud to Mrs Betty Higden, and she comments on the accomplishments of his reading (I. chap. 16). Towards the end of the book, Sloppy amplifies the comment: 'I used to give Mrs Higden the Police-news in different voices!' (II. chap. 14).
47. *L*, i. 456.
48. *L*, i. 364.
49. *L*, i. 329.
50. *L*, i. 309.
51. *L*, i, 353.
52. *The Family Reunion, CPP* 289.
53. *L*, i. 355.
54. *L*, i. 366.
55. See *L*, i. 364, 366 and 391.
56. *L*, i. 465.
57. See Lawrence Rainey, *Revisiting The Waste Land* (New Haven, 2005), pp. 200–1.
58. See *L*, i. Illustration 31.

59. Cf. VivE describing TSE under pressure of work in 1917: 'always behind hand, never up to date – therefore always tormented' (*L*, i. 185).

60. 'Conclusion', *UPUC* 144.

61. See *L*, i. 495. Cf. too, from October 1917, *L*, i. 200.

62. *L*, i. 480.

63. Cf. TSE's comment in March 1917 about 'a Satirist' – 'no man of genius is rarer' – who might show 'that the heroic couplet has lost none of its edge since Dryden and Pope laid it down' ('Reflections on Vers Libre', *TCTC* 189). By 1933 he had changed his mind: 'you cannot write satire in the line of Pope' (*ASG* 24).

64. 'Conclusion', *UPUC* 144.

65. *CP* 74.

66. *WLF* 13, 15.

67. *L*, i. 584.

68. Seymour-Jones 543.

69. *CP* 82 n. 218.

70. E.g. 'Well now that's done: and I'm glad it's over'; 'By Richmond I raised my knees / Supine on the floor of a narrow canoe' (*CP* 72, 74).

71. 'Beyle and Balzac' [1919], quoted *VMP* 208 n. 3.

72. Gordon 201.

73. *L*, i. 484.

74. Letter from Abigail Eliot (12 June 1965), quoted in programme of *Tom and Viv*, Seymour-Jones 379. Abigail Eliot (b. 1892) saw TSE and VivE in London

on a number of occasions between December 1919 and
September 1920 (cf. *L*, i. 348, 353–4, 400, 408).

75. 'Company' as late as the 16th century had the meaning
of 'sexual connexion' (*OED* 3.).

76. John Xiros Cooper states that 'In the tense bedroom
scene, "the game of chess" represents their painful,
blunted desire, resulting in mechanical sex where "ivory
men make company," bloodless pieces on a predestined
board, markers of the sterility of their love-making'
(*T. S. Eliot's Orchestra: Essays on Poetry and Music*,
2000, p. 59). This changes the meaning by ignoring the
awkward 'company between us'. Carole Seymour Jones
says that the line is 'revealing of marital incompatibility'
(*Times Higher Education Supplement*, 26 October
2001) but does not reveal what is revealed. Donald C.
Childs states that the line 'functions as a complaint by
the Tom-figure against the Viv-figure. He would suffice
as company for her; she would not suffice as company
for him. Since the complaint is articulated by the man,
the assumption will be either that the woman does not
want children or that she cannot have them because she
is barren' (*Modern Eugenics: Woolf, Eliot, Yeats and the
Culture of Degeneration*, 2001, p. 119): a reading handy
for his argument, but having nothing to do with what
TSE wrote. Ricks acknowledges the problem but only
comments that ' "Between" becomes an impediment,
admitted in the marriage of untrue minds' (*T. S. Eliot
and Prejudice*, p. 212).

77. See *WLF* 126.
78. Seymour-Jones 365.
79. '"Elegy" is another confession of the emotional tensions of Eliot's first marriage ... religious emotions are associated with remorse for a terrible wrong done to a woman or womankind' (Lyndall Gordon, 'The Waste Land Manuscript', *American Literature*, xlv. no. 4, January 1974, 560); Seymour-Jones 365.
80. Harry Trosman, 'T. S. Eliot and *The Waste Land*: Psychopathological Antecedents and Transformations', *Psychoanalytic Studies of Biography*, ed. George Moraitis and George H. Pollock (Chicago, 1987), p. 202.
81. Moody, *Ezra Pound*, p. 401.
82. Ibid., p. 402.
83. Ibid., p. 403.
84. See e.g. EP's comments on 'Whispers of Immortality' and other poems in *IMH*, Appendix C.
85. *L*, i. 502.
86. See the argument by Jim McCue in his review 'Editing Eliot' in *Essays in Criticism*, 56.1 (2006), 1–27.
87. *L*, i. 480 n. 1; TSE declared himself suffering from 'an *aboulie*' too (*L*, i. 486).
88. D. H. Lawrence had heard OM's account of Vittoz's treatment and included in *Women in Love* a reference to 'A very great doctor' who has taught the character Hermione Roddice (a recreation of OM) to 'use the will properly': 'by learning to use my will, simply by using my will, I *made* myself right' (ed. David Farmer,

Lindeth Vasey and John Worthen, Cambridge, 1987,
pp. 139–40).

89. *L*, i. 486.

90. *L*, i. 573.

91. TSE to Paul Elmer More ('Shrove Tuesday' 1929):
Soldo 141–2.

92. Ackroyd 52–3 is excellent on this.

93. On 25 May 1937; Tomlin, *T. S. Eliot: A Friendship*, p. 88.

94. *The Annotated Waste Land*, ed. Rainey, p. 38.

95. 'Conclusion', *UPUC* 151.

96. 'Henry James', *Selected Prose of T. S. Eliot*, ed. Kermode,
p. 152.

97. 'The Three Voices of Poetry', *OPP* 101.

98. *L*, i. 608.

99. TSE to BR (15 October 1923), *WLF* 129: *The
Autobiography of Bertrand Russell*, ii. 173.

100. VW, *Diary* (16 March 1935), iv. 288.

101. *L*, i. 496: 'I don't know if it holds together'.

102. 'Housman on Poetry', *Criterion*, xiii. no. 50 (October
1933), 154.

103. 'The "Pensées" of Pascal', *SE* 405.

104. 'Wordsworth and Coleridge', *UPUC* 69.

105. TSE's first use of 'The Waste Land' comes on a page
which he typed between 17 and 22 January 1922;
EP first used the title on 24 January 1922 (*L*, i. 497,
misdated '24 December 1921'). EP would call it 'Waste
Land' in August 1922 and TSE would carefully correct
him (*L*, i. 567).

106. *CP* 76.

107. *CP* 79, 78.

108. *CP* 78, 79, 86.

109. *WLF* 8–9, *CP* 70, 79.

110. *CP* 79.

111. Jim McCue has queried whether the 'purple ribbon' of these pages is, in itself, a sufficient proof that it was EP's typewriter which TSE was using. In itself, it is not; but Part V was typed on the double foolscap which EP habitually used, and at the start of the MS of Part IV EP wrote 'Bad – but / cant attack / until I get / typescript' (*WLF* 54–5), which shows that Parts IV and V were typed following EP's initial survey of the poem; therefore either after TSE had left Paris in November or after he returned from Lausanne. The latter seems more likely, given the links between the composition of Part V and Lausanne.

112. *L*, i. 496–7.

113. *L*, i. 498.

114. See *WLF* 24–5.

115. Conrad's description of the last words spoken by Kurtz in *Heart of Darkness* (1899), chap. 3.

116. *L*, i. 497. Although it is not possible to be certain which of the various typescript pages EP had in mind, the 19 pages making up the poem were – employing the editorial page numbering in *WLF* – perhaps 6, 8, 10, 12, 14, 24, 26, 30, 32, 34, 36, 48, 50, 52, 68, 82, 84, 86,

88. That would have given EP a text from 'April ... to shantih' (*L*, i. 497).

117. *L*, i. 504.

118. VW, *Diary* (23 June 1922), ii. 178; 'tensity' is 'The quality of condition of being tense; a state of tension' (*OED*).

119. VW, *Diary* (12 March 1922), ii. 171.

120. In June 1922 she told EP about colitis, temperature, increasing mental incapacity, physical exhaustion, insomnia and migraines (*L*, i. 533).

121. VW, *Diary* (23 June 1922), ii. 178; the friend was Mary Hutchinson.

122. Conrad Aiken, *A Reviewer's ABC* (New York, 1958), p. 177.

123. 'John Ford', *SE* 203.

124. *L*, i. 466.

Chapter 6

1. Ackroyd 125.

2. Jason Harding, *The Criterion: Cultural Politics and Periodical Networks in Inter-War Britain* (Oxford, 2002), p. 9.

3. Ibid., p. 12.

4. Ibid., p. 228.

5. EP to John Quinn (21 February 1922): *The Selected Letters of Ezra Pound to John Quinn 1915–1924*, p. 206.

6. I.e. *606 ideal* or *606 hyperideal*, proprietary names for the arsphenamine that could cure syphilis, first synthesised by Paul Ehrlich in 1907 and later sold under the name *Salvarsan*.

7. EP to John Quinn (4–5 July 1922): *The Selected Letters of Ezra Pound to John Quinn 1915–1924*, p. 210.

8. See e.g. TSE to EP (27 December 1925), Yale.

9. See TSE to BR (7 May 1925), *The Autobiography of Bertrand Russell*, ii. 174.

10. EP to John Quinn (4–5 July 1922): *The Selected Letters of Ezra Pound to John Quinn 1915–1924*, p. 210. EP had crossed out the sentence about 'T's nerves' in his letter and replaced it with the sentence which follows.

11. *L*, i. 544.

12. *WLF* xxvii.

13. VW, *Diary* (17 July 1923), ii. 256; VW, *Diary* (8 November 1930), iii. 331; VW, *Diary* (21 June 1924), ii. 304; VW, *Diary* (2 September 1932), iv. 123.

14. Seymour-Jones 364.

15. TSE to Paul Elmer More ('Shrove Tuesday' 1929): Soldo 141–2.

16. Seymour-Jones 278.

17. VW, *Letters* (18 May 1923), iii. 38.

18. VW, *Diary* (17 July 1923), ii. 256.

19. VivE to Sydney Schiff (31 March 1924), British Library.

20. It has been stated (Seymour-Jones 340) that VivE also 'wrote under the name of her close friend, Irene Fassett' (TSE's secretary) though Seymour-Jones 360 partly

contradicts this by saying that 'the two women began to collaborate on those reviews published under the name "Irene Fassett"'; the source given for the assertion (VivE to Sydney Schiff, 31 March 1924, British Library) however contains no reference to Irene Fassett. The *Criterion* included five book reviews by 'I. P. Fassett' (*Criterion*, iii. no. 9 (October 1924), 137–9; no. 10 (January 1925), 321–2; no. 10 (January 1925), 330–1; no. 11 (April 1925), 474; no. 11 (April 1925), 475) but their style is rather different from those by VivE, and there seems no reason to link VivE with them. Seymour-Jones 346–7, following Loretta Johnson's 'A Temporary Marriage of Two Minds: T. S. and Vivien Eliot', *Twentieth Century Literature*, xxxiv (Spring 1988), 50, states that the piece 'On the Eve', published as by 'T. S. Eliot' (*Criterion*, iii. no. 10 (January 1925), 278–81), was actually by VivE and only edited by TSE (an argument first put forward by Russell Kirk, *Eliot and His Age: T. S. Eliot's Moral Imagination in the Twentieth Century*, New York, 1971, p. 118). The financial and political discussion in the piece is different from anything else VivE ever wrote, but appropriate for a man still working in a bank.

21. 'Thé Dansant (*A fragment*)', *Criterion*, iii. no. 9 (October 1924), 78.

22. VivE to Sydney Schiff (?April 1924), British Library.

23. VivE to Sydney Schiff (31 March 1924), British Library.

24. See TSE to BR (7 May 1925), *The Autobiography of Bertrand Russell*, ii. 174.

25. TSE to Ellen Thayer, quoted in Michael Hastings, 'Introduction', *Tom and Viv*, p. 33.

26. *Criterion*, iii. no. 12 (July 1925), 498–510, 529–42, 557–63.

27. 'Frederic Manning' – also publishing in the *Criterion* 1924–5 – was, in spite of the coincidence of initials, a real person: Australian poet, novelist, reviewer and short-story writer (1882–1935).

28. The suggestiveness of the original ('Aroused from dreams of love and pleasant rapes') is replaced by 'Aroused by dreams of love in curious shapes', while the lines about Fresca slipping 'to the needful stool' where a novel 'Eases her labour till the deed is done' have no equivalent.

29. See *WLF* 22, 26, 38, 40.

30. *WLF* 22–3. Jean Giraudoux (1882–1944), French short-story writer and novelist, who became a playwright in his forties; *Suzanne et la Pacifique* (1921) would have been appropriate for Fresca's original reference to 'a clever book by Giraudoux', and *Siegfried et le Limousin* (1922) for 'another book by Giraudoux'.

31. F. M., 'Letters of the Moment – II', *Criterion*, ii. no. 7 (April 1924), 360–1.

32. Ibid., 360.

33. Ibid., 362. The *'Boutique'* is the ballet *La Boutique Fantasque* by Ottorino Respighi (1879–1936), first

performed in 1919 by the Ballets Russes in London, and in the repertoire of Léonide Massine, with décor and costumes by André Derain. See *L*, i. 523 and n. 1, Schuchard 110–11 and n. 27.

34. *CP* 17. TSE himself drafted '(pencil holograph in a black exercise book)' a version of these lines, 'ending with a parody of *Prufrock*: ' ... if one had said, yawning and settling a shawl, "Oh no, I did not like the *Sacre* at all, not at all"' (*WLF* 127).

35. VivE to Sydney Schiff (31 March 1924), British Library.

36. Harding, *The Criterion*, p. 12 n. 15. According to Harding, the magazine's standard rate was £1 for 500 words and £1. 1. 0. for a page of verse.

37. See *The Letters of D. H. Lawrence*, vol. v., ed. James T. Boulton and Lindeth Vasey (Cambridge, 1989), 86 n. 1.

38. 'Books of the Quarter', F. M. [review of *A Man in the Zoo* by David Garnett and *The Voyage* by John Middleton Murry], *Criterion*, ii. no. 8 (July 1924), 483–6, and 'Books of the Quarter', Feiron Morris [review of *Mr. Bennett and Mrs. Brown* by VW], *Criterion*, iii. no. 10 (January 1925), 326–9.

39. VW, *Diary* (20 September 1920), ii. 68. The Hogarth Press had published 'Sweeney Among the Nightingales' in 1919 in *Poems*.

40. 'The Poetic Drama', *Athenaeum*, (14 May 1920), p. 635.

41. 'But at my back from time to time I hear / The sound of horns and motors, which shall bring / Sweeney to Mrs. Porter in the spring' (*CP* 70).

42. See Barbara Everett, 'The New Style of "Sweeney Agonistes"', *The Yearbook of English Studies, Satire Special Number. Essays in Memory of Robert C. Elliott 1914–1981*, xiv (1984), 247. See too Schuchard 98.

43. *WLF* xxix.

44. *The Journals of Arnold Bennett 1921–1929*, ed. Newman Flower (1933), p. 52. TSE's essay 'The Beating of a Drum' – insisting that 'we have lost the drum' – had been published in the *Nation and the Athenaeum* (6 October 1923), pp. 11–12.

45. 'The wind sprang up at four o'clock' [using part of 'Song for the Opherion', *WLF* 98–9], 'This is the dead land' [part III of 'The Hollow Men'], 'Eyes that last I saw in tears' [*CP* 147], printed together in *Chapbook* 39 ([November] 1924), 36–7. See Gallup 158a.

46. Two ended up in *CP*; the third only in a letter TSE wrote to Hallie Flanagan in the early 1930s, reprinted in a number of places: e.g. Carol H. Smith, *T. S. Eliot's Dramatic Theory and Practice from 'Sweeney Agonistes' to 'The Elder Statesman'* (Princeton, 1963), pp. 62–3 n. 40.

47. A. Walton Litz, *T. S. Eliot: Essays from the* Southern Review, ed. Olney, p. 10.

48. See Gordon 202.

49. 'Clark Lecture V', *VMP* 142.

50. Cornford, *The Origin of Attic Comedy*, p. 106.

51. *The Origin of Attic Comedy* had described 'what is now generally called the Agon, a fierce "contest" between the

representatives of two parties or principles, which are in effect the hero and villain of the whole piece' (p. 2).

52. See 'Marie Lloyd', *SE* 456–9.

53. *CP* 113.

54. VW, *Diary* (12 November 1934), iv. 261.

55. *CP* 44.

56. See Smith, *T. S. Eliot's Dramatic Theory and Practice*, p. 62; *CP* 130.

57. 'Turnbull Lecture III', *VMP* 289.

58. *CP* 134.

59. *CP* 131.

60. *CP* 131. Matthews argued that 'Sweeney wouldn't talk that way: he would never say "copulation" ... Eliot knew what word Sweeney would have used but could not bring himself to use it' (109). Constraints on publication in the 1930s cannot be dismissed so cavalierly. 'Fucking' – the word Sweeney would presumably have used (and which TSE used in his obscene poetry) – would have made the piece unpublishable. The fact that Matthews did not use the word either (in a book published in 1974) demonstrates how little it had been a matter of TSE not being able 'to bring himself to use it' in 1932.

61. 'English Letter Writers' (1933), unpublished lecture given at Yale, noted down and quoted by F. O. Matthieson, *The Achievement of T. S. Eliot* (1947), p. 90.

62. 'Sweeney Agonistes', *CP* 131.

63. Ibid. 135.

64. 'Conclusion', *UPUC* 153.

65. *Paris Review* interview with TSE by Donald Hall, reprinted in *T. S. Eliot: Critical Assessments*, i. 90.

66. The preceding lines had run 'If you lak-a-me lak I lak-a-you / And we lak-a-both the same, / I lak-a-say, / This very day, / I lak-a change your name; / 'Cause I love-a-you and love-a you true / And if you-a love-a me'. The song had been written by the African-American musicians John Rosamond Johnson and Bob Cole, who used the tune in their popular vaudeville act. It was interpolated in the Broadway musical *Sally in Our Alley* (1902), introduced by Marie Cahill, who used it again in her next show, *Nancy Brown* (1903). It finally appeared as a song and dance duet shared by Judy Garland and Margaret O'Brien in the film *Meet Me in St Louis* (1944).

67. *CP* 131–2.

68. Cyril Connolly hosted the party, and read *Sweeney Agonistes* 'at a late hour' with TSE and JH (Connolly, 'Revolutionary Out of Missouri', p. 38).

69. VW, *Diary* (12 November 1934), iv. 261.

70. TSE to Paul Elmer More (8 April 1936): Schuchard 99–100.

71. Ackroyd 145.

72. See Glendinning, *Elizabeth Bowen: Portrait of a Writer*, p. 80.

73. VW, *Diary* (19 December 1923), ii. 278.

74. 'English Letter Writers' [1933], unpublished lecture, quoted F. O. Matthieson, *The Achievement of T. S. Eliot* (1947), p. 90.
75. VW, *Diary* (30 May 1938), v. 146.
76. VW, *Diary* (19 April 1934), iv. 208.
77. VW, *Diary* (21 November 1934), iv. 262.
78. Monk 539: 'Colette O'Niel' was the stage and (to some people) personal name of Lady Constance Malleson.
79. 'Clark Lecture VIII', *VMP* 221.
80. 'Doris's Dream Songs' printed just one of the final 'Hollow Men' sections ('This is the dead land', no. III), framed by two other short poems ('Eyes that last I saw in tears' and 'The wind sprang up at four o'clock'), *Chapbook* 39 ([November] 1924), 36–7. See Gallup C158a. Two months later, the *Criterion* published 'Three Poems', consisting of two new 'Hollow Men' sections (nos. II and IV) and one of the old poems (iii. no. 10, January 1925, 170–1); in March 1925, the *Dial* published a three-poem version with two of the old sections (nos. II and IV) but a brand new one (no. I), arguably choral, at the start (Gallup C162).
81. VivE to Sydney Schiff (*c.* March 1925), British Library.
82. Conrad, *Heart of Darkness*, chap. 2.
83. Ibid., chap. 3.
84. Bush 97.
85. *CP* 147.
86. Gordon 215.

Chapter 7

1. Frank Morley, in *T. S. Eliot: A Symposium*, ed. Marsh and Tambimuttu, p. 67.
2. Charles Powell, *Manchester Guardian* (31 October 1923); *Times Literary Supplement* (20 September 1923).
3. *VMP* 8.
4. Frank Morley, in *T. S. Eliot: A Symposium*, ed. Marsh and Tambimuttu, p. 61.
5. Seymour-Jones 293. The quotation is taken from an analysis of TSE offered by Dr Harry Trosman, but Trosman does not specify Lausanne, nor the writing of 'The Waste Land' for the occasion of such feelings, nor does he suggest that TSE was 'flooded' with such feelings at any time, nor does he refer to 'longings'. He simply says that 'It is likely that ... unacceptable homosexual interests were activated' (see 'T. S. Eliot and *The Waste Land*: Psychopathological Antecedents and Transformations', p. 202).
6. Trosman, 'T. S. Eliot and *The Waste Land*: Psychopathological Antecedents and Transformations', p. 202.
7. Ibid. p. 202.
8. Seymour-Jones 211.
9. See Seymour-Jones 435.
10. He would assume that 'The Waste Land' 'had been begun in earnest at Margate' (Sencourt 85) – it had been in progress at least six months earlier – and would state confidently that, after TSE left England in

September 1932, he never saw VivE again 'except on the other side of a solicitor's table' (122), when she actually confronted him in 1935.

11. 'Introduction', *UPUC* 34.

12. See e.g. the title given chap. 6: 'TRIPLE MÉNAGE: BERTIE, VIVIEN AND TOM' (Seymour-Jones 104).

13. Seymour-Jones 192–3.

14. Seymour-Jones 365.

15. Seymour-Jones 309.

16. Seymour-Jones 359.

17. Seymour-Jones 362.

18. Seymour-Jones 366.

19. Seymour-Jones 379.

20. VW, *Diary* (12 March 1922), ii. 171; the anecdote came via Mary Hutchinson.

21. VW, *Diary* (27 September 1922), ii. 204.

22. Seymour-Jones 349.

23. Fanny Marlow [VivE], 'Fête Galante', *Criterion*, iii. no. 12 (July 1925), 558.

24. Seymour-Jones 329. The sentence continues by saying that the ill-fitting mask 'had now become an intolerable burden': a metaphor too far.

25. John Peter, 'A New Interpretation of the Waste Land', *Essays in Criticism*, 2 (July 1952), p. 245: Seymour-Jones 615.

26. Seymour-Jones 417.

27. Seymour-Jones 417.

28. *CP* 218.

29. 'Religion and Science: A Phantom Dilemma', *Listener*, vi (23 March 1932), 428–9 (429).

30. 'Religion and Science: A Phantom Dilemma', *Listener*, 429.

31. He had been baptised as a Unitarian, but that meant he had not been baptised 'in the Name of the Father, and of the Son, and of the Holy Ghost'.

32. TSE, *For Lancelot Andrewes* (1928), p. ix.

33. TSE to Paul Elmer More ('Shrove Tuesday' 1929): Margolis, *T. S. Eliot's Intellectual Development*, p. 142.

34. TSE to Paul Elmer More (2 June 1930): Schuchard 129. See too TSE's reported rebuttal of S. S. Koteliansky's accusation that it was 'a cowardly desire for comfort' which made him turn to Christianity. TSE insisted that his faith had 'forced him to face the full dangers of the human predicament, not just in this life but for eternity; and it had burdened his soul with a terrible and hitherto unrealised weight of moral responsibility' (David Cecil, *Lady Ottoline's Album*, ed. Carolyn G. Heilbrun, 1976, p. 13).

35. 'The Relationship between Politics and Metaphysics', Jain 23.

36. 'The Lesson of Baudelaire', *Tyro* (9 April 1921), quoted *The Annotated Waste Land*, ed. Rainey, p. 144.

37. *ASG* 57.

38. 'Baudelaire', *SE* 380.

39. Since 1925, 'that Kruschen feeling' had been an advertising catch-phrase: see *OED*.

40. TSE to EP (3 January 1934): Seymour-Jones 524 prints an unreliable text.
41. Seymour-Jones 524.
42. Cf. 'Ode on the Death of the Duke of Wellington' (1852), ll. 201–2, by Alfred Lord Tennyson.
43. First recorded as 'US, 1927': 'a tough, often sadistic male homosexual, especially as a casual sex partner' (*New Partridge Dictionary of Slang and Unconventional English*, 2006). *OED* records from 1935.
44. *VMP* 40, which declares the lines 'Untraced; possibly remembered from a music-hall or ragtime lyric'. Ira Gershwin's lyrics to 'Treat Me Rough' may have something to do with them: 'Treat me rough / Pinch my cheek / Kiss and hug and squeeze me / Till I'm weak / I've been pampered enough, baby / Keep on treatin' me rough / Keep on beatin' me / Keep on treatin' me rough'.
45. *ASG* 60.
46. 'In Memoriam', *SE* 337.
47. Paul Elmer More to Austin Warren (11 August 1929): Arthur Hazard Dakin, *Paul Elmer More* (New York, 1960), p. 269.
48. *CP* 116.
49. VW, *Diary* (29 April 1925), iii. 15.
50. See 'A Commentary', *Criterion*, iii. no. 11 (April 1925), 341.
51. TSE to BR (7 May 1925): *The Autobiography of Bertrand Russell*, ii. 174.

52. 'Little Gidding', first draft (7 July 1941): Gardner 228.

53. Jain 297 n. 81, summarising TSE to Leonard Woolf (May 1925). M.D.: *Medicinæ Doctor*, doctor of medicine.

54. VivE to EP (?14 December 1925): Seymour-Jones 411.

55. Seymour-Jones 465.

56. VivE to OM (n.d. [January 1928]): Sandra Jobson Darroch, *Ottoline: The Life of Lady Ottoline Morrell* (1976), p. 276.

57. TSE to E. Martin Browne (19 March 1938): Browne, *The Making of T. S. Eliot's Plays*, pp. 107–8.

58. Ibid., p. 107.

59. 'Baudelaire', *SE* 428–9.

60. I.e. 'Dante's … brave attempts to fabricate something permanent and holy out of his personal animal feelings', 'Shakespeare and the Stoicism of Seneca', *SE* 137.

61. *ASG* 42. The quotation is derived from the misquotation ('The poor benefit of a bewildering minute' instead of 'The poor benefit of a bewitching minute') from Tourneur's *Revenger's Tragedy* which TSE justified making in 1931 ('Cyril Tourneur', *SE* 192); for his purposes, 'bewitching', with its suggestion of magic, was not as appropriate a word as 'bewildering' for the sexual experience.

62. *CP* 115.

63. *CP* 218 (a phrase at one stage unfortunately 'been and done': Gardner 193–4).

64. 'Critical [Note]', *The Collected Poems of Harold Monro*, p. xvi.

65. 'Turnbull Lecture I', *VMP* 259.
66. 'A Musical Instrument' (1860), ll. 38–42; TSE's memory of the poem was recalled by ValE in 1972.
67. ValE, *Observer* (20 February 1972), p. 21.
68. 'Wordsworth and Coleridge', *UPUC* 68.
69. 'Dante', *SE* 251.
70. 'Turnbull Lecture II', *VMP* 268.
71. TSE to JH (5 August 1941): Gardner 173.

Chapter 8

1. The phrase appears on a draft of 'Perch' io non spero'; TSE took it from the gramophone record 'The Two Black Crows' (1927) by the blackface artists Moran and Mack (Schuchard 148).
2. See Gallup C238 (as 'Salutation'), C249 (as 'Perch' Io Non Spero'), C294 'Som de l'escalina'), A15 (as a signed and limited edition costing 31s 6d).
3. *Ash-Wednesday* (Faber & Faber, 1930), p. [ix]. The dedication was one of the casualties of the poem's reprinting in 1936 in *Collected Poems 1909–1935*, but most of TSE's dedications and acknowledgements in individual volumes were dropped when the poems were collected: the dedication to his father in *Poems 1909–1925* (Faber & Gwyer, 1925), p. [3], e.g., disappeared, as (rather later) did TSE's acknowledgement to JH for his contribution to *Four Quartets* (1944), p. 5. The exceptions were the

dedication of *Prufrock and Other Observations* to Jean
Verdenal in 1917, which remained in print, extended
('Mort aux Dardanelles'), in *Poems 1909–1925*, p. 7,
and the dedication of 'The Waste Land' to EP, which
was first inscribed by hand ('miglior fabbro') on a
presentation copy given to EP in 1922 but which later
appeared in print (as 'il miglior fabbro') in *Poems
1909–1925*, p. 63.

4. Helen Gardner, *The Art of T. S. Eliot*, 6th impression
   (1968), p. 113.

5. Sencourt 112; Sencourt stayed with TSE and VivE in
   April 1930 ('just after publication of *Ash-Wednesday*'),
   and was in a position to have accurately recorded VivE's
   remark.

6. It did not appear in *Collected Poems 1909–1935*,
   published on 2 April 1936 (Gallup A32).

7. Schuchard 151.

8. According to Sencourt, they went to the French Riviera
   (Sencourt 119); a photograph survives of them abroad
   (Seymour Jones, II, 8). 1930 was the year Sencourt
   actually stayed with TSE and VivE, and he may well
   have heard them discussing the visit; OM, however,
   refused to believe in the affection when TSE told her
   about it in mid-November 1930 (Seymour-Jones 464).

9. Gardner, *The Art of T. S. Eliot*, p. 122.

10. *CP* 95.

11. *CP* 97–8.

12. *CP* 104.

13. *CP* 102: 'horn' in the sense of 'an erect penis ... *to have (get) the horn*, to be sexually excited' (*OED* 6.c.).

14. *CP* 95.

15. Bush xi, summarising TSE to William Force Stead (10 April 1928), Yale.

16. Matthews 102.

17. 'Yeats', *OPP* 253.

18. 'A Commentary', *Criterion*, xiii. no. 52 (April 1934), 452.

19. JH to Frank Morley (January 1941): Gardner 19.

20. Moody, *Ezra Pound*, p. 376.

21. 'In Memoriam', *SE* 336.

22. VW, *Letters* (7 June 1928), iii. 508; Seymour, *Ottoline Morrell*, p. 389.

23. VW, *Diary* (8 November 1930), iii. 331.

24. VW, *Diary* (12 February 1935), iv. 279.

25. Bush 102.

26. VW, *Diary* (29 April 1929), iii. 223.

27. VW, *Letters* (6 February 1930), iv. 133.

28. The Eliots had not of course used the Church of England 'Solemnization of Matrimony' service in 1915, but TSE would certainly now have sworn allegiance to the way they should have given 'their troth to each other'.

29. VW, *Diary* (10 September 1933), iv. 178.

30. *CP* 97–8.

31. ValE, *Observer*, 20 February 1972, p. 21.

32. *L*, i. 479.

33. *L*, i. 422.

34. Matthews 48.
35. Seymour-Jones 463.
36. VW, *Letters* (6 November 1930), iv. 133.
37. VW, *Diary* (8 November 1930), iii. 331.
38. Ibid. Seymour-Jones has suggested (473–4) that VW's question was ridiculous (how could the Eliots keep bees in London?) and that VivE's answer was sardonic. That is not how either question or answer can be read in the *Diary*, nor in the version VW supplied to her sister in a letter (VW to Vanessa Bell, 8 November 1930, *The Letters of Virginia Woolf*, iv. 250).
39. VW, *Diary* (2 September 1932), iv. 123.
40. Seymour-Jones 477.
41. Seymour, *Ottoline Morrell*, p. 389.
42. Ackroyd 184.
43. Sencourt 121.
44. Ackroyd 193.
45. VW, *Diary* (8 November 1930), iii. 331.
46. Raine, *T. S. Eliot*, p. 121.
47. VivE to Mary Hutchinson (29 September 1928): Seymour-Jones 461.
48. Seymour, *Ottoline Morrell*, p. 388.
49. VW, *Letters* (7 June 1928), iii. 508
50. Glendinning, *Elizabeth Bowen: Portrait of a Writer*, p. 80.
51. VW, *Letters* (7 September 1932), v. 100.
52. VW, *Diary* (2 September 1932), iv. 123.
53. VW, *Letters* (16 September 1932), v. 107.

54. VW, *Diary* (2 September 1932), iv. 123.

55. *CP* [121]. The epigraph had actually first appeared both in the October 1926 and the January 1927 *Criterion* printings of the two fragments.

56. Sencourt 122; Sencourt wrote that TSE described this to him, and quoted *Julius Caesar* II. i. 63–5.

57. Scott Fitzgerald to Edmund Wilson (March 1933): *VMP* 242.

58. TSE to OM (14 March 1933): Schuchard 179.

59. I.e., 'ever since he had learned of her affair with Russell, he had found her morally repugnant' (Schuchard 178). That is exactly what TSE is *not* saying.

60. 'The Principles of Modern Heresy', described in *For Lancelot Andrews* as a book that 'will not be ready for a considerable time', p. ix-x.

61. *CP* 153. See Childs, *T. S. Eliot : Mystic, Son and Lover* for a discussion of TSE's attitude towards Lawrence's mysticism (pp. 130–41, 176–85).

62. 'London Letter', *The Dial*, lxxiii (September 1922), 331.

63. See *L*, i. 617.

64. 'Le Roman Anglais Contemporain', *La Nouvelle Revue Française*, Mai 1927, xxviii, 671.

65. See 'Books of the Quarter' [review of *Son of Woman: The Story of D. H. Lawrence*], *Criterion* x. no. 41 (July 1931), 772.

66. Forster's letter was in *Nation and Athenaeum*, xlvi (29 March 1930), 888; TSE's response in xlvii (5 April 1930), 11; Forster's reply to TSE in xlvii (12 April 1930), 45.

67. 'Baudelaire', *SE* 429.
68. 'Books of the Quarter' [review of *Son of Woman: The Story of D. H. Lawrence*], *Criterion* x. no. 41 (July 1931), 771. That review was – apart from his four, quarterly 'Commentaries' – TSE's only contribution to the magazine for the whole of volume x, suggesting the fascination which Lawrence continued to have for him.
69. 'English Literature from 1890 to the Present Day' (Spring 1933): Ellmann, *The Poetics of Impersonality*, p. 48.
70. *ASG* 60, 61, 58, 58, 37.
71. See Gordon 274.
72. See 'Religion and Literature', *SP* 40.
73. *NTDC* 15.
74. *ASG* 39.
75. See e.g. 'To Criticise the Critic', *TCTC* 24–5. In 1939, Lawrence came in for a patronising offer to explain and justify his life (and excuse 'his aberrations') when TSE suggested that Lawrence failed in his attempt 'to look at the world with the eyes of a Mexican Indian' (*ICS* 62). The reference to the 'Mexican Indian', if meant seriously, must apply to *The Plumed Serpent* (1926), to which TSE had apparently referred in 1927: 'In his series of splendid, but extremely ill-written novels – each one vomited from the press before we have had time to finish its predecessor – there is nothing to relieve the monotony of the "dark passions" which cause his Males and Females to tear themselves and each

other to pieces' (*D. H. Lawrence: The Critical Heritage*, ed. R. P. Draper, 1969, p. 276). *The Plumed Serpent* had actually appeared in 1926, three years after its predecessor, *Kangaroo*; but TSE may have had in mind 'The Woman who Rode Away', which he had himself published in two instalments in the *Criterion* in 1925 and 1926.

76. Although TSE's Statement of Evidence (at UN, La R 4/5/2), prepared with the solicitors for Penguin Books, Rubinstein, Nash and co., spends a great deal of time explaining (and abandoning) the position on Lawrence which he had taken in *ASG*, he had made remarks denigrating Lawrence in a number of other places, and on the witness stand he might have done the defence more harm than good. He was not used, in the event.

77. See p. ooo [Chapter 5 last paragraph]. [#]

78. See 'The Function of Criticism', *SE* 27.

79. See *ASG* 60. What had upset TSE more than anything had been the revelation in 'The Shadow in the Rose Garden' not just that a recently married woman had a lover before marriage, but that she admits it to her new husband when he questions her: '"Do you mean to say you used to go – the whole hogger?" he asked, still incredulous. / "Why, what else do you think I mean?" she cried brutally.' TSE saw her answer as 'something nearly approaching conscious cruelty' (*ASG* 36) and took it as proof that Lawrence was speaking up for the 'dæmonic powers' (*ASG* 60): a matter of articulating

the sexual desires of women who 'bestow their favours' indiscriminately on 'plebeians' or 'savages' (*ASG* 61).

80. William Empson recalled TSE saying this: see 'My God, man, there's bears on it' [1972], *Using Biography* (1984), p. 199. Gardner (55 n. 51) is also a witness to the phrase appearing in the draft Statement of Evidence ('which I saw') that TSE would have used at the *Lady Chatterley* trial in 1960 (see note 76). The quoted words do not appear in a copy of the document surviving at the University of Nottingham, but were cut off it before it was deposited, when TSE made some deletions and additions, and removed most of the last page(s). TSE's original remark about Lawrence as a 'very sick soul' had appeared in 'Books of the Quarter', *Criterion* (July 1931), 772. See too TSE to EP (28 December 1959).

Chapter 9

1. *CP* 221.
2. *CP* 98.
3. Ackroyd 188.
4. *CP* 209. See too 'Yours is no better. / They have seen to that: it is part of the torment', *The Family Reunion*, *CPP* 309.
5. *The Family Reunion*, *CPP* 315; cf. too 'In which all past is present, all degradation / Is unredeemable', *CPP* 294.
6. F. R. Leavis, *The Living Principle* (New York, 1975), p. 158.

7. Gordon, *Eliot's New Life*, pp. 14–15.

8. Emily Hale to Willard Thorp (24 August 1963): Gordon 425.

9. See *VMP* 232.

10. *VMP* 244.

11. Darroch, *Ottoline*, p. 276.

12. See e.g. his letter to EP (?24 May 1933), Yale, in which he warned EP how difficult he would be to trace once he had returned to England.

13. VW, *Diary* (21 July 1933), iv. 169.

14. VW, *Diary* (20 July 1933), iv. 168.

15. VW, *Letters* (6 September 1933), v. 99 [editorially misdated to 1932].

16. VW, *Diary* (10 September 1933), iv. 178.

17. VW, *Diary* (10 September 1933), iv. 178.

18. A word from the sub-culture vocabulary of 'Polari', used extensively in the gay and theatre worlds, especially between the 1930s and the 1960s: 'slap' has made some inroads into standard English but other words (e.g. 'cottage') have been accepted into the *OED*.

19. VW, *Letters* (3 September 1933), v. 222; see too VW, *Diary* (20 July 1933), iv. 168. For the photograph, see p. 201.

20. Gordon 300.

21. *L*, i. 239.

22. Patmore 91.

23. See Seymour-Jones 553–4.

24. Gordon 199. Both there and in Gordon, *Eliot's Early Years* (p. 124) the quotation is used to represent VivE's state in the middle 1920s, but it comes from her 1934 Diary.

25. TSE to Mary Trevelyan (28 October 1954): Gordon 291.

26. VW, *Diary* (10 September 1933), iv. 178.

27. Seymour-Jones 533.

28. VW, *Letters* (*c.* 6 December 1935), v. 450.

29. Gordon 300, from VivE's diary.

30. Seymour-Jones 539.

31. *CP* [123].

32. *The Family Reunion, CPP* 306.

33. *The Family Reunion, CPP* 308.

34. 'Elegy', *WLF* 116–17.

35. VW, *Letters* (31 December 1933), v. 266.

36. Seymour-Jones 558.

37. Seymour-Jones 559.

38. Michael Hastings, 'Introduction', *Tom and Viv*, p. 21.

39. Seymour-Jones 559.

40. Gordon 311.

41. Seymour-Jones 554.

42. VW, *Diary* (10 September 1933), iv. 178.

43. 'T. S. Eliot: a friendship', *Listener*, xcvii (28 April 1977), 543.

44. TSE to E. Martin Browne (19 March 1938): Browne, *The Making of T. S. Eliot's Plays*, p. 108.

45. Blake Morrison, *Too True* (1998), pp. 139–40, information from ValE: Seymour-Jones 561.

46. *CP* 156.

47. VW, *Diary* (24 August 1933), iv. 174 n. 7.

48. Bush 209.

49. *CP* 209.

50. *Paris Review* interview with TSE by Donald Hall, reprinted in *T. S. Eliot: Critical Assessments*, i. 77.

51. 'Yeats', *OPP* 257–8.

52. 'In Memoriam', *SE* 334.

53. *CP* 189.

54. *CP* 189.

55. *CP* 190.

56. *The Family Reunion, CPP* 307.

57. *CP* 194.

58. *CP* 190.

59. *CP* 191.

60. *CP* 191, 195.

61. A photograph survives taken by TSE of the road from West Coker to East Coker (see Gordon no. 27). It was probably a Sunday, as the sexton at St Michael's church later recalled to his son how 'that summer's evening' TSE arrived 'and sat in a pew behind the font'. Mr Foot commented how Eliot 'Seemed a nice kind of bloke. Quite religious, you could tell'. 'A few days later the vicar told dad he knew the visitor had wanted a look at the church. A Mr Elliott or something like that. A bit of

a writer' (David Foot, 'When dad had T. S. Eliot caught behind the font', *The Guardian*, 22 July 2008, p. 12).

62. *CP* 199–200.

63. *CP* 196.

64. *CP* 200.

65. *CP* 201.

66. *CP* 202–3.

67. Samuel Beckett, *Proust and Three Dialogues with Georges Duthuit* (1965), p. 103.

68. JH to Frank Morley (February 1940): Gardner 17.

69. *CP* 203.

70. *CP* 203.

71. *CP* 212.

72. *CP* 210.

73. *CP* 214

74. *CP* 214.

75. *CP* 209.

76. *CP* 209.

77. *CP* 213.

78. *CP* 213.

79. *CP* 218.

80. TSE to JH (19 September 1942): Gardner 194.

81. *CP* 219.

82. *CP* 219.

83. *CP* 200.

84. *CP* 219.

85. TSE to JH (5 August 1941): Gardner 67.

86. Bush 200.

87. *CP* 218: 'Since our concern was speech, and speech impelled us / To purify the dialect of the tribe'. TSE is paraphrasing Stéphane Mallarmé: 'donner un sense plus pur aux mots de la tribu' (see Bush 158–9).

88. See 'The Three Voices of Poetry', *OPP* 101.

89. See Herbert Howarth, *Notes on Some Figures Behind T. S. Eliot* (Chatto and Windus, 1965), pp. 278–80.

90. *CP* 215.

91. Bush 226.

92. TSE would hope that it was still 'Driven by dæmonic, chthonic / Powers' (*CP* 213).

93. *CP* 214.

94. *CP* 223.

95. Leavis, *The Living Principle*, p. 253.

96. TSE, 'Introduction' to Paul Valéry, *Le Serpent* (1924), p. 12: quoted Bush 5.

97. Robert Lowell, quoted in 'Eliot's Life', *Listener*, lxxxv (14 January 1971), 50.

98. 'Shakespeare and the Stoicism of Seneca', *SE* 137.

Chapter 10

1. See 'Defence of the Islands', *CP* 227–8; 'A Note on War Poetry', *CP* 229–30; 'To the Indians who Died in Africa', *CP* 231; 'To Walter de la Mare', *CP* 232–3.

2. I.e. 'The Cultivation of Christmas Trees', *CP* 117–18; 'A Dedication to my Wife', *CP* 234.

3. Frank Morley, in *T. S. Eliot: A Symposium*, ed. Marsh and Tambimuttu, p. 68.

4. Ibid., p. 65.

5. Ibid., p. 68.

6. Ibid., p. 66.

7. Mairet, 'Memories of T. S. E.', *T. S. Eliot: A Symposium for His Seventieth Birthday*, ed. Braybrooke , p. 40.

8. Ibid., p. 39.

9. *NTDC* 43.

10. See Schuchard chap. 2. Schuchard does not, however, make the link between TSE's and Hulme's enjoyment of the adoption of extreme positions.

11. *ASG* 19–20 ... see too Chapter 4 note 46.

12. Denis Donoghue, *Words Alone* (2000), p. 213.

13. The image is not mine; see 'He was gifted with a light touch: he was also cursed with a heavy hand' (D. J. Enright, 'A Haste for Wisdom', *New Statesman*, 30 October 1964, reprinted *Conspirators and Poets*, 1966, p. 100).

14. *ASG* 28.

15. The Elliot and Fry photographic studio (1863–1965) was at 55 Baker Street, London. See Nuzhat Bukhari, 'The Distinguished Shaman: T. S. Eliot's Portraits in Modern Art', *Modernism/modernity* 11.3 (2004), 373–424.

16. *CP* 141. TSE refers not only to the famous essay 'Zum ewigen Frieden' (1795) by Immanuel Kant, normally

translated as 'Perpetual Peace', but to the ideals (and
tortuous negotiations) of the League of Nations.

17. VW, *Diary* (19 December 1938), v. 193.

18. TSE to Paul Elmer More ('Shrove Tuesday' 1929):
Margolis, *T. S. Eliot's Intellectual Development*, p. 142 ...
CP 95.

19. VW, *Diary* (2 February 1935), iv. 277.

20. *CP* 218 ... *CP* 117.

21. VW, *Diary* (16 February 1940), v. 268.

22. 'Poetry and Drama', *OPP* 85.

23. Raine, *T. S. Eliot*, p. 124 ... VW, *Diary* (22 March 1939),
v. 210.

24. Mary Trevelyan, quoted Gordon 472.

25. *The Cocktail Party*, *CPP* 438.

26. Ibid. 439.

27. VW, *Diary* (16 February 1940), v. 268.

28. Sencourt 152.

29. *The Family Reunion*, *CPP* 327.

30. Gordon 462. Cf. W. H. Auden's memory of asking
TSE why he liked playing patience: 'Eliot reflected
gravely for a few moments and then replied, "Well, I
suppose it's because it's the nearest thing to being dead"'
(Stephen Spender, *T. S. Eliot*, 1975, p. 240).

31. *CP* 207 ... VW, *Diary* (5 February 1935), iv. 277.

32. Sencourt 154; the information must derive from JH,
who told TSE the news.

33. See *CP* 40 ... 'Critical [Note]', *The Collected Poems of
Harold Monro*, p. xvi.

34. Matthews 138.
35. See Ackroyd 306, Gordon 466.
36. Ackroyd 229 ... Seymour, *Ottoline Morrell*, pp. 521–2.
37. Tomlin, *T. S. Eliot: A Friendship*, p. 218. Tomlin had talked at length with Theresa Eliot in 1959.
38. Quotations from the letter Emily Hale wrote to her friend Lorraine Havens (7 August 1947): Gordon 411–12.
39. Tomlin, *T. S. Eliot: A Friendship*, p. 219.
40. Gordon 466 ... *L*, i. 598.
41. *WLF* [1]; see too TSE to Thomas McGreevy (14 February 1931), Dublin: Harding, *The Criterion*, p. 203.
42. Cf. Nietzsche, *Beyond Good and Evil*, 'Maxims and Interludes' no. 68: ' "I have done that," says my memory. "I cannot have done that" says my pride, and remains adamant. At last –memory yields.'
43. EP may have been first with the first: see his letter of 4 November 1922 and its passing comment 'she's right, mon POSSUM' (*L*, i. 589). TSE's friends in the 1930s knew him as 'Elephant': see Ackroyd 235.
44. Ackroyd 199 ... VW, *Diary* (2 September 1933), iv. 177 ... VW, *Diary* (24 August 1933), iv. 174.
45. Cf. Coleridge's comment on Hamlet: 'O that subtle trick to pretend to be *acting* only when we are very near *being* what we act' (S. T. Coleridge, *Lectures 1808–1819 on Literature*, ed. R. A. Foakes, Princeton, 1987, i. 541).

Chapter 11

1. 'Conclusion', *UPUC* 148.
2. The only major exceptions, I think, are the children 'whimpering in corners' at the start of 'Prufrock's Pervigilium' (*IMH* 43), the odd outdoor children in 'Ash-Wednesday' who 'will not go away and cannot pray' (*CP* 103), who sound more like souls in limbo than laughing children, and the damaged child of 'Animula' (*CP* 113–14).
3. See Leonard Unger, *Eliot's Compound Ghost* (Pennsylvania State University Press, 1981), p. 89. Within the garden can be heard 'the uncontrollable laughter of children who were trying not to be heard' (Frances Hodgson Burnett, *The Secret Garden*, Leipzig, 1912, chap. 27, p. 281).
4. See Illustration 12 in Bush; Soldo 151.
5. Bush 189.
6. *IMH* 383. The children sing a lyric used constantly in Catullus, no. 61: an invocation to the God of marriage from a poem celebrating sexual desire and happiness. The children however sing either to or about a female demon, drawn from the bowels of the earth, who is supposed to have intercourse with men in their sleep.
7. *CP* 115.
8. *CP* 152.
9. *CP* 190, 195.
10. *CPP* 335.
11. *CP* 201.

12. *CP* 222.

13. TSE to JH (5 August 1941): Gardner 29.

14. 'The wild thyme unseen, or the winter lightning / Or the waterfall' (*CP* 213).

15. Bush 167.

16. *CP* 69.

17. Matthews 192.

18. *L*, i. 88.

19. Seymour-Jones 449.

20. TSE to JH (29 November 1939): Seymour-Jones 449.

21. *CP* 152. Schuchard quotes the lines as evidence of TSE's 'revitalized' emotional life with EH, 'twenty years after their love began' (179).

22. Philip Larkin, 'The Winter Palace', *Collected Poems* (1988), p. 211.

23. See e.g. Illustration 15 in Bush; Janet Adam Smith, *T. S. Eliot: Essays from the* Southern Review, ed. Olney, pp. 213–26.

24. See e.g. the three splendid poems in his letter to VW of 3 February 1938, quoted Lee, *Virginia Woolf*, pp. 451–2, and his verse address to Clive Bell quoted in *T. S. Eliot: A Symposium*, ed. Marsh and Tambimuttu, p. 17.

25. *CPP* 226–7.

26. *CP* 116 (my italics).

27. The poem's epigraph quotes Seneca portraying the maddened Hercules at the moment of discovering that he has slaughtered all his own children.

28. Tomlin, *T. S. Eliot: A Friendship*, p. 157.

29. Gordon, *Eliot's New Life*, p. 243; Gordon 497 removes the reference to 'a disciple'.
30. ValE quoted in 'Eliot's Life', *Listener*, lxxxv (14 January 1971), 50.
31. TSE discovered, just before the wedding, that Jules Laforgue had got married – also to an English woman – in the same church.
32. For JH's various versions of the event, see Matthews 159–61.
33. Cf. *CP* 218.
34. I can supply no trustworthy source for this remark: I have found it in a number of places.
35. ValE quoted in 'Eliot's Life', *Listener*, lxxxv (14 January 1971), 50.
36. ValE, *Observer*, 20 February 1972, p. 21.
37. See TSE to EP (11 November 1961). On the other hand, on 29 November 1939 he had told JH that the years since he left VivE had been 'the only happy years of my life' (Seymour-Jones 564).
38. *CP* 211.
39. Robert Lowell to Valerie Eliot (12 April 1965): *T. S. Eliot: Essays from the* Southern Review, ed. Olney, p. [130].
40. *OPP* [5].
41. *CP* 194, 202.
42. *CP* 234.
43. *CP* 104.
44. *CP* 234.

45. *CP* 234.
46. 'Baudelaire', *SE* 428.
47. *CP* 28; 'Whispers of Immortality', *IMH* 370; *WLF* 22–23.
48. *CP* 234.
49. *The Elder Statesman*, *CPP* 583.
50. TSE, *Knowledge and Experience in the Thought of F. H. Bradley* (1964), p. 10.
51. TSE became a British citizen in 1927, though VivE seems to have been against it: 'I never wanted him to get naturalised' (Seymour-Jones 536); see *The Guardian*, G2, 19 November 2008, p. 21.
52. *Sunday Times*, 7 February 1965, p. 35. One rumour did however circulate at the time that he had said 'I couldn't not have come'.
53. *WLF* [vii].
54. Cf. 'To whom I owe the leaping delight / That quickens my senses', *CP* 234.

Afterword

1. 'John Ford', *SE* 203.
2. 'Virginia Woolf', *Horizon*, iii. 17 (May 1941), 313. As recently as 1937, TSE had written about Byron's 'charlatanism', his 'reckless raffish honesty' and his 'vanity of pretending to disreputability', but had nevertheless insisted that such qualities were 'important

in estimating his work: not his private life, with which I am not concerned' ('Byron', *OPP* 206)

3. 'Virginia Woolf', *Horizon*, iii. 17 (May 1941), 314. Michael Hastings quotes the passage in the 'Introduction' to his play *Tom and Viv* (pp. 13–14) but omits the words 'and coherently' (p. 14).

4. In the 7 July 1941 draft of 'Little Gidding', the phrase was 'Every poem its own epitaph' (Gardner 232); in the 1942 (and published) version of the poem, 'Every poem an epitaph' (*CP* 221).

Index